INTRODUCTION TO COMPUTER SYSTEMS: ANALYSIS, DESIGN, AND APPLICATIONS

INTRODUCTION TO COMPUTER SYSTEMS: ANALYSIS, DESIGN, AND APPLICATIONS

John A. Aseltine
Walter R. Beam
James D. Palmer
Andrew P. Sage
George Mason University
Fairfax, Virginia

WILEY

A Wiley-Interscience Publication

JOHN WILEY & SONS

New York / Chichester / Brisbane / Toronto / Singapore

Copyright © 1989 by John Wiley & Sons, Inc.

All rights reserved. Published simultaneously in Canada.

Reproduction or translation of any part of this work
beyond that permitted by Section 107 or 109 of the
1976 United States Copyright Act without the permission
of the copyright owner is unlawful. Requests for
permission or further information should be addressed to
the Permissions Department, John Wiley & Sons, Inc.

Library of Congress Cataloging in Publication Data:

Introduction to computer systems: analysis, design, and applications /
    John A. Aseltine . . . [et al.].
        p.   cm.
    "A Wiley-Interscience publication."
    Bibliography: p.
    ISBN 0-471-63704-1
    1. Computers.   2. System analysis.   3. System design.
    I. Aseltine, John A.
    QA76.I63   1989
    004—dc19   89-5683
                                                          CIP

Printed in the United States of America

10 9 8 7 6 5 4 3 2 1

PREFACE

The objective of this text is to provide a basis for the development of computer understanding, as needed for further study in information systems and related areas. It is directed principally toward individuals who have not had formal exposure to computer understanding which is now characteristic of undergraduate education in computer science, electrical engineering, or systems engineering.

We assume that the reader is familiar with the use of carefully structured diagrams for the explanation of interrelationships between objects, elements, or individuals. Although no prior familiarity with programming languages is required, the reader is expected to understand the basic elements of natural language (i.e., parts of speech, syntax, and semantics). Modern high-level computer-programming languages are increasingly designed to emulate the natural languages which we use in writing and conversation, though computers require a precision of expression seldom found in personal communication.

A certain familiarity with mathematics is expected, though this is limited to algebra or elementary calculus. What is most important, in this respect, is the ability to recognize the nature of numeric problems and to be able to express them in a symbolic, generally algebraic, form. Once this step is accomplished, the transformation into a computer programming language is relatively straightforward. Although much computer programming deals with logical rather than numerical relationships, and current directions of computer technology development emphasize symbolic manipulation more heavily than numerical manipulation, there is a need for algebraic type of expressions as precursors to producing a program.

This is not simply a computer literacy text. Many such efforts have aimed solely at imparting a modest knowledge of programming in some particular language (in the past, FORTRAN; at present, typically BASIC or Pascal). Our objectives are more ambitious. We believe that understanding something about the systems level architecture of computers, including the limitations of computers as a function of this architecture and the nature of software and programming languages, is essential to modern managers and technologists. This is especially the case in those areas in which information technology applications for productivity enhancement are under consideration.

Insofar as actual programming is concerned, nothing is better than actual practice in working with problems that are potentially important to the individual and/or the organization with which the individual is affiliated. We will emphasize this hands-on experience (via the ubiquitous IBM-PC), first by use of the DOS-provided DEBUG utility to get at the internal elements. Then we will introduce the C language as a means to our programming ends.

We choose this approach for several reasons. We feel that C provides the close connection with the hardware and architectural features necessary for an appropriate level of real machine understanding. At the same time, C incorporates the advantages of portability and documentation that most modern high level languages provide. Learning C on the PC also provides skills that are useful for mini- and mainframe computers. As we proceed in communicating about computers, we will also provide some discussions in Pascal, as another common high level language. The emphasis, though, will be on the C programming language.

It is perhaps much more likely that some of our readers will need to understand the workings, at a system level, of modern word processor or database management software, or to integrate several software packages, rather than be able to create application programs. There is a need to understand the way computers work if we are to perform other than very simple routine operations on them. Participation in the computer age is better enabled through a working knowledge of computer system fundamentals. Thus, to better understand the use and utility of modern application software, understanding how computers operate becomes very important.

We have chosen to take a complete contemporary computer system, actually a "family" of such computer systems—the computers deriving from IBM's Personal Computer—as the "standard" for our exposition. This family has come to include the PC, XT, AT (and more recently PS/2) versions of IBM's products, along with a wide variety of computers which are compatible in the sense of being able to execute most or all of the programs executable on the IBM machines and to use the same hardware circuit boards as the IBM-PC. We have chosen a microcomputer rather than a larger "mainframe" computer system, in large part because of their ready availability. However, these "micro" computers currently possess most of the features previously found only on the larger systems. Modern microcomputers exceed the capabilities of "big" mainframe computers of just a few years ago. With the advent of local area networks, the microcomputer workstation is rapidly becoming the computer used by the vast majority of information system professionals, as these machines are able to establish linkage to most mini- and mainframe systems.

Access to an IBM-PC or compatible computer is really essential to appreciation of the material presented here. For the learner, this usage will reinforce our presentation considerably. The best way to learn about computers is to use one.

We recognize that there are other popular microcomputer systems, of which the Apple MacIntosh is an example. The reader should be pleased to know that, although there are many detailed incompatibilities at the level of applications software transportability across machines, there is much more in common at a conceptual level. In a high level language like C, it is generally an easy matter to "port" source code to and from a large variety of microcomputers and mainframes.

The organization of the books is as follows. We begin with an introduction to number systems and computer organization and architecture. Some of this is written from a historical perspective. Beginning in Chapter 4, we introduce the architecture of the classic IBM-PC. Chapters 5 and 6 continue with this theme. There is a very brief introduction to the micro channel architecture (MCA) for the new IBM PS/2 System. These systems are covered in Part I of the book, which is basically concerned with computer organization, architecture, and elementary programming.

Chapter 7 continues Part I of the book, and is devoted to elementary data operations and an introduction to programming in C. The focus of our exposition is on data operations; and the C programming language is introduced as the language to enable these, in what we feel is an understandable and natural way. Chapter 8 continues our work with C and introduces some simple concepts concerning data structures and data pointers. These concepts will be used often throughout the remainder of the text as we examine some of the basic aspects of database and information systems. Computer decisions and logic are the topic of Chapter 9. Logic calculations enable the computer to make elementary decisions and are the special feature of computers which differentiates them from their antecedents.

The application of elementary computer decisions and logic on numbers and symbols, program path decisions, and a change in activities is termed flow control. This is covered in Chapter 10 which begins Part II and our study of computer peripherals and elementary applications. We cover the flow of computations that may be repetitive and involve loops, branching opportunities, and other forms of flow control.

Next, in Chapter 11 we introduce the notion of computer peripherals. Having discussed the C programming language and the various attributes of that language, it is desirable to be able to examine how these operations are connected to the outside world. Peripherals may be connected to the computer so as to appear as an integral part of the "iron" or may be as remote as thousands of miles away. Chapter 12 continues this discussion by examining more general forms of input and output.

Chapter 13 begins our exposition of the use of the programming language C to show how jobs might be done. The approach that is taken is to look at elementary programming applications of importance around the office or factory by use of menu design.

Chapter 14 represents what might initially appear to be an aberration in our progression. This chapter alone comprises Part III of the text and is devoted to operating systems. The MS-DOS or PC-DOS operating system is described almost exclusively, although we do briefly introduce Operating System II and Unix in the concluding portion of this chapter.

Chapters 15 through 17 comprise Part IV of the text, which concerns data structures and advanced topics in C. The emphasis here is on database management-type applications. As is the case in earlier chapters we also explain some of this material in a Pascal setting. This will benefit those who wish to approach this material from a bilingual perspective, C and Pascal. One of the principal topics covered in this part is an introduction to popular data sorting algorithms, together with appropriate elementary programs. These algorithms form the basis for most database management systems and are, therefore, very important for information system development. Chapters 18 and 19 examine numerical computing and computational complexity considerations. Even the most rudimentary spreadsheet and financial analysis applications require numerical calculus and algebra procedures. We base our discussions almost entirely on a Taylor series approach and illustrate some of the more commonly used numerical algorithms.

Chapter 19 presents an elementary discussion of generic problem solving approaches and related computational complexity considerations. Our emphasis in this is certainly on the pragmatic aspects of problem formulation and how various algorithmic search procedures may be implemented in C.

As the material presented is introductory, we have not provided a plethora of references. A few important ones, often historical, are noted in the various chapters. There is a very brief bibliography at the end of the book. There are many other topics which could be considered. We believe that the 19 chapters contained here represent just slightly more material than can typically be covered in a one-semester course. Generally the depth and breadth of each chapter, except for Chapters 1 through 6, is such that one week is devoted to each chapter. A typical one semester course follows the following outline:

Week 1   *Chapters 1 and 2*: Computers and computing, numbers, text, and pictures and their storage

Week 2   *Chapters 3 and 4*: History, the evolution of the computer, the IBM-PC

Week 3   *Chapters 5 and 6*: Hands on the computer, processor operation

Week 4   *Chapter 7*: A high-level programming language

Week 5   *Chapter 8*: Data structures and pointers

Week 6   *Chapters 9 and 10*: Computer decisions and logic, expressions, and flow Control

Week 7   *Chapters 11 and 12*: Computer peripherals programming, input/output

Week 8   *Chapter 13*: Programming applications

Week 9   *Chapter 14*: Operating systems

As is apparent, the pace is rapid. Yet for mature students, particularly those without a formal computing background, but who have been using the IBM-PC in their daily work experiences, the course is *very* doable in one semester.

Various drafts of this book have been used in an introductory graduate level course in the School of Information Technology and Engineering at George Mason University. This course is offered primarily to students with undergraduate degrees in nonengineering areas who intend to enroll in Masters degree programs in information systems, but who lack a specific knowledge of modern computing. Students have come from a variety of backgrounds. The course, while it does carry graduate credit, is an articulation course and extends the minimum plan of study requirements for a graduate degree by three semester hours. The course has demonstrated that a sophisticated understanding of principles necessary for further study in information systems can be obtained by mature students without specialized technical preparation. The authors would like to thank the many students who contributed to this book through their use of it and by their suggestions.

We hope that this text fills what we feel is a significant void in enabling an educationally mature individual without significant computer background to advance rapidly to the point where the contemporary literature and practice in computer and information systems is accessible.

JOHN A. ASELTINE
WALTER R. BEAM
JAMES D. PALMER
ANDREW P. SAGE

Fairfax, Virginia
August 1988

CONTENTS

INTRODUCTION TO COMPUTER SYSTEMS: ANALYSIS, DESIGN, AND APPLICATIONS

PART I

COMPUTER ORGANIZATION, ARCHITECTURE, AND ELEMENTARY PROGRAMMING

1

COMPUTERS AND COMPUTING—
REPRESENTATION OF NUMBERS

1.0 INTRODUCTION

In this chapter we provide an initial, primarily historical, overview of the development of the modern stored-program digital computer.

1.1 REPRESENTING DATA, AND NUMBERS, AND INFORMATION AND KNOWLEDGE

People in western societies are now immersed in a sea of information. This information is so complex and varied, and in such great quantity, that most of us deal with it in the aggregate, sometimes counting on repeats of important messages to alert us to important events or facts. This contrasts sharply with life a few hundred years ago, when most of the populace were limited to knowing about their own family's experiences, and activities such as reading or performing arithmetic were pursuits of scholars.

As clever as we are about noting and storing for later use that information which appears to affect us, most of us have had little or no need to understand information at the primitive and precise level at which computers must operate. To appreciate the capabilities and limitations of computers, which will enable us to put them to work in an effective and efficient way, we need to see information as data input to, internal within, and output from computers.

Numbers are one form of data that may ultimately become information. They represent the kind of information for which computers were originally built. Generally, it is improper to use the term information when referring to numbers.

3

Numbers really only represent data. This data may become information when it is associated with contextuality. We will often refer to numbers as information here, we do so by noting that these numbers are taken out of the information context in which they are embedded. Even though this usage is improper, it is very common.

Numbers may take on many forms, such as integers, which may be written with or without a plus or minus sign. *Real numbers* are often written using an implied decimal representation. The number 12.01 is real. Often numbers are expressed in scientific or *floating point* notation, as 1.201 times ten to the first power. This may be written into or displayed on a computer (or pocket calculator) as 1.2 E1. The hardware of a simple computer may be limited to dealing with integers. Through the use of software, almost any computer can deal with real (noninteger) numbers even if it is limited in hardware to dealing only with integers.

Numbers of practical importance may appear singly, as, for example, the annual salary of an employee or the velocity of an aircraft. They may also appear as numbers representing value and direction, called vectors, or in *arrays* of many dimensions. For example, a pair of numbers may represent a ship's position in latitude and longitude. A three-dimensional array of numbers, in which each number corresponds to the count of a population for a particular occupation, age, and sex, comprises what is often called an array or a vector of dimension three. Some of the very fastest computers, the so-called *supercomputers,* have hardware which is set up to perform particular arithmetic operations on each element of vectors that contain many numbers.

Text material is often written in a nonnumeric language. The text of this book was prepared using computers and *word-processor* programs, for example. This is another form of information. In handling this kind of information, the computer and its program typically have no awareness of the meaning or the correctness of the information that is being represented. To a *word processor,* which is a computer program for helping us write letters or other documents, the text is merely a sequence of characters. Whether or not these characters represent numbers is really immaterial. These programs may be simplistic or highly complex as to features that are provided. Some programs or specialized word processing systems contain *spelling checkers,* which can determine if a typed word is in their "dictionary." If it is, the word is declared to be spelled correctly. Others provide for numerical calculations or synonym presentation through use of a thesaurus.

How do computers operate on *information?* All of us are familiar with many operations which we can carry out using sets of numbers. Addition, subtraction, multiplication, division, and comparison are the principal ones. Letters of the alphabet, or combinations of letters forming *words,* however, are *symbols* which can have far richer meanings than simply numbers. A very reasonable question is: can the computer manipulate them?

We can easily envision limited manipulation of letters and words. One of these is the process of putting letters, or words, into alphabetical order. In the computer world, this is usually referred to as *sorting*. However, unlike the central role of addition in the world of numbers, sorting plays a limited but important role in our dealing with text material. Sorting is used, for example, in alphabetizing entries for an *index* in a book. In our most common intuitive activities involving the use of words to communicate with others, we act as if we were formally applying rules of grammar and syntax. These rules are more complex than the simple rules of mathematics. Unlike the universal rules of mathematics, human language "rules" are subject to personal and regional variations in usage.

In everyday life, we often deal with other complex forms of information, for example, in the form of *pictures*. A picture is a two-dimensional representation of a real or envisioned physical object. These may exist in many forms, for example, line drawings, paintings, or photographs. We do not readily envision characteristic manipulations of two- or three-dimensional objects such as we easily accomplish with those arithmetic operations so familiar to us. However, a computer can be programmed to perform special operations on this "spatial" type of information. For example, programs have been written to analyze satellite photographs. They can extract information from them about geological formations seen by a special television camera a hundred miles above the earth.

And how about *knowledge?* In the last few years, there has been increased attention to broadening the capabilities of computers to deal not merely with data, or with data imbedded in contextuality to form information, but with knowledge. Knowledge is purposeful information. In a true sense, any computer program which manipulates data is an encapsulation of knowledge by the programmer. But most computers deal with programs very differently than they deal with data. Depending upon the level at which one examines knowledge or information, it may appear to a computer as if the knowledge or information is only data.

1.2   NUMBER SYSTEMS: DECIMAL AND BINARY

The decimal number system is a very natural system for us, but only because ten is the number of fingers on human hands. Had humans been four-fingered, the *octal* number system (counting in eights, rather than tens) would no doubt have prevailed. Even when we use a computer, we generally insist on the computer output that is presented to us being in the form we most easily comprehend, that is, counting by orders of ten. Computers lack hands. They generally make use of "off-on" counting circuits, which deal with counting by twos rather than tens. To appreciate the internal, and some external, operations performed by computers as they deal with numbers, we must understand the *binary representation of numbers*.

First, let us remark that the numerals

$$1 \quad 2 \quad 3 \quad 4 \quad 5 \quad 6 \quad 7 \quad 8 \quad 9$$

are only *symbols* representing counts of one, two, and so on. We might as easily have used symbols such as I, II, III, and so on. In fact, the Romans did just this. They realized, however, that such symbols took too long to write for large numbers. Hence they devised abbreviations: V for five, X for ten, L for fifty, C for one hundred, D for five hundred, and M for one thousand.

The Roman numeral system, though still in use today to add a touch of classicism to book prefaces or subsections of a document, has at least one very serious flaw. It lacks a consistent rule for generating larger numbers, and for such elementary operations as counting. To do either requires a number system with a fixed base, or *radix*, and an understanding of the meaning of *zero* when used in this context. Our decimal system uses a radix of ten.

If we use a number system with radix ten, we must identify symbols for counts from one through nine, and one additional symbol to represent a full count of ten. It remained for the Arabs, in the burst of innovation that followed establishment of the Islamic religion, to discover that numbers of any size can be represented by adding a special symbol (zero) to the representation. Thus while 1 through 9 represent counts of one through nine, the number 10 represents a full count of ten ones. The number 100 represents ten counts of ten, and so forth, such that we can obtain as large a number as is required. Most real-life numbers can be represented by a modest number of *digits,* or as symbols. For example, $2,000,000,000,000 is the approximate value of the national debt of the United States of America as of 1986. In natural speech and writing, we might say "two trillion dollars" to represent this number, since this is easier to say than "two million million dollars." The nicknames for different orders of ten (thousand, million, billion,[1] etc.) or in scientific usage the prefixes kilo- and mega-, however, are not generally understood by computers.

If we use the notation of separating trios of digits by commas, such as in 1,000,000, then the computer must be programmed to understand the meaning of the comma. We use the comma for convenience, only to designate multiples of 10^3, as an aid to our visual interpretation. We could just as well use the period and write 1.000.000, as any European would surely do! The computer, being a device for which counting by twos is natural, uses internal binary representations instead. In *binary* representations we need only *two symbols:* the first to represent a count of *one,* and the other to represent a count of *zero.* Alternately, we could say that this second number represents counts of two in the same way that zero represents counts of ten in the base-ten system. Unfortunately, mathematicians chose to use the familiar symbol 1 to represent a count of one in binary, and the symbol zero to represent repeated counts of 2. We say this is unfortunate only because numbers expressed in binary (base two) form might be confused with decimal numbers. The number 1001 can be said to represent one thousand and one if, and only if, we are using a decimal system for counting.

The reason for using base two in a computer lies in the way numbers may

---

[1] Some U.S. readers may be surprised to learn that most Europeans refer to 10^{12} rather than 10^9 as a *billion,* using the term "one thousand million" for what in the United States is referred to as a billion.

easily be physically represented by internal switches in the computer. An open (or *off*) switch can represent 0, and a closed (or *on*) one can represent 1.

Consider[2] the binary number 10 1001. Were we unaware that this is supposed to be a binary number, we might mistake it for "one hundred and one thousand and one." To avoid this problem, which would occur if we use binary numbers and decimal numbers in the same computer program without any special notation to indicate the difference, we are usually required to write the binary number in some special way, such as 101001B, to let us know that it is a binary number. What does this number "mean?" The answer to that question depends on whether one is familiar with binary numbers. If you were asked what the decimal number 243 means, you might answer "two hundreds plus four tens plus three units." But if we are using base five, the number 243 is equal to $2 \times 5^2 + 4 \times 5^1 + 3 \times 5^0$ or seventy three in decimal notation.

With this same contextual relationship for "means," the binary number 10 1001 "means" one "10 0000" plus one "1000" plus one unit. This answer, however, is probably not what the person asking the question intended. Assuming that the individual was only conversant in decimal numbers, he or she probably wanted to know the decimal equivalent of the binary number. To find the decimal equivalent, we need to know the decimal equivalent of the binary numbers 1, 10, 100, and so on. Then we can simply add them up.

No matter what number system we use, there is only one underlying meaning: *the number of objects represented.* If we say 10 decimal (one zero decimal) or "1010 binary," the various ways of communicating the count value have the same meaning. The word "ten" is equivocal, however, unless we know we mean base 10. If we use the word ten to imply the symbol 10, then ten means two (decimal) if we are in the binary system or eight (decimal) if we are using the octal system. Perhaps we should use words like two, thirteen, or twenty to represent numbers whose base is ten. Then we will use numerals only if we are in some other base. Given this, 1010 is equivocal but "one thousand and ten" is not. It can only mean 1010 to the base ten (decimal). We will do this! We recall that 10 in the decimal system means ten, or //////////. In the binary system 10 means two or //. Likewise the binary number 100 means "two twos," or four. We can make a table of binary decimal equivalents:

Binary	Decimal
1	1
10	2
100	4
1000	8
1 0000	16
10 0000	32
100 0000	64
1000 0000	128

[2]We will add spaces to make the binary numbers more readable. We will insert a space after every four binary digits, counting from the right. Thus, 11101 will become 1 1101.

Then, if we want to find the decimal equivalent of 10 1001, we refer to the table and look up the decimal equivalents of 10 0000, 1000, and 1 and add them, decimally of course, to obtain

$$
\begin{array}{rr}
100000 & 32 \\
1000 & 8 \\
1 & 1 \\
\hline
101001 & 41
\end{array}
$$

Therefore, we see that the decimal equivalent of 10 1001 is forty one.

It should be immediately obvious, even though we have two hands and two feet, why the binary system did not develop as the natural one for humans. Many more *digits*[3] are required to express a number in binary form than in decimal form. However, the "addition" and "multiplication" tables for binary digits are *extremely* simple. We have, for example:

$$
\begin{array}{cc}
1 & 1 \\
+1 & \times 1 \\
\hline
10 & 1
\end{array}
$$

and no elementary school student should have difficulty memorizing these tables! Let us add two binary numbers:

$$
\begin{array}{lll}
\text{c c c} & \text{c} & \text{c} \\
101 & 1110 & 0001 \\
+110 & 1101 & 1001 \\
\hline
1100 & 1011 & 1010
\end{array}
$$

Here, we have placed a c to indicate a *carry* above each digit for which a carry was generated.

If we attempt to add a large set of such numbers at once, such as in

$$
\begin{array}{ll}
1011 & 1 \\
1101 & 0 \\
1011 & 0 \\
1101 & 0
\end{array}
$$

we notice that multiple carries may be produced at any given column. If we are working the problem on paper, it is quite possible that we will count the "ones" in the column in our natural decimal style. Clearly this means we will have to make multiple conversions between decimal and binary to cope with the multiple carries as we go along. This is surely not a logical way to proceed. A computer

[3]The term *bit* is used universally within the computer field, as an abbreviation for *binary digit*.

would do all of these operations in the binary system only. For the example considered we obtain 1 as the right-most column result, and 100 for the second column. Thus we have a carry which jumps over two columns.

It should be comforting to know that computers never attempt to add a long column of binary numbers in one step. Instead, the problem is decomposed into many simple problems involving the addition of only two numbers at a time. The operation proceeds as follows. The first two binary numbers are added. A third binary number is then added to the sum of the first two, and so forth.

Subtraction of one binary number from another is also very similar to the decimal equivalent. We *borrow* one unit from the next digit to the left when needed. A typical example is:

```
 bb  bbbb  bbb
 10  0011  1100
-01  1111  1111
 ─────────────
 00  0011  1101
```

We must often borrow from the more significant digit to enable subtraction, as in the foregoing example. As with all addition-subtraction problems, we can check our answers by adding the difference to the number subtracted. For the example just considered, we obtain

```
 01  1111  1111
+00  0011  1101
 ─────────────
 10  0011  1100
```

The fact that we obtain the initial number proves the correctness of our subtraction procedure, at least for the example considered. When this is the case for many examples, we have an inductive proof that we have found a correct procedure.

Multiplication and division of two binary numbers follow the same principles that we know and use so well in dealing with decimal numbers. For example, we might multiply two binary numbers together:

```
      1  0111
     ×1  1001
     ─────────
      1  0111     Partial product
   1011  1        Partial product
 1 0111           Partial product
 ────────────
 10 0011  1111
```

We need to but copy the top number, *shifted,* and add it to the other *partial products* at each level. In this case it might appear that the computer cannot *avoid* multiple carries, as we may have to add more than two binary numbers to get the final answer. Since the computer can only add two binary numbers at once, however, it finds the partial sum of each product with the previous partial sum before determining and adding the next partial product. In other words, the computer might add numbers as in

$$
\begin{array}{r}
1 \ \ 0111 \\
1011 \ \ 1 \\
\hline
1100 \ \ 1111
\end{array}
$$

and then add this last number with the (missing) partial product

$$
\begin{array}{r}
1100 \ \ 1111 \\
1 \ \ 0111 \\
\hline
1 \ \ 0011 \ \ 1111
\end{array}
$$

to get this correct answer.

Division is easy in the binary system. Just as in our decimal experience, the divisor (denominator) is subtracted from the numerator and shifted. The manual division process is left to the reader to explore (see problem 1.13).

If we divide one binary number by another large one, the result must be a number less than unity. Thus far we have been dealing only with numbers as counts. Division, however, requires the invention of "the decimal point," or, in this case the "binary point." Thus we might represent the decimal number 1.5 as binary 1.1, or 1.25 as binary 1.01. That is, 0.1 (binary) represents one divided by two, 0.01 represents one divided by four, and so forth. None of this is the sort of alchemy that it might appear at first glance. When we write a number e d c b a (B), where the symbol B is used to represent the base, what we mean is

$$
a \ [x] \ B^0 + b \ [x] \ B^1 + c \ [x] \ B^2 + d \ [x] \ B^3 \\
+ e \ [x] \ B^4
$$

Thus the number 6 4 1 (8) would be interpreted as

$$
1 \ [x] \ 8^0 + 4 \ [x] \ 8^1 + 6 \ [x] \ 8^2
$$

It is "natural" for us to give a decimal interpretation to this although this is not at all needed. We could just as well give it a hexadecimal (or base 16) interpretation, which would require us to note that $8^0(H) = 1 \ (H)$, $8^1(H) = 8$ (H), and $8^2(H) = 40 \ (H)$. In our usual decimal system we have 641(8) $= 1 \times 8^0 + 4 \times 8^1 + 6 \times 8^2 = 417 \ (10)$.

Numbers less than one are represented in precisely the same way. We formally define the binary system for numbers less than one as a b c d e (B) = a [x] B^{-1} + b [x] B^{-2} + c [x] B^{-3} + d [x] B^{-4} + e [x] B^{-5}. Again, it is convenient to use decimal number equivalents for the B^{-n} terms on the right hand side of the foregoing example, but any base is acceptable. If we think in terms of decimal fractions, binary numbers less than one are simple, and are easily obtained from the foregoing relation:

Decimal	Decimal	Binary
0.5	$1/2=(2)^{-1}$	0.1
0.25	$1/4=(2)^{-2}$	0.01
0.125	$1/8=(2)^{-3}$	0.001
0.0625	$1/16=(2)^{-4}$	0.0001
0.03125	$1/32=(2)^{-5}$	0.00001
0.015625	$1/64=(2)^{-6}$	0.000001
0.0078125	$1/128=(2)^{-7}$	0.0000001

Thus decimal 1.50 may be represented as $1\,(10^0) + 5\,(10^{-1})$, and in a binary-to-decimal conversion table yields the binary number $1.1B$.

Actually, modern computer programs convert the decimal numbers we enter into binary numbers and then reconvert the results of computations to decimal numbers before providing them as output for a human to view. We need to be conscious of internal conversion of numbers only when we want to understand what is happening inside the computer. For those concerned with the detailed inner workings of a computer, such as computer scientists and assembly-language programmers, this knowledge is needed. The many ones and zeros get cumbersome, however, and another representation is used in dealing with both personal computers (PCs) and larger computers: the hexadecimal (radix 16) number system. The hexadecimal (or hex) number system provides a rationale for use of, as well as a symbol for, each group of four binary digits.

1.3 HEXADECIMAL NUMBERS

In hexadecimal representation, fifteen count-symbols and the equivalent of zero are required. The common symbols used for this representation are: $0,1,2,3,4,5,6,7,8,9$, with A,B,C,D,E,F representing ten through fifteen counts.[4]

A typical hexadecimal number might be $10A3$. In the case of hexadecimal numbers, which, in general, may contain a A,B,C,D,E or F, an H is added after the number, such that we have $10A3H$. This is a very good convention and we use it throughout this book. Henceforth any number not in base ten must have the base written after the number.

[4]Purists who believe it would have been better for entirely new symbols to be used rather than some symbols which are well known decimal numbers must, however, face the question: "How could we remember all those strange symbols?" Hence there is after all a good argument for reuse of familiar symbols, though it makes it possible to mistake a number in one base for that in another.

Once we have learned the binary equivalent of the hex symbols `zero` through `F`, the binary representation of a number is easy to write down in groups of four binary digits. For the number `10A3H`, we have

```
    1    0    A    3
  0001 0000 1010 0011
```

What is the decimal equivalent of `10A3H`? We find out in a very straightforward way; we have

```
3 units                                    3
plus A times "sixteen" (A[x]16)          160
plus 0 times "sixteen-squared"             0
plus 1 times "sixteen-cubed"            4096
so the decimal value is                 4259
```

In a somewhat more formal way, we write

$$10A3(H) = 3 \times 16^0 + 10 \times 16^1 + 0 \times 16^2 + 1 \times 16^3 = 4259$$

Often we find zero with a line through it used to distinguish zero from the letter oh. In this text the zero is simply thinner than the oh and, on occasion, care must be taken to tell them apart. So, please try to distinguish between 0 and O.

Before we rush to convert hexadecimal numbers to decimal and later back again to hex, we should first determine whether the decimal equivalent is really *needed*. Often a simple addition or subtraction or a mere comparison of two hex numbers, is all that is required. Many experienced computer professionals don't even think of the decimal equivalents of hex numbers, since these numbers usually relate only to the internal workings of the computer and its programs and never need be compared with external decimal values. In Chapter 3 we will use the utility program DEBUG to examine the IBM PC's internal contents. DEBUG uses *only* hex numbers and special hand-held calculators are used by machine-level programmers who need to make frequent conversions.

The real value of hex numbers lies in the ease with which they allow conversion from binary numbers, together with the accompanying abbreviation achieved by being able to represent four binary bits by one hex number. There is nothing esoteric about individual `ones` and `zeros`.

For example, the out-of-paper condition of a printer is signaled to the IBM-PC by changing a single binary digit from a `0` to a `1`. Conversion can be done easily from the binary number partitioned into four-digit segments.

Here is the subtraction problem we considered in an earlier part of this chapter. We now accomplish the subtraction in binary and in hex to obtain

$$
\begin{array}{rr}
10\ 0011\ 1100 & 23\text{C} \\
-01\ 1111\ 1111 & -1\text{FF} \\
\hline
00\ 0011\ 1101 & 3\text{D}
\end{array}
$$

In the foregoing, the transition from 0011 to 3 is simple, and so is that from 1100 to C if we remember that 1100 is 8 + 4, or 12 decimal. The hex representation C comes from remembering that 10 decimal is A hex. Thus 11 in decimal corresponds to B in hex and 12 in decimal equates to C in hex.

In a sense, dealing with different number systems is like learning a new human language. As we first learn a new language, we often continue to think in the one initially learned. We convert many inputs and outputs between the two languages. Later, as we gain familiarity with the new system, we may convert to thinking about numbers directly in the new language.

We have not mentioned *octal* (radix eight) number representation. The same basic principles apply. We use symbols 0, 1, 2, 3, 4, 5, 6, 7. Octal representation was commonly used in dealing with computers which stored numbers internally in groups of 12, 24, and 36 binary digits. The IBM System 360 used 32-bit internal storage and represented characters with 8 bits, as do many contemporary computers. Thus, hexadecimal representation is commonly used today.

1.4 NEGATIVE NUMBERS IN COMPUTERS

Before leaving our discussion of number systems, we point out that the concept of *negative numbers* is a sophisticated one. It had no experiential basis in the origin of numbers (counting objects in everyday life). Having "minus one apple" is not a simple concept, except perhaps to a commodities dealer! Negative numbers take on physical meaning only when we refer to *relative* situations or shortfalls: the age of siblings relative to a midlitter brother or sister; the time of the second-place runner relative to the winner; the accounting idea of assets and liabilities; or the temperature in Minneapolis on an early February morning relative to the temperature at which water freezes.

One way to represent a negative number is to attach a symbol (e.g., a dash, -) to such a number. If we do this, however, we must carry the dash into the computer representation in order that the number be treated correctly inside the machine. Early computers actually used a special marker, which had to be introduced into the computer to signify a negative number. Modern computers use a simpler scheme which, however, occasions possible traps for the unwary. The scheme is simply this: a number is positive if its most significant bit is zero, otherwise it is negative. That is, the binary number 101 1111 1110 would be defined as negative, while the number 011 1111 1111, of similar length in bits, would be positive. Note that the very definition assumes that the number representation has a fixed and known number of bits, else there would be confusion over the value. This is the pitfall just noted.

The simplest way to determine the proper value for a certain n-bit negative number in this system is to find the n-bit positive number to which it can be added to produce a result with n zeros in the resulting n-bits. Thus, using 8-bit numbers, the negative number 1011 0110 can be added to the positive number 0100 1010 to produce the result 1 0000 0000, having 8 zero bits. A quick way to find the negative of a binary number is to

(1) invert each digit of the original number, then
(2) add 1 to the result.

The intermediate result obtained after step (1) is called the *ones complement* of the original number, while the final result is referred to as its *twos complement*. Arithmetic accomplished using addition to represent negative numbers is referred to as *twos complement arithmetic*. It can be shown that arithmetic performed on numbers formed in this way follows the same rules as for positive numbers. Hence the computer hardware for both positive and negative numbers is the same.

Suppose we wish to subtract the number 32 from the number 75. Each number is to be represented binary. It will take 6 binary bits to represent a number as large as 75, and we need one more for a negative sign. We have

$$75(10) = 0100101\ 1$$
$$32(10) = 0010000\ 0$$

We write the twos complement of 32 and add it to 75. We get

$$\begin{array}{rcl} -32(10) &=& 11100000 \\ 75(10) &=& \underline{01001011} \\ && 00101011 \end{array}$$

Thus the answer is

$$1 + 2 + 8 + 32 = 43$$

which we know is correct.

A potential trap into which one can fall when using computers to manipulate numbers via twos complement arithmetic is that all numbers, including the results of intermediate calculations, must be kept within the range of numbers which the computer can represent. For example, consider a very simple 4-bit representation (in which 0000 to 1111 is the range). Notice that there are 2^4 possible values which the 4-bit representation can assume. We will use 0000 for zero, of course, and 0001 will be one. We can count up to only seven with positive numbers (0111 = seven), and the combinations 1000 through 1111 must represent negative numbers. By following the procedure given above, 1000 is complemented bit by bit to 0111, and then we add a bit to find the positive equivalent of the largest negative number. The result, surprisingly, is eight (1000 - 0111 + 0001 = 1000). In using n bits to represent a signed integer number in this way, the largest positive number which can be represented is $2^{n-1} - 1$, and the largest negative number is -2^{n-1}. For example, in 16 bits we can represent numbers from -32768 (decimal) to $+32767$ (decimal).

A helpful way to think of this is in terms of a line segment along which we measure numbers, as below (for a 3-bit representation):

$$100 \quad 101 \quad 110 \quad 111 \quad 000 \quad 001 \quad 010 \quad 011$$

We notice that the largest positive number is three, but the most-negative number is negative four. When we add 001 to the largest positive number we obtain the most-negative number (and a carry into a nonexistent fourth bit position!). Hence, if we attempted to use this system to add the two positive numbers two (010) and two, we would end with the result negative three! Clearly, precautions are needed.

1.5 FLOATING POINT NUMBERS

Computers can represent values as *floating-point numbers,* known also as *scientific notation* numbers. Recall that any real number can be written in the form of a decimal number between 0.0 and 0.99999..., multiplied by ten to some power. (The number 12345.6789 can be expressed as 0.123456789 times 10^5.) If we limit the range of the mantissa (the first part, 0.123456789 in the example) to a limited number of bits, we can continue to use twos-complement notation to represent the number's sign. Similarly, the exponent (5 in the example) may be represented by an additional number of bits, in twos-complement form. However, this again results in a limitation on the range of numbers representable, but the limitation is on the range of values of the exponent. A similar limitation is familiar to all who have used an electronic pocket calculator, which may, for example, be limited to representing numbers between $9.9999 \ 10^{-99}$ and $9.9999 \ 10^{+99}$. In most *computers,* the number is usually *not* represented in terms of a power of ten, but a power of *two* or of *sixteen.* Seldom do we need to deal with these *internal representations* of numbers in computers; as yet there is no standardization of representation between computers built by different manufacturers. Accordingly, floating point numbers are generally *always* converted to decimal equivalents when entering and leaving a computer. Floating-point numbers are needed in many applications, such as in computation of interest on a loan or mortgage payments. While the applications programmer may never specifically deal with number conversions, awareness of limitations associated with these numbers must be kept in mind.

1.6 SUMMARY

In this very introductory chapter we have examined some simple number representation concepts. All of this is very elementary and it is essential if we really wish to examine the inner workings of computers at a microlevel.

PROBLEMS

1.1   Define a set of ten features or attributes, describing a *person*, to which you can assign a single range of *numeric or symbolic values*. (Suggestions: physical dimensions are one class of feature, colors are another.)

1.2   Even though physical dimensions or other features can have infinitely many values, for practical purposes we find it convenient to limit the numbers of those values with which we must deal to "standardized" values.

(a) Discuss how this principle is applied, in respect to ready-made clothing, mechanical parts such as nuts and bolts, cosmetics, and currency.

(b) Define some other attributes (of a person, place, or thing) which we do not attempt to standardize, but which can still be described completely adequately by brief descriptions or measures.

1.3   Identify three attributes of a person, place, or thing about which any two individuals might easily disagree on a value or description. Discuss how these attributes might be defined by (or "coded into") a limited set of numbers or symbols.

1.4   In computer terms, *arrays* of numbers or symbols usually consist of numbers or symbols all of the same type, for example, a one-dimensional numerical array (also called a *vector*) consisting of the salaries of all employees of a company, or a two-dimensional numerical array defining the distances between a set of cities, such as is often found printed on a map. The characters on a typed page or computer display can be (and often are) treated as a two-dimensional array of alphanumeric symbols. Give examples of one-, two-, and three-dimensional arrays of numbers or symbols which might be of interest in computer data manipulation.

1.5   Determine the decimal equivalents of these unsigned binary numbers:

110 0011 1101
     1111 0000
101 0101 0101

1.6 Determine the decimal equivalents of these hexidecimal numbers: 12345, 4FF0, and AAAAA1.

1.7 Determine the decimal equivalents of these *octal* numbers: 23776, 10234, and 670732.

1.8 Add the *radix-7* numbers 230146 and 304560 and determine the decimal equivalent of the sum.

1.9 Multiply the unsigned binary numbers 110 0111 and 1011, thereby finding the binary product, and verify your result by using decimal equivalents.

1.10 Divide the unsigned binary number 1110 1100 by 1011 and carry the result to four "binary places," checking by the decimal equivalents. (The process can be identical to that you use for decimal "long division.")

1.11 When the two's complement notation is used to represent *signed* binary numbers, the number must usually be represented using *all of* its digits, and mention made that it is *intended to represent* a signed number. Demonstrate that subtracting 0101 1000 from 0111 1000 produces the same 8-bit result as adding the signed integer representation of *minus* 0101 1000 to 0111 1000.

1.12 Shifting an unsigned number to the right by one digit is equivalent to dividing its value by the value of the radix. Show that this is also true for signed negative binary numbers, provided, however, that a 1 is "shifted into" the left-most digit to keep the number of bits constant.

1.13 Prepare a brief but reasonably complete discussion of division in the binary number system.

2

REPRESENTATION OF NUMBERS, DATA, TEXT, AND PICTURES

2.0 INTRODUCTION

In Chapter 1 we concentrated on the way a computer stores and deals with numbers. Now we turn our attention to the question of storage of more general forms of information.

2.1 ENCODING OF SYMBOLS

The storage of numbers, text characters, or images in a computer requires various numbers of bits, depending on the *form of representation* that is used. Prior to about 1965, most computers represented only uppercase alphabetic and numeric (alphanumeric) characters and were able to store only a few punctuation symbols. This required only *6 bits* per character and resulted in $2^6 = 64$ possible combinations, which will not quite allow both upper- and lowercase alphabetic characters and a few needed punctuation symbols. Thus a 6 bit computer would be just a bit inadequate for many uses.

A 7 bit computer will allow $2^7 = 128$ characters to be represented. The standard character representation is based on a 7 bit binary representation, as are most telecommunication protocols. Eight bits are physically more possible to realize than seven. The eighth bit is generally used for error control or other purposes.

The need for a comprehensive computer character set resulted in several 8-bit character sets being established. EBCDIC (*Extended Binary Coded Decimal Interchange Code*) was first used by **IBM** in its System/360 computers. Several

18

other 8-bit character sets were once in use. Other computer manufacturers out-voted IBM in U.S. standards committees, however, and ASCII (*American Standard Code for Information Interchange*) became a standard. Table 2.1 shows the hex 7-bit representation of 128 characters for the symbols represented by these codes. These 128 characters are number codes for characters and for orders to perform actions like carriage return or line feed. The first 32 of these are action orders. For example, hex representation 0d corresponds to cr or return, and 07 to bel or ring the bell (if there is one). The remaining 96 characters represent the upper- and lowercase letters, the numbers from 0 through 9, and punctuation. Table 2.2 presents a complete ASCII table. The ASCII characters corresponding to decimal 037 to decimal 127 is the *normal* English or American characters. The symbols above 127 represent the extended ASCII character set. These represent a variety of occasionally useful symbols, such as symbols for line drawings, greek characters, and a variety of European accented characters and mathematics symbols. Many printers are not capable of printing other than the standard USA alphabet of symbols from 037 to 127.

The ASCII table uses only half, or 128, of the 256 characters made possible by 8 bits or 2 hexidecimal numbers. As we have noted, the other bit can be used as desired. It is used in multiple ways. In the popular word-processing system Wordstar it is used to send microjustification commands to printers. This will make typed copy look *somewhat* like professional typesetting for those printers that could accomplish the adjustment of space between characters. This micro-

TABLE 2.1 ASCII and EBCDIC 8-Bit Codes.[a]

EBCDIC CODES[b]

4567	00	01	10	11	00	01	10	11	00	01	10	11	00	01	10	11
0000	NUL	DLE	DS		SP	8	−									0
0001	SOH	DC1	SOS				/		a	j			A	J		1
0010	STX	DC2	FS	SYN					b	k	s		B	K	S	2
0011	ETX	DC3							c	l	t		C	L	T	3
0100	PF	RES	BYP	PN					d	m	u		D	M	U	4
0101	HT	NL	LF	RS					e	n	v		E	N	V	5
0110	LC	BS	EOB	UC					f	o	w		F	O	W	6
0111	DEL	IL	PRE	EOT					g	p	x		G	P	X	7
1000		CAN							h	q	y		H	Q	Y	8
1001		EM							i	r	z		I	R	Z	9
1010	SMM	CC	SM		c	l		:								
1011	VT				.	$	,	#								
1100	FF	IFS		DC4	<	×	%	@								
1101	CR	IGS	ENQ	NAK	(	)	−	'								
1110	SO	IRS	ACK		+	;	>	=								
1111	SI	IUS	BEL	SUB	!	−	?	"								

TABLE 2.1   ASCII and EBCDIC 8-Bit Codes.[a] **(Continued)**

ASCII CODES[c]

b7	b6	b5	b4	b3	b2	b1	COLUMN → ROW ↓	0 000	1 001	2 010	3 011	4 100	5 101	6 110	7 111
			0	0	0	0	0	NUL	DLE	SP	0	@	P	`	p
			0	0	0	1	1	SOH	DC1	!	1	A	Q	a	q
			0	0	1	0	2	STX	DC2	"	2	B	R	b	r
			0	0	1	1	3	ETX	DC3	#	3	C	S	c	s
			0	1	0	0	4	EOT	DC4	$	4	D	T	d	t
			0	1	0	1	5	ENQ	NAK	%	5	E	U	e	u
			0	1	1	0	6	ACK	SYN	&	6	F	V	f	v
			0	1	1	1	7	BEL	ETB	'	7	G	W	g	w
			0	0	0	0	8	BS	CAN	(	8	H	X	h	x
			1	0	0	1	9	HT	EM	)	9	I	Y	i	y
			1	0	1	0	10	LF	SUB	*	:	J	Z	j	z
			1	0	1	1	11	VT	ESC	+	;	K	[	k	{
			1	1	0	0	12	FF	FS	,	<	L	\	l	|
			1	1	0	1	13	CR	GS	–	=	M	]	m	}
			1	1	1	0	14	SO	RS	.	>	N	^	n	~
			1	1	1	1	15	SI	US	/	?	O	_	o	DEL

NUL	Null, or all zeroes	DC1	Device control 1
SOH	Start of heading	DC2	Device control 2
STX	Start of Text	DC3	Device Control 3
ETX	End of Text	DC4	Device Control 4
EOT	End of Transmission	NAK	Negative Acknowledge
ENQ	Enquiry	SYN	Synchronous idle
ACK	Acknowledge	ETB	End of transmission block
BEL	Bell, or alarm	CAN	Cancel
BS	Backspace	EM	End of medium
HT	Horizontal tabulation	SUB	Substitute
LF	Line feed	ESC	Escape
VT	Vertical tabulation	FS	File Seperator
FF	Form feed	GS	Group Seperator
CR	Carrige return	RS	Record Seperator
SO	Shift out	US	Unit Seperator
SI	Shift in	SP	Space
DLE	Data link escape	DEL	Delete

[a]Note differences in layout and in control codes between EBCDIC and ASCII.
[b]Most significant bit termed bit 0.
[c]Recommended USA Standard Code for Information Interchange (USAASCII) X3.4 - 1967. © 1967 USA Standards Institute. Reprinted by permission. Most-significant bit is termed bit 7.

justification allows fixed-pitch type to look somewhat as if it were proportionally spaced.

The use of eight bits for an alphanumeric symbol suggests very strongly the use of *multiples* of 8 bits for ease of access of stored information. Computers are distinguished by their *word length,* among other features. This word length is usually defined as *the number of bits which are accessed in parallel in a single operation from the computer's internal memory.* Thus a computer with an 8-bit

TABLE 2.2   ASCII Table

Dec	Hex	Code	Symbol
000	00	nul	
001	01	soh	•
002	02	stx	•
003	03	etx	•
004	04	eot	◆
005	05	enq	•
006	06	ack	•
007	07	bel	•
008	08	bs	•
009	09	ht	○
010	0A	nl	•
011	0B	vt	•
012	0C	np	•
013	0D	cr	•
014	0E	so	•
015	0F	si	•
016	10	dle	▶
017	11	dcl	◀
018	12	dc	↕
019	13	dc3	‼
020	14	dc4	¶
021	15	nak	§
022	16	syn	•
023	17	etb	•
024	18	can	↑
025	19	em	↓
026	1A	sub	→
027	1B	esc	←
028	1C	fs	•
029	1D	gs	↔
030	1E	rs	▲
031	1F	us	•
032	20	sp	
033	21	!	!
034	22	"	"
035	23	#	#
036	24	$	↑
037	25	%	%
038	26	&	&
039	27	'	'
040	28	(	(
041	29	)	)
042	2A	*	*
043	2B	+	+
044	2C	'	'
045	2D	–	–

TABLE 2.2   ASCII Table (Continued)

Dec	Hex	Code	Symbol
046	2E	.	.
047	2F	/	/
048	30	0	0
049	31	1	1
050	32	2	2
051	33	3	3
052	34	4	4
053	35	5	5
054	36	6	6
055	37	7	7
056	38	8	8
057	39	9	9
058	3A	:	:
059	3B	;	;
060	3C	<	<
061	3D	=	=
062	3E	>	>
063	3F	?	?
064	40	@	@
065	41	A	A
066	42	B	B
067	43	C	C
068	44	D	D
069	45	E	E
070	46	F	F
071	47	G	G
072	48	H	H
073	49	I	I
074	50	J	J
075	51	K	K
076	4C	L	L
077	4D	M	M
078	4E	N	N
079	4F	O	O
080	50	P	P
081	51	Q	Q
082	52	R	R
083	53	S	S
084	54	T	T
085	55	U	U
086	56	V	V
087	57	W	W
088	58	X	X
089	59	Y	Y
090	5A	Z	Z
091	5B	[	[

TABLE 2.2   ASCII Table (Continued)

Dec	Hex	Code	Symbol
092	5C	&	&
093	5D	]	]
094	5E	^	^
095	5F	–	–
096	60	`	`
097	61	a	a
098	62	b	b
099	63	c	c
100	64	d	d
101	65	e	e
102	66	f	f
103	67	g	g
104	68	h	h
105	69	i	i
106	6A	j	j
107	6B	k	k
108	6C	l	l
109	6D	m	m
110	6E	n	n
111	6F	o	o
112	70	p	p
113	71	q	q
114	72	r	r
115	73	s	s
116	74	t	t
117	75	u	u
118	76	v	v
119	77	w	w
120	78	x	x
121	79	y	y
122	7A	z	z
123	7B	{	{
124	7C	|	|
125	7D	}	}
126	7E	~	~
127	7F	del	1

word length extracts 8 bits in parallel from memory. One with a 16-bit word length extracts 16 bits in parallel from memory. Some of the largest scientific computers have 64-bit word lengths. One advantage of a large word length computer is speed. The more bits in parallel, for a given memory cycle time, the greater the rate at which data (or program instructions) may be accessed. Of course, for an operation like word processing, there is little need for more than 8 bits.

As we have noted, word length is customarily defined in terms of the number of bits of each parallel memory access. Some computers, of which the original IBM is an example, "fetch" data from memory at one level of parallelism (16 bits for the PC). This was a very natural architecture to adopt as the 16-bit microprocessor. The original IBM-PC was a transition machine from the 8-bit PC world that existed up to that time. The faster IBM-PC/AT is fully compatible with programs written for the original PC, but fetches or stores 16 bits per memory access. The IBM System/370 and later mainframe computers intended for large businesses or offices are 32-bit word machines, but may bring *64 or more* bits from the computer memory in each fetch operation. Large-size words are now appearing in microcomputers. The generation of 80386 machines use 32-bit words.

2.2 BCD: DECIMAL NUMBERS IN A BINARY MACHINE

A special, but important, use of computers is for the processing of information about decimal numbers, such as financial currency. Decimal quantities are common (dollars and cents), but sums and differences are always carried to exactly two decimal places. Unless one is very careful, use of a nondecimal machine may result in strange round-off errors. Since binary arithmetic does not fit this round-off requirement the way decimal arithmetic does, there are reasons to use a special coding for this kind of calculation. This coding is called *binary coded decimal* (BCD), and the relationship between BCD and decimal digits is shown in Figure 2.1.

The natural occurrence of binary arithmetic comes about because computers are constructed of special electronic circuits that can operate stably and reliably

BINARY DIGIT	DECIMAL DIGIT
0000	0
0001	1
0010	2
0011	3
0100	4
0101	5
0110	6
0111	7
1000	8
1001	9

FIGURE   2.1 Binary-coded   decimal (BCD). (1011 —> 1111 sometimes symbolizes sign or decimal point.)

(1010 —→ 1111 sometimes symbolizes sign or decimal point)

in only two *states*. A circuit's output voltage may be "high," just below the DC power supply voltage, or "low," just above the ground level of the power supply voltage. This favors the use of binary number systems, and binary *representation* of nonnumerical symbols for use in computers. Computers generally represent each decimal digit in a number by a 4-bit BCD internal representation that allows decimal numbers of virtually any length to be handled. Since only 10 of the 16 (2^4) possible 4-bit values are needed to represent 0–9, the other 6 can be used to represent a decimal point, the sign of the number, and other "markers."

With BCD representation of numbers, computers must do arithmetic in *serial* fashion: digit by digit. They usually "pack" two BCD digits per (8-bit) byte in order to provide compact storage. The essential advantage of BCD is that the representation is accurate "to the penny" in such operations as addition, or in other operations that involve amounts in the billions (of dollars or yen).

Computers that store real numbers in a *floating point* representation must necessarily round-off to some particular number of digits. This number depends, of course, on how many bits are used to represent the number. In business *accounting* calculations, the BCD scheme must be used to avoid this round-off problem. This usually poses no performance problem, since most business calculations are relatively simple. For large scientific or engineering calculations, "scientific" computers use floating point numbers to add all of the bits of two binary numbers in *parallel*. This is inherently a faster process than could be achieved with BCD arithmetic.

The elementary BCD addition process is illustrated below for BCD digits. There is a potential need for special precautions to insure a proper carry. The number that follows a nine (1001) should be a zero (0000), and this is obtained by adding a six (0110). Then the next occurrence of a one, or higher number, will produce the correct result and also yield a carry. These "decimal correction" steps following addition are frequently carried out in hardware.

```
Decimal    BCD
────────────────
   9       1001
  +4       0100
────────────────
  13       1101    If result nine (1001),
                   then add six

           ──────
           10011   To get correct BCD digit
                   plus carry
```

2.3   COMPUTER MEMORY ADDRESSING

Data and programs must be stored in a computer memory through use of some scheme whereby they can later be fetched for use by, or as, a program. The most widely used scheme is that of establishing a *numeric memory address* for each word or, in some systems such as the IBM PC, each 8-bit *byte* of memory. This numbering scheme is, with some variations, universal in modern computers. If the data word or a program instruction[1] in the computer's memory at a specific address is needed by a program, the program specifies that specific address, which is then forwarded to the memory. Circuits in the memory next *translate* the numerical address into a physical location in the storage circuits. This enables the computer to find the data stored at that physical location and return it to the processor. All of this typically occurs in a fraction of a *millionth* of a second (10^{-6} sec $= 1$ μsec).

If a computer memory contains a very large number of words, so that the computer can have access to large programs or large arrays of data, the number of memory addresses must be correspondingly large. To address only 1024 ($= 2^{10}$) words of memory requires a numerical address of 10 bits. To address $(1024) \times (1024)$ words requires 20 bits. Here is where the value of a *large computer word length* becomes apparent. If the computer word length is 24 bits, $16 \times (1024)^2$ words may be accessed directly by an address whose length is equal to the word length, since $16 \times (1024)^2 = 2^4 \times 2^{20} = 2^{24}$.

It is common usage to find terms such as "640K of memory" or "40 kilobytes of memory." In most science and occasionally elsewhere, K refers to the prefix kilo-, a factor of one thousand. For computers, the prefix *kilo-* prefers to a multiplier of 1024, which is very close to 1000, but is an *exact power* of 2, as $1024 = 2^{10}$. When individuals refer to "640K of memory," they are mixing several number systems. The 640 means a *decimal* six hundred forty. The K refers to 1024. The units, if not specified, are normally *bytes,* or sets of *8 bits.* Likewise, *megabyte* refers to a factor 1024^2, not one million, as in most of science. A *quarter megabyte* would, accordingly, refer to 256 kilobytes.

Computers vary widely in the direct and indirect ways that they address memory, as we shall see in a later chapter. Processing a sequence of instructions of a program, a paragraph of text, or the elements of a pictorial image will generally involve repeated memory access to successively incremented addresses. A convenient description of computer memory locations is by the numbered *pigeonholes* or addresses in which numbers are stored. A given piece of information may extend over a large number of memory addresses. The *modularity* of memory, which must consist of a finite number of bits per address location, permits a wide variety of types of data to be stored in a fixed-memory structure.

The opening of Lincoln's Gettysburg address, as it might be stored in a computer's memory beginning at memory location 103 (hexadecimal), is shown below:

103	104	105	106	107	108	109	10A	10B
Four	sco	re a	nd s	even	yea	rs a	go,	our

---

[1] In Chapter 3 we will discuss the storage of data and instructions together in memory. This idea is fundamental to computing and is due to von Neumann, after whom the principle is named.

Memory locations in this case each hold 32 bits, or four characters, of information. The actual storage is binary, of course.

2.4   THE PUSH-DOWN STACK

In most cases the most convenient form of memory access is through numbered addresses. Some information, however, is characteristically stored and reused in a particular order which lends itself to a storage method which is, in some ways, simpler than that just described. The so-called *push-down* stack can be envisioned as similar to saucer storage in a restaurant. Each saucer placed in a well in the counter causes a spring to depress further, so that many saucers can be stored and the top one is always at counter height.

A push-down stack, when receiving a word of data, stores the data (pushes it). When data is needed from the stack, the most recently *pushed* data is *popped*, and returned, after which the next previously pushed information may be popped. Another term for such a stack is last-in, first-out (LIFO). The importance of stack organization in storage and access from computers will become clearer in a later chapter, when we show that the successive addresses needed to call and to return from subroutines can be ideally manipulated by a LIFO stack.

A simple analogy is Hansel and Gretel, who dropped bread in their path through the woods and followed the marked path on the way home; bread-eating birds did them in when they tried it again! In our computer the losing track of our reference pointers to the stack has the same effect.

2.5   STORAGE OF PICTORIAL INFORMATION

Information which represents imagery must be subdivided for computer storage. A typical method for two-dimensional images is to divide the image into a Cartesian array of small areas that are usually square in shape. These are referred to as *pixels* (for *picture elements*). Each pixel is assigned a value, which may be a compound value to represent different intensities. For example, if the picture is in color, three different sets of bits may describe the intensity of red, blue, and green as averaged over the area of the pixel. These three sets of bits may be grouped into a single group and stored in successive addresses in computer memory. This would generally be done in the same order in which the pixels are displayed in an image created from the pixel data in a conventional television *raster*. Alternatively, the data representing red may be stored as one array of data in memory and that for green and blue as other arrays.

Picture information may require very large amounts of storage, often 64 kilobytes or more. The amount of storage depends on the *number of pixels* into which the picture is separated and the *number of bits required to represent each pixel*. Clearly, the number of bits required to represent a pixel might be anything from *one,* if a binary (black and white) image is required, to 32 or more, if each of three colors is to be represented by a large number of different intensity levels. Generally, providing 256 different intensity levels (8 bits for monochrome, or for each color) is sufficient to portray real-life images such that the human eye cannot distinguish boundaries between different levels of shading.

If we want to generate a picture with the typical amount of detail (level of resolution) characteristic of standard U.S. television pictures, we would need to break the displayed image into approximately 263×350 pixels. With one byte (8 bits) per pixel to produce a monochrome image, we would require $263 \times 350 \times 8 = 73,640$ bytes of memory—about 74 kilobytes—to store this image.

If this appears to be a great deal of memory, remember that a consumer TV image will not display more than perhaps 16 lines of 40-character readable alphabetic text. If alphabetic information (i.e. text) is stored in coded (ASCII) form, at 1 byte per character, the same information can be stored in only 640 bytes! Storing the character code rather than the shape of the letter is $73,640/640 = 115$ times more efficient.

Computer graphics efforts involve using a computer to produce visual images on a display. The term "computer graphics" often refers to the ability to define, store, and display arrays of pixels. In every case, the number of pixels available is limited not only by the software, which manipulates the stored images, but also by the videographics hardware, which actually generates the display images.

A television picture is actually comprised of 525 *lines,* each of which can distinguish about 350 values. Since it is as high as it is wide, a TV pixel is somewhat wider (1/350 of screen width) than it is high (1/525 height), that is, its physical width to height ratio is $2:1$. For practical purposes, the pixel might best be considered to raster lines high, in which case it is square in shape.

The most common cathode-ray tube displays used as computer displays, as on PCs, will typically display 25 lines of 80 easily readable characters each, for a total of 2000 characters. These are not stored as a group of pixels. Rather, the display is produced using a special *character generator* chip. This chip can read the 7-bit characters which are input for each character output that is to be displayed. The extremely high frequencies (several times higher than in a standard TV picture) in the dots that form each character only need to be transmitted from the *character generator* chip to the display. The display is limited to images which can be expressed as a binary dot pattern in an array typically 7 dots (pixels) wide and 9 pixels high. Thus, if the character patterns include segments of horizontal and vertical lines, these character-generating displays can produce simple line drawings limited to vertical and horizontal lines. This simple form of graphics should not be confused with true computer graphics, in which each pixel can be *separately* defined.

When the IBM-PC is in the character mode and 2000 characters are to be placed on the screen, each screen position is separately addressable as a memory location. This is called a *memory-mapped* display. Actually, 4000 bytes of storage are used for this purpose: one byte of each position for the character ASCII code, and the other for an *attribute* byte which controls color, intensity, blinking, and so on. (In Chapter 5 we will move the character codes of letters into the screen memory positions to form messages.)

This does not in any way complete the list of possibilities for image storage and display. If an array of individual pixels is stored in the computer and displayed as a beautiful scene or drawing, we may be limited in our ability to *manipulate* the image. For example, in some cases we might wish to change the size, shape, or color of an object depicted as part of the image. This is a common need when using computer graphics to design artwork and in engineering design of machinery. If this is a necessity, the data for the image must generally be stored in the computer in a form other than pixel intensity values.

Each line of a line drawing, or the pixels representing each of a number of *objects* depicted in the image, may be stored using a description that allows it to be easily changed. For example, a circle might be stored as a set of data words which identify its *center* (in display-screen coordinates), its *radius,* and its color or the nature of its outline (solid line, dotted line, etc.). Each time the circle must be moved or altered in shape or color, the new display must be *computed.* This is a lot more easily accomplished, however, using object representations, than a location map for thousands of pixels. This is how the ubiquitous video-arcade games are displayed. As an object in the picture, say "an attacking space ship," is intended to move, its present image is erased from the "pixel map" which is displayed, a new image location is calculated, and the pixels forming the object are written into new locations. In this type of simple display, the *background* pixels uncovered by the movement of the object must then be restored to complete the effect. More advanced storage schemes used to represent moving objects in a computer display may employ a portion of memory to represent the pixels of an (unchanging) background, while images of moving objects are in another memory area which can take precedence and *overlay* the background. As in most computer tradeoffs for speed or programming convenience, there is a penalty: in this case, additional memory is necessary to avoid the need to recompute background information.

It should be clear that image information, when used in a computer, will be stored in a form which depends strongly on the objectives of the display: monochrome or color, line drawing or fill-in regions, binary (black-white only) or near-continuous intensity scale, a fixed and limited set of colors or a wide range of color values, static images or images which must change as in a motion picture. Computer graphics is an important subfield of computer application which will become increasingly more valuable because of the ease with which humans can understand complex concepts in pictorial form.

2.6 SUMMARY

We have provided an introduction to how words and symbols can be represented as numbers. Essentially all of this chapter applies to any digital computer system as well as the PC.

PROBLEMS

2.1 Two BCD digits are packed into each of two 8-bit storage locations. Each half-byte may have the values 0000 through 1001 (zero through nine decimal). If the two bytes are added by normal binary addition, describe the conditions and the steps which must be taken in a following operation to adjust all 8 bits to indicate the correct BCD sum. (NOTE: adders intended for BCD operations will note if a carry occurred in adding the four right-most bits, as well as normal carry from the 8-bit result.)

2.2 What is the *highest* address value (in hexadecimal notation) of a computer whose memory contains 64k bytes? 640 kbytes? (Observe that the lowest address is zero, hence the highest address will be *one less than* the memory length.)

2.3 Using an analogy of an automobile trip in which a series of proper turns at intersections must be made, show how one might make a series of notes to oneself and put them on a *stack* of notes, so that on return the directions for proper turns at each intersection would be in the proper order.

2.4 A graphic computer image is made up from an array of 400 × 600 pixels, each pixel having red, green, and blue intensity components, each component being defined by 4 bits.

(a) How much memory, in kilobytes, is required to store the pixel image?

(b) How many different *color combinations* can theoretically be produced, and for each color, in how many different intensities? (Watch out for this one!)

(c) If a computer requires execution of five instructions, each requiring 1 μsec (10^{-6} sec) to display *one pixel,* how much time may it require to display *the entire image?*

2.5 If the character generator for an alphanumeric display can use only 5 (wide) × 7 (high) pixels for a single character, using graph paper lay out the dot patterns which it might use for the upper- and lowercase letters A, B, C, D, E, and F.

3

HISTORY: THE EVOLUTION
OF THE COMPUTER

3.0 INTRODUCTION

In Chapters 1 and 2, we provided a very brief glimpse of the sort of detailed activity which is carried out in making simple arithmetic manipulations on data that has been stored, in the form of binary numbers, in a digital computer. Merely understanding that these operations were possible using digital or switching circuits was an early step in the evolution of the *digital computer*. In this chapter we review some important historical events that surround, and have determined perspectives for, the modern-stored program digital computer. Figure 3.1 provides graphic insight into the rapid development of the modern stored program digital computer, beginning with the first true stored program device and continuing to parallel architecture in common use today.

3.1 EARLY HISTORY—THE "VON NEUMANN" MACHINE

Before World War II, simple digital electronic circuits had begun to exist. In large part, these were due to efforts at Bell Telephone Laboratories that initially involved switching circuits for telephone exchanges. During World War II, a high priority was placed on the development of *computing engines*. It was then realized that certain key military needs, most particularly improved artillery-based ballistics computations, were strategically dependent upon the availability of high-speed computational capabilities.

During that war several major computing devices were designed and built for artillery problem solving. The usual approach was based on organizing large

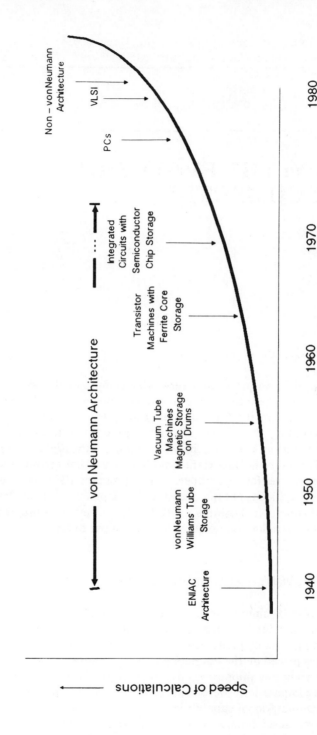

FIGURE 3.1 Computer technology growth in speed of correction.

numbers of electromagnetic relays in order to open and close sets of contacts and thereby to implement binary logic and arithmetic functions. The relays closed or opened a set of contacts when current was applied to their coils. A schematic of a primitive, normally closed relay is shown in Figure 3.2.

The fundamental binary logic functions were, therefore, easy to implement. Two relays with normally open contacts connected *in series* would form an **AND** circuit, if we define a "zero" as corresponding to an open circuit and a "one" to a closed circuit or contact. This is the case, since both relay coils would need to be energized in order to close the series circuit. Likewise, two relays with normally open contacts *in parallel* formed an **OR** circuit, as shown in Figure 3.3. The **NOT,** or *inversion* function, needed in binary arithmetic and logic is formed by using a relay with a pair of contacts that are normally closed. One side of the relay contact is connected to a supply of voltage. The output at the other side represents the inverse of the signal which supplies current to the relay's coil. We see that a potential difficulty with this relay arrangement is that the contacts need to be able to carry the full amount of current necessary to energize the relay. If we do not allow for this, we must maintain the sort of logical separation between input and output that makes interconnection and cascading of logic arrangements very difficult. We will return to the binary logic operators in Chapter 5.

As we have noted, relay schemes for binary logic derived from early telephone network-switching efforts at Bell Telephone Laboratories in the 1940s and 1950s. At that time, IBM primarily manufactured punched-card-handling

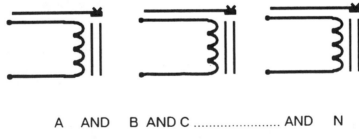

A   AND   B AND C .... AND   N

FIGURE 3.2   Schematic of a closed relay.

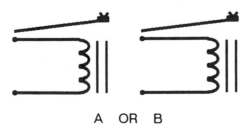

A   OR   B

FIGURE 3.3   Schematic of an open relay.

equipment. To support this equipment, for business data processing purposes, they constructed a massive relay-based calculator that had been initially designed at Harvard University. This relay calculator was far faster than the human-operated mechanical calculators of the day, and it could perform a lengthy sequence of operations. Typically, these machines were programmed through use of punched paper tape, like that of a player piano or the door key of certain hotel rooms, or by plugging a set of wire connectors into a patch panel. Each relay operated within about 1/20 of a second after current was initially applied. This represented a very slow operation indeed, compared to what we now associate with computer operation. For a fascinating and detailed account of these historical developments, the reader is referred to Keister et al. (1951) and Caldwell (1958). It is very interesting to note here that textbooks dated in the latter half of the 1950s are now historical!

Most of these early digital computing machines were operated *asynchronously*. That is, when an operation was completed by one set of relays, the closing (or opening) of a final relay caused the sequencer to advance in order to begin the next computation. It was believed at the time that this would always be the most efficient way to operate a computing engine since there was no wasted time. This belief was doubtlessly correct in that relay based digital computers were best operated in an asynchronous mode. With the arrival on the scene of much more complex, and much faster, all-electronic computing machines, most operations began to be carried out *synchronously*. In these computers, and all modern ones, computer operations are timed by a clock, which serves much the same purpose as a band-master keeping time with a baton. In a relay based system, there is no need at all for a clock and, consequently, no need for synchronous operation. In Figure 3.4 we show some comparative differences between a series of synchronous and asynchronous events.

The electron vacuum tube was known to be able to turn electrical current flow on or off in a time period of only about one *microsecond*. This was approximately 50,000 times faster than that obtainable with relays. Consequently, there was great interest in the development of digital computers or circuits in which as many operations as possible were carried out using vacuum tubes rather than relays.

John von Neumann,[1] an applied mathematician, is generally credited with defining the basic structure used for almost all present-day computers. This first appeared in a classified memorandum written during World War II. Perhaps von Neumann's greatest contribution to digital computer architecture and design was to suggest that *programs* which controlled the sequences of computer operations, along with the *data* being manipulated, should *both* be kept in a *single* set of numerically addressable registers that comprised the computer's *memory*. This was a great departure from the tradition that existed at the time in which data would be either stored on tape or cards or in a wire program board.

---

[1]Pronounced von noy'-man.

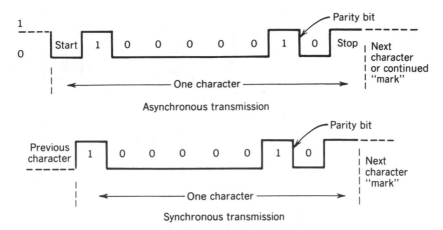

FIGURE 3.4 Asynchronous and synchronous transmission of the ASCII "A" character. In asynchronous transmission there is a start and stop at the end of one and the start of the next character, even if the next character follows immediately, while in synchronous transmission, three is no start–stop.

He proposed that the other elements needed to form a complete digital computer were:

1. An *arithmetic (and logic) unit* capable of performing the actual numerical or logical operations on the data;
2. A *control unit*, whose function is to interpret the stored commands (now called instructions) and thereby control the operations of the arithmetic and logic unit;
3. An *input unit*, whereby data (and programs) could be introduced from the outside world;
4. An *output unit*, which would transmit the results computed and stored in the memory to the computer's user; and
5. A *timing unit* or *clock*, which controls the rate at which the operations of the computer are sequenced.

This simple structure is shown in the block diagram of Figure 3.5.

3.2 EARLY COMPUTING MACHINES

The first computing machine that was constructed using most of von Neumann's concepts was built at the University of Pennsylvania. It was completed near the end of World War II and called *ENIAC*, which stands for Electronic Numerical Integrator and Calculator. In its earliest form, programs were stored in a mem-

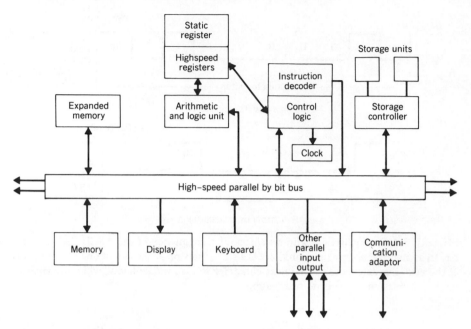

FIGURE 3.5   Elements of a typical digital computer.

ory that consisted of fixed memory—banks of 10-position hand-operated switches, and in accumulators. These accumulators were equivalent to electronic file cabinets, which could store a 10-place decimal number as well as add or subtract another number.

Initially, programs were set up using a set of connecting cables that linked together in an appropriate way, as called for by stored programs, the many semi-independent units that comprised the computing machine. Later, programs were set up in hand-switched memory banks.

Another great contribution made by von Neumann was the concept of program *branching*. This concept led to the ability of the stored-program computer to alter its sequence of operations *in response to the result of a previous operation on data*. This logic capability is taken for granted today. At the time, however, it was a great conceptual leap forward.

von Neumann also realized the important notion, which the ENIAC had implemented from the start, that the input and output mechanisms did not have to operate at as fast a speed as the all-electronic control, arithmetic, and memory units.

For the most part, modern computers still use the basic architectural forms proposed by von Neumann. This von Neumann architecture comprises:

- memory,
- control,

- arithmetic/logic unit (ALU),
- clock, and
- input and output units.[2]

Figure 3.6 presents a simple illustration of this von Neumann architecture.

Through most of the 1950s, electron tubes formed the high-speed binary logic and adder units then found in computers. These gave way to *transistors,* and later to *complexes* of transistors which were called *integrated circuits.* Integrated circuits are constructed as a monolithic unit on the surface of a single thin, flat rectangle of silicon. They are, typically, a small fraction of an inch on a side. An integrated circuit may contain the detail workings of thousands, or hundreds of thousands, of discrete components. A modern PC uses a single integrated circuit which forms its central processing unit (CPU), and integrated circuits which comprise its memory. In the case of the PC, the presently available memory units are capable of storing 2546K *bits* of data. Larger memory units are in early stages of realization. The PC of today is clearly a direct derivative of von Neumann's initial architectural concepts.

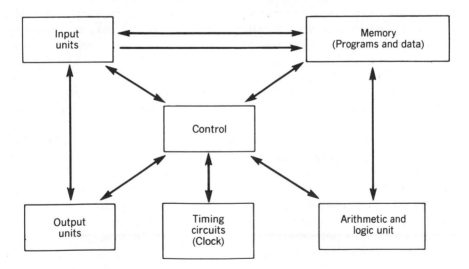

FIGURE 3.6   Elements of the "von Neumann" computer architecture.

---

[2]The combination of control and ALU, and those parts of the input output circuits which operate in conjunction with the high-speed computer operations, is usually referred to as the Central Processing Unit or CPU. This includes everything in the von Neumann model except memory and the actual input and output devices or subsystems.

3.3 MEMORY

Contemporary needs require the solution of very complex problems in a variety of application areas. As programs and data have grown in volume and complexity, the amount of data and instructions which need to be stored in the computer's memory has greatly increased. In 1952 von Neumann's own first computer was then at the Princeton-based Institute for Advanced Studies. Now it is housed at the Smithsonian Institution. The memory consisted of only 1024 words, with each word containing 32 bits. This would today be referred to as 4 *kilobytes* of random access memory. Present-day large computers may typically contain 16 *megabytes* (4000 times greater) or more of random access memory. Contemporary PCs may contain this amount, generally in the form of expanded memory. The early von Neumann computer used a set of 32 cathode-ray tubes for its memory. These stored data in the form of electrons that adhered to 1024 small areas on the inner surface or face of the tubes in what is called a "Williams tube" memory. Today, a 256-K ram chip is about the size of a conventional stick of chewing gum.

Memory technology first evolved from an early bulky form to the form of small doughnut-shaped "cores" of magnetic ferrite material whose magnetization could be reversed from one circular direction around the core to the other. Core memory technology was prevalent in computers until about 1970. At that point in time, semiconductor integrated circuits became economical. Even into the 1970s, computer users might often refer to a main memory as containing "256 kilobytes of core." Once semiconductors took over the memory role, the numbers of bits storable on a single chip grew from 128 bits in the early 1970s to 1 megabyte in the mid-1980s and continues to increase today. This reduction in memory cost has allowed and is the primary reason, to a large degree, why the overall cost as well as physical size and electrical power consumption of computers to shrink dramatically over the years.

The growth of the *size* of memory, generally expressed in bits, has also led to specialization in memory functions. The earliest computers contained a set of *registers* in their CPUs. These were individual memory units, with each usually capable of containing a *single computer word*. Some of these registers might be used by the program to hold the intermediate results of data manipulation without the need to store them in active memory. Usually, these memory registers are only accessible to a programmer who is writing code in its most primitive or "machine language" form. Unlike addresses in the main memory, these registers are not numbered. They are usually given symbolic identifiers: the A register, B register, and so on. Registers like these, which may be used by the program for any temporary storage purpose, are usually called *general purpose registers*. A schematic layout of the registers within the processor of the most common PC will be shown in Chapter 4 after a more detailed discussion of this topic.

Some of the memory registers may be assigned special functions. The register that has been assigned the most important function is referred to as the *program counter,* or sometimes as the *instruction pointer,* to describe the function performed. This register has the key role of containing the main-memory address of the *next instruction* is to be executed by the computer. Normally, at the completion of one instruction by the computer, the instruction pointer register is automatically incremented *in sequence* to the address of the next instruction. Occasionally, the program must branch or jump out of sequence to an instruction that will place the address of the first instruction of the new sequence to be followed in the instruction point register. The instruction pointer indicates to the control unit where to obtain the next instruction. The jump will occur naturally when the control unit seeks the next instruction. This sort of operation is called an *absolute go-to.* It is doubtlessly unavoidable at the level of machine language programming. Generally, it is regarded as something to be avoided in higher level programming language use, as we will indicate in Chapter 10 and elsewhere.

One of von Neumann's many contributions was to observe that instructions and data could be intermixed in memory. To do this, there must exist an instruction pointer which keeps track of the place where the next instruction to be executed is stored.

3.4   THE STACK

A register called a *stack pointer* will be found in many modern computers. A stack is a set of memory locations which are accessed in a particular manner. When we *push* a word of data onto a *stack,* it is stored in a particular memory location. This storage location is the location at the top of the stack. The address of that location is kept in the stack pointer. Similarly when we pop data out of the stack, we fetch the data pointed to by the stack pointer.

To keep order in the process, we might *decrement* the stack pointer *before* storing the pushed word; and then *increment* it *after* fetching the popped word. Any other consistent and reasonably efficient scheme would also work. It is reasonable to ask, "What if the pushing were to continue until the stack extended below the lowest address in memory that has been set aside for stack storage?" An answer is that, in most computers, the programmer is responsible for making certain that enough memory locations are set aside for pushed data at addresses below the initial value of the stack pointer. If this precaution is not taken, other data or program information may be overwritten.[3]

---

[3]The popular Hewlett-Packard digital hand-held calculators use a stack which is used to hold in its two "nearest" locations the values to be combined in addition, subtraction, multiplication, or division. Many of these calculators have only four stack locations for holding numbers, yet surprisingly large problems can be dealt with, without the need to reenter intermediate results.

3.5 MAIN MEMORY

We have already referred to the large storage area that is usually known as main memory. It is distinguished from the registers through the presence of numeric addresses that are used to store and fetch information. A computer user, or even a programmer using a typical high-level programming language such as Pascal or Fortran, will generally never need to deal with the actual physical memory addresses and their specific location in the computer. Many high-level programming languages do, however, provide some way to store or fetch data from these *absolute* addresses. To the computer itself, however, these numerical memory addresses are not distinguished in any way. Thus any address may be used to store a piece of data or a piece of an instruction. When used with modern operating systems that simplify a user's task of working with the computer, portions of memory may be set aside *by the operating system* for various functions. These may include the user's program, special program routines for passing data to or from input or output devices, and of course the operating system program itself. For the most part, this memory management activity is carried out without the user being aware of it. If insufficient memory remains for a large program or data, warnings may be given or the operating system may merely refuse to load the program.

The amount of memory available was usually small in early computers. The number of bits required to numerically address any word or byte in the memory was generally no greater than the length of the word that was used by the central processor. As a consequence, machines dealing with 16-bit words could easily access 2^{16} bytes (or 64 kilobytes) or words.[4] But if these 16-bit-word computers are to be able to address *more than* 64K bytes (or words), some way to deal with addresses more than 16 bits in length must be found.[5]

Designers have handled this problem in several different ways for various computers. The most straightforward approach is to allow addresses to be *more than one computer word* in length. By using a 32-bit address, it is then possible to address 232 bytes or 4 gigabytes of memory![6] Computer designers have shunned this apparently simple approach. Such an approach requires that all

---

[4]Some computers use memory addresses which count memory locations by byte (usually 8-bit chunks of storage), while others address only at a word-length level (16 bits, 32 bits, or more). In the former, if the memory hardware is designed to deliver data to the CPU only in two-byte or larger portions, and the program specifies a byte address which is not at a "word boundary," usually the memory will need to be accessed two times, since the word delivered will actually come from parts of two words in the actual memory hardware. This can slow down operations substantially, unless the system software is designed to minimize this wasteful operation.

[5]This problem is most apparent in computers using 8- or 16-bit words. When the computer word length reaches 32 bits, the amount of memory addressable is large enough to satisfy the memory size required for most modern applications.

[6]By the usual computer-world convention, if kilo means "times 1024" and mega means "times 1024 squared", then giga means "times 1024 cubed."

computer *instructions* that also contain a memory address must be an additional word in length.

Some computer designs have overcome the address-length limitation by switching the computer operation from one 64-kbyte bank of memory to another. The limitation of this approach is that a *program* in one bank cannot routinely deal with data in another bank. This is a limitation that cannot be overcome easily. The compromise taken in the IBM PC will be discussed in Chapter 4.

3.6 BUFFERS

The word *buffer* is often used, sometimes in the plural. The context generally suggests that it has something to do with computer memory or storage. The term buffer denotes a portion of the computer's memory that is being used as a *temporary storage location*. Buffer storage is often used for data which is being sent to or received from an external input or output device. As we will discuss in more detail later, many computers have circuitry which allows external devices to fetch or store information. This is accomplished by using the computer's main memory and what is called *direct memory access* (DMA). By placing a portion of the output data into a buffer, the main program can call upon the services of the operating system to affect an input or output transfer in a more efficient way than would otherwise be possible. We will return to DMA in our discussion of interrupts later in this chapter.

It is current practice to call *any* memory that is used for temporary storage a buffer. The principal need for such way stations for data entering or leaving the machine is the much faster operation of the fully *electronic* computer that is thereby made possible. The fast-response computer is made to see only a fast response buffer, as contrasted with the mechanically limited input and output equipment. When systems programs expect buffered data to be in fixed-size portions,[7] a part of memory may be set aside for buffer use. If three of these portions are allocated, a programmer might refer to three buffers as being available.

3.7 THE CPU: CONTROL AND ARITHMETIC FUNCTIONS

As we have noted before, the CPU of today is largely an evolution of the fundamental architectural structures proposed in 1945 by von Neumann. We now examine the elements that comprise this architecture, their connectivity, and the reasons they are present.

At the heart of most processors is an arithmetic and logic unit (ALU). This

---

[7]For example, the amount of data written to or read from a disk in a single operation, or 512 bytes in the case of the usual personal computers.

unit takes input from two registers and provides output to a third. Until recently, even in relatively large mainframe computers, there was only a single full-width ALU. There is, or was, a very good reason why this is the case. An adder for two 32-bit or larger binary numbers is a fairly complex circuit. Suppose that we used full adders to add such a long number and pass the carries from one stage to the next more significant bit. There would be a considerable delay since the carry might have to propagate from the least to the most significant bit. This is overcome by adding complexity to the carry circuits. (Try adding 0000 0001 to 1111 1111, for example!). A common scheme is to *precompute*, for each group of 4 or 8 bits, the carries that would be applied if the carry fed to the rightmost of those bits were a zero, and also if it were a one. Now the process of propagating carries can take place much faster. This is possible because the carry to be passed along to the next more significant group of bits can be determined almost immediately upon arrival of the carry from the next less significant group.

The various functions of an ALU will usually include logical as well as arithmetic combination of two binary numbers. If the Exclusive-OR[8] function is required, for example, it is only necessary to "turn off" the carry operation completely. Subtraction may be performed by complementing all of the bits in that one of the two registers feeding the ALU which is to be subtracted. Adding a carry at the least significant bit completes the operation of two's complementation, thereby making the number which actually enters the adder the negative of the one which was placed there from memory. The ALU then simply performs its usual addition operation. Half-adder operations are shown in Figure 3.7.

This same ALU is also used for *address calculations* in many machines. As we will see in the next chapter, the process used by the IBM-PC of segmenting memory requires addition to find the true address. In programs addressing arrays of numbers, the address of a desired number may be found by adding a base address containing the start of the *array* to an index address containing the location within the array. Where a processor has a large and fast ALU for its program computations, it makes sense to also use this for address computations. This is much more effective than, for example, using a slower address-computing circuit which would slow up program execution.

3.8 THE MICROPROGRAM

Another principal part of a modern computer is the control function. In many, if not most, modern processors this takes the form of a relatively simple control coupled to a *microprogram memory*.

A natural question is: "Why microprogram?" It should be clear that a number of operations, for example, multiplication and division, require many se-

---

[8]The EXCLUSIVE OR operator applied to corresponding bits of two words returns zero if the bits are the same, and one if they are different.

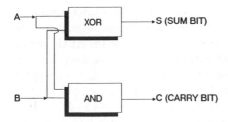

FIGURE 3.7 A half-adder. A half-adder combines two bits to form a sum bit and a sum bit and a carry bit. If AND and XOR gates are available, it can be implemented using only one of each.

quential operations that use the ALU. In early computers these sequences were carried out using arrays of logic circuits and a simple timer. Some modern computers use a primitive "program" called the *microprogram* to direct these sequences. Availability of high-speed memory for microprogram storage makes this operation feasible.

All *synchronous* computers employ a high-speed timer circuit which produces a series of precisely spaced pulses. There may be a *major clock cycle* of 1 μsec (or less), and within that time period, a fixed number of *minor clock cycles*. Each provides a series of pulses. The microprogram store to memory usually performs one fetch operation per minor clock cycle. A typical cycle length is 50–100 nsec (nano seconds or billionths of a second). An example of a typical timing sequence for phase-shift-keyed transmission is shown in Figure 3.8.

In executing a simple instruction, such as *adding* two numbers stored in main memory, the first microprogram step might be to determine the address for one of the two *operands* of the instruction, and the next to request that operand from memory. The following microprogram steps would establish the second address and request the second operand. An additional step would transfer the two num-

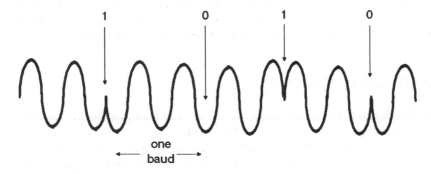

FIGURE 3.8 Time variations of a phase-shift-keyed transmission. Time variations of a phase-shift-keyed (PSK) transmission from one modem to another. At the end of each baud, the electrical phase of one tone may shift by 180 degrees or not at all (binary PSK). If the interpretation is that a shift represents a 1, no shift a 0, the signal is referred to as "differential PS" (this is the common method). Amplitude level may also be changed at the end of each baud, allowing additional bits to be signaled in a single baud-time.

bers, all bits in parallel, into the two registers feeding the ALU. After waiting, if necessary, for the ALU to finish propagating carries into its output register, the final step(s) would be involved with transferring the result from the ALUs output register to some register into which the instruction is supposed to pass the sum.

Microprogram-controlled computers use a wide variety of design concepts in the way they operate. Some, for example, have large numbers of bits in *each word* of the microprogram, which will usually contain only from 1 to 4K of these words. Many bits from the long microprogram word may simply be fed to gates which open to allow data to move from one internal register to another. Other bits will select the mode of the ALU (ADD, AND, etc.).

A chief advantage of the microprogram-control concept is that it allows the computer's operation to be altered. For example, it is possible to create a new microprogram which will allow a computer to *emulate* a computer of another design. The emulating computer is capable of responding to instructions written for the other computer. There are limitations to emulation however. The machine which is doing the emulating should have *enough registers* to represent all those of the machine being emulated. The word length of the machine doing the emulation should be at least as long (in bits) as that of the machine being emulated. And of course, the manipulations possible using the microprogram must include all those needed to manipulate data and addresses in the same way as the machine being emulated. The microprogram control concept also affords the computer designer the opportunity to debug or optimize the computer. By changing only the microprogram, it is possible to change the way it operates. Of course, if there is a logic error in the ALU, nothing can be done to overcome it using the microprogram!

The microprogram is generally invisible to the user of the machine. This person generally accepts the machine as it is, as defined by its microprogram. Only the machine's designers have access to the microprogram. For example, the instruction ADD may be used by programmers of an IBM-PC; the microcode which is set into the Intel 8088 chip to accomplish ADD is not adjustable, and can only be changed for the next chip design by the Intel engineers.

3.9   OTHER FEATURES

Another feature, found increasingly even on microcomputers but characteristic of only the largest scientific computers of 25 years ago, is *instruction look-ahead.* Since the instructions are executed in direct sequence of addresses in memory until a branch (or jump) instruction causes a change in the sequence, it is possible to save time by reading the next instruction (or several instructions) from memory, well ahead of their execution. This is done by providing registers which can contain one or more instructions. As instructions are needed, they are directed to the control unit. When a branch/jump instruction requires a shift to a new starting address for the next sequence of instructions, however, the look-ahead device must be informed (by the control) as to where to find the next instruction. In even more advanced computers, *both* the direct and jumped instruction sequences may be preloaded so that there is no delay, even if a program branches to an out-of-sequence instruction address. In simpler machines, the entire look-ahead may consist of fetching only one instruction in advance, and discarding it if a jump is made. Most modern computers have some sort of *memory controller*. This may consist of nothing but registers to contain the address and data for a store or fetch, or may be as complicated as the mechanism to manage a multilevel *virtual memory,* including a set of registers containing the addresses of the pages currently being stored in the high-speed level of the memory and mechanisms to keep track of usage of each page. A page will often not be *written to;* such as when the page contains a program or input data only, rather than output data. Then, if the page is no longer needed, it may be replaced without writing it back to the next level of memory.

An essential register (or set of registers) in any processor is the status register. This includes, for example, bits which signify whether the last instruction resulted in a negative result or produced a carry in the ALU. Other bits may indicate which of a number of users has control of the processor. Or these bits may indicate variable information which is used to control the flow of action by the computer.

3.10 INTERRUPTS

Most computers have a scheme which allows the processor to be *interrupted* upon completion of an instruction. This can be triggered by an input or output device signaling on a binary input wire. When an interrupt occurs, the processor usually:

1) saves the status register(s), and
2) fetches its next instruction from a special address or addresses that have been designated for interrupts.[9]

There is clearly an enigma if one interrupt is followed immediately by another. To cope with this, the interrupt-handling process usually includes *disablement* of additional interrupts. This disablement continues until the necessary housekeeping is taken care of, thereby ensuring orderly procedures.

The processor interrupt process is central to the connection of the processor to the "outside world," and is an important part of the input/output subsystem. If a keyboard is connected to the processor, each keystroke produces an interrupt. Devices such as disk drives usually interrupt the processor only when they have

---

[9]One such scheme relies on the input or output device to transmit to the processor the address to which the processor should jump. In other schemes, the processor jumps to a fixed address, at which a program is located which is able to determine the source of the interrupt and decide on a course of action.

completed an assigned task, such as positioning a read-head on a specified track. The *interrupt handling routines* or programs are generally kept as short as possible to avoid wasting time on basic housekeeping chores. Many processors have the ability to prioritize interrupts. Sometimes these are realized merely by providing a group of wires on which the interrupt is signaled, and by responding to each interrupt on the basis of which wire it signals through. Interrupts may be masked, which means that the interrupt signal will not be responded to. This provides a way to prevent less important matters from interrupting more critical ones.

Typically, in a priority interrupt scheme, the highest priority is assigned to those *input* devices that cannot be held up, for example, remote data inputs over a telephone line. In some processors, another part of the input/output structure is what is termed a "direct memory access (DMA) controller." This is a device attached to the processor, to which a program can send an address and a word (or byte) count. Then the controller may wait until a time at which the memory is ready to be accessed but the processor does not need to access it. This may be true for 50% or more possible accesses of memory! At this point, the DMA controller accesses memory. It keeps its own count of the bytes/words stored or fetched, and interrupts the processor when the count reaches zero. Such a controller must also be attached to an input or output device, receiving data from it or sending data to it in response to control signals. In this way, it is possible to make data transfers between main memory and input/output devices (including magnetic storage devices) in a way which is almost totally transparent to the processor.

3.11   COMPUTER SPECIFICATIONS

Our very brief and necessarily incomplete history of the digital computer has led us to a discussion of computer specifications. The technical description of a computer usually contains certain key information. At a minimum, this includes the following:

1. A description of the set of registers which are accessible through execution of instructions including the program counter, stack pointer, and status register(s);

2. A description of the instructions which the processor is capable of performing: what they do, in what sequence, under what conditions they cause bits in the status register to change, and by what binary code the instruction is represented;

3. A description of the bus structure, if the computer uses one. This bus constitutes a single set of wire connections whereby memory as well as many input or output devices may all be connected to the processor. It usually includes address and data lines as well as control and signaling lines. Proc-

essors which do not use a bus concept usually have a separate memory interface to the processor, together with special input/output control devices. Bus signals generally must conform to rigorous pulse-timing requirements;

4. A description of the interrupt handling processes in the processors; and

5. A description of any error detecting and signaling processes of which the processor is capable, for example, if an error in its own operation is detected, or if lower power-supply voltage implies the possibility of the occurrence of errors.

Such a description is usually contained in the documentation for the machine. In the case of the IBM PC the document is called *Technical Reference Manual*.

PROBLEMS

3.1   The von Neumann stored-program computer model described in the text deals with a computer at a particular *level of detail* in which control, arithmetic unit, memory, input, and output were discernible elements. Describe an automobile as a system at a level of detail including five major parts, showing a block diagram and at most a single connection between each pair. Then take one of those parts (with which you should be somewhat familiar) and describe it (only) by a schematic (block) diagram, at a finer level of detail, indicating what comprises each of the actual *interface* connections between that part and one of the other major parts. Make sure that the average reader will understand what each of your components is intended to represent.

3.2   For a trigonometry problem in which two sides of a *right triangle* are provided and the length of the hypotenuse is to be determined (using Pythagoras' well-known theorem), assume that a computer has addition, multiplication, and square root instructions, and a small set of high-speed registers. The two known values are initially moved into registers from memory. By laying out steps of the process, assuming each instruction can operate on data held in registers, *how many registers* must be used to avoid the need for reading from or writing to main memory before obtaining the answer?

3.3   Many computers have 4, 8, or 16 general-purpose registers. In terms of the layout of binary instruction codes, what advantages does this give?

3.4   Assuming a hypothetical computer which adds 8-bit numbers, but contains only a 4-bit adder with two 4-bit registers for input value and a 4-bit register and carry register for the results, along with 8-bit registers which can be used to hold 4- or 8-bit results, lay out a series of microprogram steps for accomplishing the 8-bit addition. In one step you can move bits from any registers to any others (but not in and out of the same register in the same step), or obtain a result from numbers entered into the adder in the *previous* step. How many microprogram steps will you require? What is the most complicated step?

3.5   The interrupt process observed in computers has many analogies in real life. Describe at least three of them, including for each: (1) what causes the interrupt, (2) what steps are taken to make it easy to return to the task previously underway, and (3) what interrupt processing must typically be done to service the interrupt.

3.6   From reference materials in your library, obtain what you need to characterize a processor not described in this text in terms of: (a) number, size, and identification (e.g., letters) of general purpose registers and other registers which can be altered by a program; (b) number of bits which the ALU can add or perform other arithmetic/logic operations upon; (c) the maximum amount of memory (words or bytes) which can be directly addressed by an instruction; and (d) the general scheme (bus or other) whereby I/O is accessed by the processor.

3.7   Some primitive processors limited to 16-bit addresses (addressing 64K bytes directly) permit additional and separate 64K memory banks to be addressed by the processor sending output to an I/O port address. (In actuality, all this does is to switch the memory addressing to another bank which is separate from the first.) Considering that your program is executing an instruction somewhere in bank 0 which switches memory to bank 1, describe a glaring problem which must be overcome by programming. How might you make use of bank 1?

3.8   Describe four existing or potential computer applications in which different data is processed in exactly the same way, so that a single-instruction-stream parallel processor might be used. Comment, if you can, on the difficulty of presenting the required data to a large number of processors *simultaneously*.

4

THE IBM PERSONAL COMPUTER

4.0 INTRODUCTION

Personal computer concepts emerged in the late 1970s when complete 8-bit-word length CPU units on a single semiconductor chip first became readily available. The term *personal* was applied because all previous computers had been *institutional,* in the sense that they were generally owned and used by companies, universities, and so on, rather than by individuals. Since the early 1960s there had been computer *terminals*. These generally were comprised of a keyboard and a display that were placed on a user's desk. These units were connected by means of telephone-line-like connections to a central computer that was located elsewhere. These *keyboard display combinations* were often called *dumb terminals,* and they were dumb in the sense that they had no computing capability whatever if separated from their mainframe host.

The PCs, as originally and still defined, includes not only the CPU and associated memory, but also a *keyboard* data entry, a cathode-ray tube, or other type of *display*, and some *permanent* medium in which to store data and programs. Such a device is shown in Figure 4.1. Usually, this storage medium involves a flexible disk of magnetic-oxide-coated plastic, the now-familiar removable floppy disk. It may also include a hard disk, which may be removable or nonremovable.

4.1 THE IBM PERSONAL COMPUTER AND RELATED COMPUTERS

The IBM-PC is perhaps *the* most successful computer in the history of computing, at least in terms of sales volumes. Most large computers have, during a sales

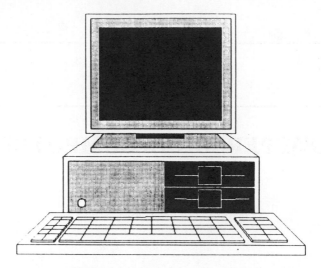

FIGURE 4.1   A personal computer.

lifetime lasting not more than four or five years because of rapid technological advance, sold in quantities of tens, hundreds, or thousands.[1] Millions of IBM-PCs have been sold. However, it should be remembered that the PC is hundreds of times lower in cost than the larger mainframe computers. Although the IBM-PC is not necessarily inferior in most performance aspects, its impact has not necessarily eclipsed those of larger computers, as there are some few large computer jobs that must be performed only on larger computers. Future trends surely call for PCs to function as workstations, networked to other PCs and large mainframes. Both will function together in an integrated way in the evolving computer environment of tomorrow.

The IBM-PC and related 16-bit machines arrived on the market several years after the first PCs. It was less well refined than has been typical of most IBM computers, and had been hurried to the market to give IBM an opportunity as a "late" competitor in an already developing market for low-cost computers. Initially, the IBM-PC must have been envisioned as a game-oriented machine for children. It had a rudimentary form of Basic in read only memory, did not need a floppy disk drive, and could have a cassette type recorder for input or output. It rapidly outgrew this initial design intent, however.

Earlier PCs had, for the most part, been 8-bit word machines. Generally, they were limited to a maximum of 64K bytes of random access memory. For the most part, but not always, they used an operating system called Control Program for Microprocessors (CPM) that was designed by the Digital Research Corporation. What made these low-cost computers possible was the "processor on a

---

[1]The largest of IBM's System/360 processors of the 1960s, the 90-series, reportedly found only 12 sales, though small versions sold by the thousands.

chip." This was a complete processor; except for memory, clock, and other than input/output facilities, which it lacked. This CPU had been designed into one semiconductor integrated circuit. Processor chips initially entered the market as 4-bit (BCD) chips for pocket calculators. These had preceded PCs by nearly a decade. The first highly successful 8-bit chip was Intel Corp.'s 8080. It was followed by Zylog Corp.'s Z80, which performed all 8080 instructions, added additional ones, and was generally faster. The Z80 was the microprocessor on which most early 8-bit microcomputers for serious business use were developed. As integrated circuit density expanded, 16-bit processors on a chip evolved, and later, 32-bit processors. Thus we have seen the Z80 followed by the 8088, the 8086, the 80286, and the 80386—all made by Intel. The Motorola 68000 family is also a powerful 32-bit chip.

Some aspects of the historical development of ever more capable chips as a function of time is shown in Figure 4.2.

The choice of a processor chip is a fundamental step in the design of a small computer. At the time IBM designed its PC, true 16-bit processor chips were available. However, IBM chose a chip which was, from the point of view of memory accesses, an 8-bit chip. This was the Intel 8088. While this chip functioned as a 16-bit chip internally, it functioned externally as an 8-bit chip. An advantage to this arrangement was that much of the 8-bit random access memory technology, and the resulting architectures, could easily be transported to the new 8088 environment.

It could be argued that IBM should have designed its own proprietary chip for the PC. This would have made it difficult, perhaps nearly impossible, for others to copy. Most probably the decision not to do so had to do with urgency. IBM

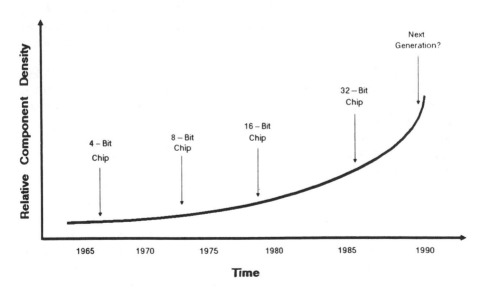

FIGURE 4.2 Evolution of computer chip density.

had no such chip designed, and that would have added many months and additional millions of dollars in design costs to the resulting product. Presumably, part of the wisdom of this selection of the 8088 was that it was part of a well-structured *family* of Intel processor chips which would be extended to faster 16-bit chips and eventually to a 32-*bit* and higher-bit chips. Even when the 8088 was chosen, the 8086 (a true 16-bit processor) was available. This led outsiders to the conclusion that IBM was following its long-established policy of entering the market with a product which could later be improved upon. And that indeed seems to be the case. The PC-XT and PC-AT, each offering significant speed and other improvements, followed at measured intervals. The more advanced PS/2 series allows some parallel computing functions to be performed using the proprietary microchannel architecture (MCA).

The IBM-PC is the most *copied* computer in history, both in the United States and abroad. There have generally never been attempts to make duplicates of larger computers, because these large computers are so complex, expensive, and specialized. There have, however, been computers designed by one manufacturer to run programs written for successful systems that were designed by another manufacturer. But this is only *part* of the objective of those who have "cloned" the PC and other members of its computer family. Another objective is to permit these other computers to use the same hardware accessories and software. Encouraging other vendors to develop hardware and software for the PC was clearly an advantage to IBM in the sense that it made the PC more useful to more people. A disadvantage for IBM was that it also made it easier to duplicate.

We do not wish to imply that the copying of the IBM-PC has necessarily flouted the laws. The choice of a processor chip, and all other chips that were readily available to others, made the design of an IBM-PC "look-alike" a relatively simple engineering task. The result of IBM's design decision has made the IBM-PC family and its imitators the most widely used computer architecture in history.

The attempts to imitate the IBM-PC, and the degree of success in so doing, have varied from one manufacturer to another. The almost universal objective in this is "100% software compatibility." This phrase means that *any* program which would run on the IBM-PC would operate *in exactly the same way* on a clone or copy. Because of minor differences, usually having to do with *input/ output* (the keyboard, display, or printer), the goal of 100% compatibility has often *not* been reached. *Most* programs, however, will execute exactly the same on the clone computer as on an IBM-PC. Although we will be describing the IBM-PC, other clone computers will differ only in *logical* aspects that do not appear at our level of description. *Physically*, however, great differences may and do exist. These reflect themselves primarily in a redistribution of internal parts, differences in numbers of slots for plug-in accessory boards, and overall dimensions of the housing. There are some machines, such as the Texas Instruments Professional computer, which was not compatible at the level of plug-in accessory slot equivalence and otherwise. In particular, it had a superior, but different, video display architecture. It was withdrawn from production in the summer of 1987. An earlier TI PC, the 99A, had been withdrawn in part because of the reluctance of TI to open its operating system to third-party applications software developers. This significantly inhibited the development of software for this otherwise excellent machine. It may well be that IBM learned a lesson from the failure of Texas Instruments in this regard.

4.2   ARCHITECTURE OF THE PC

To understand the PC and its clones, we must first understand some features of the single-chip processor which lies at the heart of the computer, in this case the Intel 8088. A diagram of its structure is shown in Figure 4.3.

The 8088 microprocessor contains a number of registers available to the programmer who is coding at the "machine-language" level.[2] These include four general-purpose registers. The generic names given are **AX , BX , CX**, and **DX**,

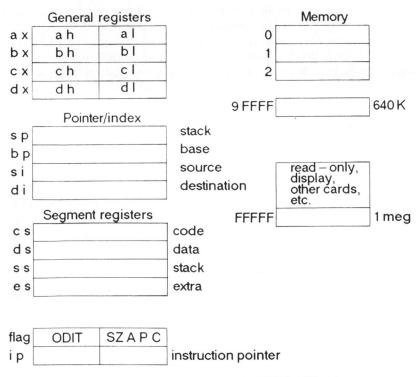

FIGURE 4.3   Architecture of the INTEL 8088 chip.

[2]We will begin writing programs at the machine-language level for the PC in our next chapter.

which refers to their use as 16-bit registers, which they really are. When used as pairs of 8-bit registers, the names A L, A H, R E P R E = t, the "low" and "high" 8 bytes of the A X register, respectively, and B H, B L, and so on. This 8-bit orientation reflects the 8080 heritage of the chip. Arithmetic and logic functions are carried out by a 16-bit ALU. Memory addresses are formed using a combination of a 16-bit address *offset* plus a 16-bit address *segment*. Four registers (C S, D S, E S, and S S) are provided whose *sole* function is to contain the segment part of addresses. They are appropriately called segment registers. To determine the actual physical address in the memory, which can be as large as one megabyte (2^{20} bytes), the segment and offset addresses are added, internally and invisibly to the programmer, with the segment portion shifted 4 bits left to create a combination of the necessary *20-bit* length. We will discuss this further in Section 4.4.

There are additional registers that perform pointer and index functions. S P uses registers with S S as a segment register to address the current stack location. D I and S I are usable for general-purpose registers functions, but are also dedicated to use in instructions which transfer data to, from, or between memory locations and are therefore also pointer/index registers. B P is a general-purpose register, but is usually reserved by the programmer for *point-to* addresses in the stack. So it is also rightfully called a pointer index register.

From the processor's point of view, both memory and input/output are represented as *addresses*. When memory is to be read or written, the address to be written to or read from is set up on a set of output pins that represent processor connections to the outside world. Additional output pins may be activated to indicate:

(1) a memory operation is required, (rather than actual I/O), and
(2) whether the output is a read or write.

The memory itself is external to the processor chip and it must respond to the signal sent by the processor chip. When input or output is required, an address similarly is set up. This occurs on the same address outputs. A *different* provision is made to indicate whether the address refers to input or output. The memory or input/output devices, which are located external to the processor, indicate the presence of data or acceptance of it. This is accomplished by signaling the processor on yet another pin. A short time *after* the address, the data is actually transferred on some of the same pins that were used to transfer the address. This multiple use of the processor's limited number of connection pins is known as *multiplexing*. It is commonly used in microprocessors in order to avoid the cost and complexity that would otherwise be associated with providing many more single-use connection points. When an address refers to inputs or output, it is usually described as that of a "port" address, principally in order to distinguish such I/O addresses from like-numbered addresses in memory. There is no possibility of the computer confusing memory and I/O addresses because of the different signals through which it signals intentions to read from or write to memory or to I/O devices. A given I/O device will *always* respond to signals that are sent to the specific I/O ports (addresses) with which it is associated.

The connection of an input or output device to a particular port or ports is easily accomplished. This is done by connecting the processor's port *address* signals, along with a signal indicating the operation to be an I/O operation, to a simple logic circuit containing a group of AND gates.[3] These gates are arranged so that only one particular port address can be activated by the output. The output signal is then connected to an *enable* input on the external device. If a given device has several control inputs, low-order *address bits* from the processor may be connected directly to these inputs. It is then possible, by *addressing* a particular port, to select the appropriate function of the input or output device. Since certain of the *higher-order* address bits may have been ignored in the port selection logic, it is unwise to assume that the port address specified for a device is unique. If a (hex) port address 02F0 is specified for a given device, it is possible that any port addresses differing only in the highest order bits (e.g., addresses 12F0, 32F0, and 42F0 etc.) will also address the same device.

When storing a series of bytes into memory, the program must advance the address each time a new byte is to be written. When transferring bytes through an I/O port to an output device, however, the port address will always be the same as the port to which that device was initially attached. The output device is responsible for such efforts as printing each byte in sequence or writing to a magnetic storage device.

4.3 CONSTRUCTION: THE MOTHER BOARD

The 8088 processor is but one of many integrated circuits in the *IBM-PC*. See Figure 4.4 for a functional layout of the mother board. In addition to this processor, the large mother board also contains a clock. This is a quartz crystal which is coupled to an electronic counter that produces the necessary timing pulses. These pulses have a rate of about 4.88 million per second in the IBM-PC. There is also circuitry for keyboard input and output. There is a connection for a video-game "joystick" and another for use of an audio cassette as a permanent storage device. Both of these are holdovers from the early era of the IBM-PC. They probably reflect its initially perceived use as a computer for children, much like the early Apple computers, and not for what was soon to be the best market for the machine, business applications. These devices do not appear on the later versions of the IBM-PCs.

Also inside the computer cabinet is a power supply. This converts the AC line power to low-voltage DC for powering the semiconductors. The small loudspeaker on the mother board can have a voltage switched on or off, under program control, so that repeated pulses of voltage produce audible tones or even crude music or voice sounds.

[3]See Chapter 9 for a discussion of such hardware.

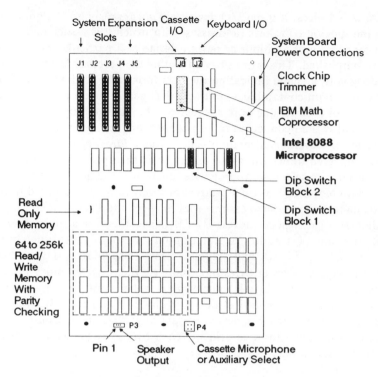

FIGURE 4.4   The main circuit board of the IBM PC. This figure illustrates the switch adjustments which a skilled user might find necessary to alter. Note how minor the role the "central processor" (shaded) would seem to play, since it is one of the many integrated circuits, although by far the most complex. (From "IBM PC Technical Reference," copyright IBM Corp). The board perpendicular to this "Mother Board" in the five expansion "slots" handles all I/O except for tape–cassette and joystick interfaces, which do not appear on more powerful machines of this sort.

A portion of the main memory is also on the mother board. Initially, this was only 64K RAM, and even now it is only 256K bytes on the IBM-PC. Some of the PC clones can contain as much as 768K bytes of memory on their mother board. The AT can contain 512K, and the 80386-based machine much larger amounts of random access memory.

4.4   MEMORY FOR THE PC

The approach to memory used in the 16-bit computer family is a rather complex one. A physical memory address is 20 bits in length, but it is kept in *two* 16-bit words. The low-order word contains address values of 0000H to FFFFH (zero to 65535 decimal), and is referred to as the *offset* address. The high-order word contains a similar range of values and is referred to as the *segment address*. In the 8088 chips, the actual memory address is *not* formed by simply appending the low-order word to the high-order word to form a 32-bit address. The segment address is shifted 4 bits left before adding it to the *offset address*. The result is a 20-bit address which can thus address 2^{20} bytes ($= 1$ megabyte).

This process is illustrated below, for a compound address consisting of segment address l F E 2 (hex) and offset address of 1 3 2 4 (hex). Note that the overlap of 12 bits is precisely *three* hexadecimal digits.

```
segment             1FE2
offset              1324
                    ────
actual  address     21144    (all  values  are
                              hexadecimal)
```

This somewhat complex scheme has the advantage that it then becomes possible to use different segment addresses to address memory as close as 16 bytes (called one *paragraph*) apart. If the two words comprising the address were simply abutted to form a 32-bit address, the memory would then be divided into non-overlapping 64-kilobyte segments. Also, segments could only start on 64-kilo-byte boundaries. With this overlap scheme, a segment can start on 16-*byte* boundaries.

It should be emphasized that this scheme is entirely internal to the 8088 and 8086 hardware, and that addresses are calculated internally from the machine code that is provided by the programmer. Later members of the family retain the (64K) segment addressing scheme, but can form addresses as long as 32 bits. The method used internally by the hardware is invisible to the user, fortunately.

If a program and its data require no more than 64 kilobytes of memory, which is often the case, the combined program and data can be assigned to a segment of memory starting no more than 16 bytes above other programs, such as the system programs that are already located in memory. Within its 64-kilobyte segment, the application program and data can be fully accessed by altering *only* the offset address, whose smallest value is zero (at the low end of the segment). Hence, if the segment address is simply ignored (by the programmer), the program can be written to use memory addresses 0000 (hex) through FFFF (hex), just as if it were written for a computer limited to 64 kilobytes.

However, if the program and data exceed 64 kilobytes, but neither alone exceeds 64 kilobytes, the program can be assigned one segment address and the data a second. The actual segment address ranges may *overlap*, depending on how much memory is needed by each. The Intel 8088 and 8086 and related processors are unusual in that the instruction counter, treated as an offset, is combined with one segment register, the C S register, as above. For fetching or storing data, the offset addresses of the data are combined with one of two other segment registers, D S or E S. A fourth segment register, S S, is combined with the stack pointer when this is needed.

At the most primitive programming levels, the manipulation of the segment register values can be very tedious. However, the addressing scheme permits a program and its data to have access to all of the available memory. In so doing, it always works with addresses of just 16 bits. Instructions which *move* information *from one memory location to another memory location* use the DS segment register for the source and the ES for the destination. By setting different values for the two, information can be moved from any specified location in memory to any other. To use a memory larger than 64K bytes, the program must occasionally change the values of segment addresses.

An important rationale for this apparently complex scheme is that the *family* of Intel processors is intended to contain not only 16-bit processors but also 32-bit processors. To retain upward compatibility, the larger processors must retain the ability to execute programs that have been written for the smaller ones. An address of up to 32 bits, made possible by combining 16-bit segment and offset addresses with no overlap, can address up to 1 gigabyte of memory. It does not matter whether these 32 bits are in one word of the 80386 or two or more words of earlier chips. Only 16 megabytes of actual (physical) memory can actually be used however.[4] This is, as in the older processors, logically separated into 64K segments.

In the next chapter we will present simple experiments which illustrate these and other features of the IBM-PC.

4.5   THE BUS

From an addressing standpoint, the commonalty of memory and I/O leads to one of the most important aspects of the PC. This is its *bus*. Many of the signal pins from the processor, along with a few others, such as the power supply voltages, are fed to a distinct set of identical connectors which are mounted on the mother board. These signals are strengthened by semiconductor "driver" chips on the mother board, so that a number of different accessory boards may merely be plugged in at right angles to the mother board. On the IBM-PC these accessory boards *always* include a *disk-controller* board, which contains the integrated circuits which operate the storage disk drives, and a second board which controls the computer display. The plugs and space for additional boards are referred to as *slots*. These slots permit the installation of a wide variety of other boards that enable various functions, including:

- *Parallel adapters* to connect to printers, transmitting one byte at a time over eight parallel wires (plus a ground wire).
- *Serial adapters* to connect to devices in which the eight bits of a byte are serialized and transmitted over a single wire (plus a ground wire).

[4]The actual process of accessing memory in this so-called "protected mode" involves using the *high* 16 bits to reference the memory table which contains the real starting address of the segment. (Fortunately, the user and programmer need not be concerned in most cases.)

- Additional *main memory*, usually limited to 384K bytes to give a total RAM of 640K, the maximum that can be addressed by the standard operating systems.
- A battery-operated *time-of-day clock*, which also (as with most digital wrist watches) keeps track of the *date*.
- A hard disk.
- A graphics board for a color monitor.
- A board with plug for connection to a *mouse*, a form of inputs device which one grasps and rolls across the desk, to move the cursor correspondingly on the display screen.
- A variety of other devices designed to interface with the PC's bus.

The standard bus is perhaps the feature which enables the great adaptability of the PC and its other family members. So flexible is the design, and so ingenious are the designers attempting to exploit that flexibility, that such accessories as a card containing a Z80, an 80386, or some other processor with its own memory can be connected to the bus. This allows the 8088-based 16-bit PC to execute programs written for the other 8-bit processors but with programs and data stored in the PC's disk storage. It turns out that this emulation can also be accomplished using software only, but at a much slower speed.

4.6   READ ONLY MEMORY (ROM)

We will discuss the *operating system* (PC-DOS) used with the PC in a later chapter. It is, however, entirely in the form of *software* and must be read into the computer each time the computer is powered up. There are certain very basic programs *in the PC itself* which are part of the hardware and stored in integrated circuit chips known as read-only memory, or *ROM* chips. One function of the *ROM* programs is to test the hardware of the PC and its attached boards each time power is turned on. A second function provided in the PC, but not provided in its imitators, is a simple BASIC interpreter which allows the computer to be used without an operating system. As we have noted, this is a holdover from an earlier era of personal computing or an earlier image of the perceived use of the PC. A third, and perhaps most important, function of the *ROM* is to implement what is called the *BIOS* (basic input-output system). This is a set of programs which isolates the operating system and application programs from the need to directly manipulate the hardware. The *ROM* is clearly hardware. Yet it contains a program which the computer exercises. Does this make the ROM equivalent to software? Some, perhaps euphemistically, call it *petrified software*.

   Our experiments in the next chapter will include the use of the *ROM BIOS*. For example, we will place a selected character at any position on the display screen with one of the *BIOS* functions. Access to *BIOS* and also to utilities provided by *DOS* is through interrupts, using a facility provided by the *8088* to simulate the interrupting event with software.

4.7   INTERRUPTS

The PC's *interrupt structure*, characteristic of the complete computer and not just the 8088 chip, contains eight "interrupt request" lines which are connected as part of the bus and designated (for identification purposes) I R Q0 thru I R Q7. Circuitry on the mother board external to the central processor arranges these signaling lines so that I R Q0, which is activated by the timer which keeps the internal clock updated, will take precedence over I R Q1, which is activated by receipt of a character from the keyboard. This makes possible the assignment of interrupt lines to the different I/O functions that are needed for cards in the PC's slots. It also permits the more important interrupt situations, such as low power supply voltage, to be given precedence over those of less urgency.

Upon receipt of an interrupt, an address is placed in the I P register. This forces control to be transferred to a dedicated memory location which is at the beginning of the physical addresses. These dedicated memory locations have additional addresses which contain the programs needed to service the interrupt. One of the software instructions simulates such an interrupt. It can be used for testing or, in the case of B I O S and D O S, for access to programs which provide utility services.

4.8   THE REST OF THE MACHINE

The PC has an attached keyboard. The original version of this was the subject of much controversy because its key placement and key sizes deviated from those familiar to IBM Selectric typewriter users. This has been largely corrected in later releases.

Electronically, the keyboard communicates with the processor as if it were a *serial I/O device*. The keyboard sends its signals over only one pair of wires and causes a processor interrupt each time a key is depressed or released. The *ROM BIOS program*, which uses a small reserved portion of memory, is responsible for keeping track of the historical sequences that result from pressing the shift key and other keys. These keys are used in combination. In this way, one-key-at-a-time signals, which the keyboard sends, can be interpreted as a wide variety of key combinations.

A wide variety of video accessory cards, which operate the display, are available. These display boards allow the support of text-only displays, monochrome graphics in which the screen is divided into pixels which are individually addressable, or color graphics. Of course, for color graphics the display itself must be color-capable. Many graphics boards will display in several shades of monochrome the images that they would display in color on a color monitor.

The Disk Drive Controller accessory card controls magnetic storage disks. In the original PC, it controls only drives for *floppy* or removable *diskettes*. However, other suppliers made possible the installation of a nonremovable *fixed* or *hard* disk drive. This drive is in addition to, or in replacement of, the original floppy drives. The disk drive controller has multiconductor *ribbon* connectors through which it supplies power to the drives themselves. It also controls data storage and retrieval and associated operations such as starting the drive motor or moving the read/write head.

In an evolutionary manner the original IBM-PC was improved upon by a hard-disk equipped version which was designated XT. The next evolution to appear was the AT (with an 80286 16-bit chip and a hard disk). In 1987 the PC, XT, and AT were all replaced by the PS/2 series. This includes, at the top of the line, a machine with a 32-bit 80386 chip. However, the architectural standard established by IBM with the PC, and more particularly the AT, is likely to remain for some time in look-alikes and work-alikes that are produced by competitors.

With most electronic appliances, the end user is usually and explicitly warned NOT to open the container. With the PC and similar computers, the end user is encouraged to take off the metal cover to install or remove accessory cards. (It is worthwhile to try it, just to have a look!) One end of such cards may connect to devices outside the computer itself and, if so, will contain electrical receptacles, into which cables are plugged. These may join the computer to a display, a printer, a telephone connection, a *mouse*, or other devices. Because the voltages used in modern computers are 12 volts or less, there is almost no danger of electric shock involved in accidentally contacting the circuit boards. The *high-voltage* parts of the power supply are separately enclosed for safety, and one should not trespass into this portion of the circuitry without good reason and knowledge of the power supply layout. As with any sensitive electronics, it is wise to turn off the power and unplug the line cord before opening the housing. This is mostly to protect the circuits, not the user. There is virtually no danger that users could hurt themselves in this manner, unless they start tampering with the power supply. When holding an accessory card to be plugged into the computer, the user-installer should touch the frame of the computer with a hand, to avoid an electrostatic charge causing damage to the semiconductors in the machine or on the card. Thus we see the truly complex architecture of the PC as an orderly set of components skillfully arranged to enable easy access.

5

HANDS ON THE COMPUTER

5.0 INTRODUCTION

We have now reached the point where some hands on assembly language programming, to illustrate some of the concepts introduced in earlier chapters, will be accomplished. Very few, if any, of us will have any significant use for assembly language programming. Yet this **is** the way computers once had to be programmed. Even today it is the way of choice, if not necessity, if we wish to write fundamental internal programs, such as operating systems, for a computer.

The IBM PC is a very powerful computer, especially in more recent configurations. Even though the PC is small, it has essentially all of the features of much larger machines. Learning about it is generally very useful, even if one intends to devote most of their efforts to mainframe computers. The complexity and capability of current PCs are fully comparable to those of *full-size* computers of only a few years ago.

Use of the computer is fundamental to learning about computers. It will interact as a patient teacher should, and will often tell us immediately if we have made a wrong move. It is virtually indestructible unless it is roughly handled. We need have no fear of easily causing damage to the machine, no matter what is typed at the keyboard.

Before turning on the machine for the first time, a new user should read the "start-up" information that comes with the machine. Programs for the machine and the operating system called DOS, for disk operating system, are initially delivered on diskettes. Each box of new diskettes contains protection stickers which can be used to cover the write-protect slot on the diskette itself. It is a good idea for a new user to protect software from damage through inadvertent writing on the disk this way, and to follow the directions that come with both the machine and software very carefully, as shown in Figure 5.1

5.1   PC-DOS, MS-DOS, AND DEBUG

The PC needs an operating system: PC-DOS or MS-DOS is normally purchased with the machine and the operating system must be available to the default drive when the machine is started.[1] Other operating systems are available, such as UNIX or PS-2. We restrict our discussions to PC- or MS-DOS. When the power switch is turned on the PC starts up from a program stored in its read-only memory. First, the machine checks its own hardware; then it looks in its disk memory for a *bootstrap* program. This is provided from a special track on the DOS disk. After successful startup, generally called *booting*, the terminal will display the DOS prompt:

A :

or perhaps

A>

depending upon the type of machine and the way some basic definitions are handled.

Without Write Protect Tab   With Write Protect Tab

FIGURE 5.1   Diskettes with write protect tab off and on.

[1]If you start without the DOS disk in place, the IBM-PC machine will start with a primitive BASIC language program running, which will not be useful for our purposes. Clones may just sit there with the floppy disk spinning.

At this point, the machine is ready to use and application programs can be run, such as a word processor like the one on which this text was written. Here we will use another application program that will allow us to gain access to the microprocessor itself. The program is called DEBUG.COM, and is furnished as a part of DOS. If it is not installed on the DOS disk in the machine you plan to use, it should be copied from one of the DOS disks to the one you plan to keep in the machine.

We assume that you have *booted* the PC satisfactorily. To check the contents of the disk, we type

```
A: dir
```

and strike the enter or carriage return button on the keyboard. A number of commands such as dir and copy are resident within or internal to the operating system. Others, such as DEBUG, are external to the operating system and separately contained on the DOS disk.

If DEBUG is not on your DOS disk, find the other DOS disk (with PC-DOS version 3.1, it is on the disk labelled "Supplemental Programs"). Place the second disk in drive B and type

```
A:copy b:debug.com
```

After hitting the *return* key DEBUG will be present on your drive A disk. Before using DEBUG we will review the architecture of the PC. Our real intent in use of this program is insight into the architecture of the PC and assembly language programming, which is very architecture dependent.

5.2 THE 8088 ARCHITECTURE

The internal register arrangement (or architecture) of the Intel 8088 microprocessor, which is used in early versions of the IBM and other PC's, is shown in Figure 5.2. Registers are all 16 bits wide. The general reisters can each hold two independent 8-bit bytes or single 16-bit words. Memory is addressed by (8-bit) byte locations. Data is moved by bytes from memory to the registers and vice versa. When a 16-bit transfer is programmed, two 8-bit transfers are executed without hesitation.

Other members of the Intel family have this same register organization. Programs written for the 8088 are upwardly compatible; that is, they will run on the later family members, such as the 80286 and 80386. The 8086 moves data to and from memory in 16-bit units, and is therefore faster than, but in other respects is like, the 8088. The 80286 used in the PC-AT PS-2 and other computers, has the same basic organization as the 8086, but adds memory management functions.

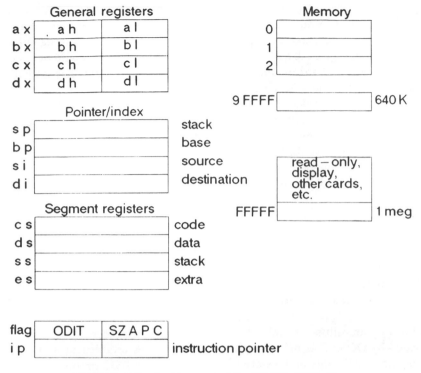

FIGURE 5.2   Architecture of the INTEL 8088 chip.

The 80386 has the 8088 registers, but they have been enlarged to 32 bits by expansion on the left. They are called EAX, EDX, and so on, with EAX including a 16-bit AX and a 16-bit extension.

The flag register contains 1-bit storage for results of operations. For example, if an operation sets a register to zero, the Z flag is set to 1. If a carry occurs, the C flag is set. These flag registers are used continually in controlling the flow of a program.

5.3   WRITING A PROGRAM

The binary number system is used internally by the computer. This corresponds to the electronic storage of numbers a bit at a time in registers. Our written communication of these binary numbers will be in hex because this representation allows us to handle the bits four at a time and avoids the long strings of ones and zeros that would be needed if a binary representation were used.

The language used at this level of computer programming is called *assembly language*. It consists of mnemonics or English-like words that are suggestive of the action to be performed. For example, to subtract **456** hex from the number present in register **bx** we write **SUB bx,456**. The answer to this calculation would be left in register **bx**. In this example a SUB is the command or *opcode*, **bx** is the destination for the memory operand (the number in which is changed by the operation), and 456 is a source number (unchanged by the operation).

There are many books available on programming the 8088/8086 and these contain tables of instructions. We will introduce the few we need for our purposes here as we go along. As our first program dealing directly with the 8088 microprocessor, we ask for the solution of a simple hex addition problem which will check the arithmetic in an example of subtraction we presented in Chapter 1. The addition problem we consider is

$$
\begin{array}{r}
1FF \\
+ \quad 3D \\
\hline
???
\end{array}
$$

We will proceed by placing **1FF** (hex) in the ax register using the **MOV** instruction; then we will add 3D to the **ax** register with **ADD**. The answer will be left in **ax**.

Our program will be assembled at offset 100 (hex[2]) in the work area segment provided by DOS. This offset is consistent with rules established by DOS for writing programs that can be stored and run from the DOS prompt; we will be writing such programs soon.

First we invoke DEBUG from the DOS prompt[3]

```
A: debug
```

Debug responds with a hyphen (its own prompt signal), and since we wish to assemble a program starting at offset 100 (hex) we type

```
-a 100
```

to which debug, which only understands hex inputs, responds with the address in *segment:offset* form at which we will start:

```
0FB2:0100
```

---

[2]Below 100 hex is an area called the program segment prefix which contains certain information about the program we are executing.

[3]DOS does not distinguish between upper- and lowercase, so we are free to mix cases here; the C language does make the distinction, and lowercase is commonly used, so we favor it when there is a choice.

The segment (**0FB2**) is provided by DOS (and will probably be different on your machine). Next we type in an instruction to move the number **1FF** hex into the ax register:

```
0FB2:0100 mov ax,1FF
```

Since we want to add **3D** hex to that register, we type in the next instruction. This starts at offset 103 since the MOV command is issued at offset 0100, the ax register location at offset 0101, and the IFF number is at 0102. Thus we see on the monitor

```
0FB2:0103 add ax,3D
```

followed by a place holder: a no-op instruction which does nothing:

```
0FB2:0106 nop
0FB2:0107
```

DEBUG then asks for the next instruction, but we simply press the < E > < R > key and end the program. To see what we have, we can use the unassemble instruction u. We enter a command that will unassemble the program that appears in locations 100 through 106. In response to the entry

```
-u 100 106
```

we obtain the result

```
0FB2:0100 B8FF01        MOV     AX,01FF
0FB2:0103 053D00        ADD     AX,003D
0FB2:0106 90            NOP
```

To run this simple assembly language program, we use g for go and specify the starting and stopping places:

```
-g=100 106
```

DEBUG responds with the contents of the registers and flags and the next instruction. We obtain on our monitor:

```
AX=023C   BX=0000   CX=0000   DX=0000   SP=FFEE
BP=0000   SI=0000   DI=0000
DS=0FB2   ES=0FB2   SS=0FB2   CS=0FB2   IP=0106
NV UP EI PL NZ NA PO NC
0FB2:0106 90     NOP
```

The answer is in location a x : 23 C hex. The nonzero flag N Z was set by the last instruction. The instruction pointer IP points at the next instruction NOP at offset 106. Now we are through, so we enter q for quit:

−q

and we return to the DOS prompt.

The problem just solved contained data in the positions shown in Figure 5.3. This figure indicates the registers and memory of the microprocessor after the last step of the program.

General registers

a x	0 2	3 C
b x	0 0	0 0
c x	0 0	0 0
d x	0 0	0 0

Memory

0100	B 8
	F F
	0 1
	0 5
	3 D
	0 0
0106	9 0

Pointer/ index

s p	F F	E E	stack
b p	0 0	0 0	base
s i	0 0	0 0	source
d i	0 0	0 0	destination

segment registers

c s	0 F	B 2	code
d s	0 F	B 2	data
s s	0 F	B 2	stack
e s	0 F	B 2	extra

flag	0010	00 0 0 0	
i p	0 1	0 6	instruction pointer

FIGURE 5.3   Numbers stored in various locations at offset 106.

We have copied the contents of the registers from the list furnished by DEBUG after the go instruction. The memory contents came from the unassembled listing.

The resolution of this problem is associated with a x and the instruction pointer points at the NOP. The assembled program is in memory starting at offset 100. The code for the MOV instruction is B8 and the operand 1FF is stored in reverse order in the next two slots. This reverse order is characteristic of the Intel 80x86 family. Not only are the two bytes of the word reversed, but a complete 4-byte address is stored with its offset portion preceding its segment portion.

The assembler does all this for us, following the rules for the 8088 microprocessor. Notice the way the instructions and data are mixed in memory; this is the way the von Neumann machine works (see Chapter 3). Some machines, for example, the IBM 360 mainframe computers, preserve boundaries so that it is easier to tell where instructions begin. In the PC no such boundaries are found. To demonstrate this, type u 101 106 and see what instructions the computer appears to have stored.

This is a good time to point out a danger in running programs like this. Notice that we provided a starting and ending address to the go instruction. Without a place to stop, the program would have continued to execute the instructions in memory beyond offset 106. But beyond our program there are no planned memory contents—those locations contain *garbage*, perhaps fragments of the previous program executed. The processor will try to execute anyway, and the results are unpredictable. The most likely result will be an endless loop in a meaningless section of programs or data, and loss of access to the machine. Depending on the type of inadvertent operations performed, the keyboard may have no effect. In this case, the machine must be turned off and on again to regain control with consequent loss of whatever we had in memory. If we are more fortunate, we may be able to restore control through what is called a *warm-boot* of the operating system. This will still result in loss of any data stored in random access memory. There are two lessons: save your work often by writing it to the disk and be very careful when dealing with the machine at this rudimentary level.

5.4   WRITING TO THE SCREEN

Now we will write another program. This one will write something to the screen. The typical PC screen is bit memory mapped, which means that each character in the display can be reached by addressing it as a memory location. There are variants to this, such as the roster or virtual mapped screen found in postscript displays or when using graphics oriented operating system shells such as the Graphics Environment Manager (GEM) or Windows program from Digital Research or Microsoft. We will, however, concentrate on the most basic DOS environment here and will not take advantage of these more advance features.

If you have a conventional monochrome display, the segment address of the character to be displayed in the upper left-hand corner of the screen is hex b000; for color it is b800. The offset address in either case is zero: 0000. If we plan to move data to the screen, the address calculation made internally by the 8088 must be with respect to this address area. Thus we will need to change the segment used for the calculation. This is done with what is called a segment override instruction: in our case ES. The screen address to be used is stored in the extra segment register.

Before starting, we type c l s at the dos prompt. This will start us with a clear screen and with the cursor at the top of the screen. The DEBUG dialog for entry of the program is

```
-a 100
0FB2:0100  mov  ax,b800
0FB2:0103  mov  es,ax
0FB2:0105  mov  bx,500
0FB2:0108  mov  ax,8f58
0FB2:010B  es:
0FB2:010C  mov  [bx],ax
0FB2:010E  nop
0FB2:010F
-g=100 10e
AX=8F58   BX=0500   CX=0000   DX=0000
SP=FFEE   BP=0000   SI=0000   DI=0000
DS=0FB2   ES=B800   SS=0FB2   CS=0FB2
IP=010E   NV UP EI  PL NZ NA PO NC
0FB2:010E 90                  NOP
```

First, the address of the screen segment (in this case the color display memory address) is moved via a x into e s. An attempt to move the address directly to es will fail, as such an operation is not allowed by any valid 8088 instruction. DEBUG will let us know this if we attempt such an operation. The fall-back to using a x is natural for an assembly language programmer as almost any operation can use a x, or a l or a h, as a source or destination.

Next b x is given the offset of the eighth line of the screen. The calculation goes like this: 8 lines times 80-characters-per-line times 2 bytes-per-character equals 1280 decimal or 500 hex.[4]

Each screen character needs two bytes for proper identification and represen-

[4]The conversion can be made with the right kind of pocket calculator or with this algorithm (procedure):

```
1280/16  = 80,  remainder = 0
80/16    =  5,  remainder = 0
5/16     =  0,  remainder = 5
```

The conversion to base 16 is the set of remainders, backward: 1280 decimal = 500 hex. This works for conversion from decimal to any base.

tation. We need an ASCII character identification code byte and another with *attribute* information. In our program the character is a capital X (code 58 hex) and the attribute is blinking high intensity. Information about the codes and attributes will be found in the IBM PC *Technical Reference Manual,*[5] and equivalent documentation for other manufacturers.

Next comes the segment override instruction. The following instruction will use the extra segment (containing the address of the screen corner) instead of the data segment in its memory address calculations.

Finally, the character/offset combination in a x is moved to the address pointed to by b x. By means of the square brackets ([b x]) the move is made not to b x but to the location whose *offset address* is contained in b x. This is called *indirect addressing.* Experienced assembly language programmers read [bx] as "location pointed to by bx." The contents of b x are used as a *pointer* to the destination of the move. We will have much more to say about pointers and their importance as we continue with our discussions of high-level languages.

The result of running the program is a blinking, high-intensity capital X at the left of the eighth line on the screen.

Let us examine what we have done by examining this assembly language program. For the 8088, the u command shows the program as assembled, and the d for dump command shows the contents of memory, including the ASCII code translation for each byte at the right. The latter is useful in reading data that has been stored in memory. We obtain

```
-u 100 10e
0FB2:0100 B800B8        MOV    AX,B800
0FB2:0103 8EC0          MOV    ES,AX
0FB2:0105 BB0005        MOV    BX,0500
0FB2:0108 B8588F        MOV    AX,8F58
0FB2:010B 26            ES:
0FB2:010C 8907          MOV    [BX],AX
0FB2:010E 90            NOP
-d 100 10e
0FB2:0100   B8 00 B8 8E C0 BB 00 05-B8 58 8F 26
89 07 90
-q
```

As a final demonstration of DEBUG using this example, we use the t (for trace) command to step through the program one instruction at a time. Five steps are asked for, starting at offset 100. We obtain in response to the command

```
-t=100 5
```

[5]The DOS technical reference manual is distinct from the technical reference manual which describes the hardware.

the screen display

```
AX=B800   BX=0000   CX=0000   DX=0000
SP=FFEE   BP=0000   SI=0000   DI=0000
DS=0FB2   ES=0FB2   SS=0FB2   CS=0FB2
IP=0103      NV UP EI PL NZ NA PO NC
0FB2:0103 8EC0              MOV     ES,AX

AX=B800   BX=0000   CX=0000   DX=0000
SP=FFEE   BP=0000   SI=0000   DI=0000
DS=0FB2   ES=B800   SS=0FB2   CS=0FB2
IP=0105      NV UP EI PL NZ NA PO NC
0FB2:0105 BB0005              MOV     BX,0500

AX=B800   BX=0500   CX=0000   DX=0000
SP=FFEE   BP=0000   SI=0000   DI=0000
DS=0FB2   ES=B800   SS=0FB2   CS=0FB2
IP=0108      NV UP EI PL NZ NA PO NC
0FB2:0108 B8588F              MOV     AX,8F58

AX=8F58   BX=0500   CX=0000   DX=0000
SP=FFEE   BP=0000   SI=0000   DI=0000
DS=0FB2   ES=B800   SS=0FB2   CS=0FB2
IP=010B      NV UP EI PL NZ NA PO NC
0FB2:010B 26                 ES:
0FB2:010C 8907              MOV     [BX],AX
ES:0500=0743

AX=8F58   BX=0500   CX=0000   DX=0000
SP=FFEE   BP=0000   SI=0000   DI=0000
DS=0FB2   ES=B800   SS=0FB2   CS=0FB2
IP=010E      NV UP EI PL NZ NA PO NC
0FB2:010E 90                 NOP

-q
```

DEBUG gives us the contents of the address pointed to by b x in the next-to-last step, just before our own move to that location is ordered. The word 0743 (which is arranged in memory with low-order byte first as 43 07) prints as the letter C (ASCII 43 hex) with normal attribute (07). bx was pointing to the letter C when we ran the program, but unless your screen had the same contents as ours, you might have something different there.

The reader is strongly encouraged to type this simple program into debug and try running it with g=100 10e. A blinking capital X is the result of executing the program.

5.5   NEGATIVE NUMBERS

Now we write a simple program to show the way negative numbers are stored in the PC. This short program subtracts 123 from 0 in register ax, then enters 123 into bx, and finally uses the operation NEG to make the contents of cx negative. The stored value of negative 123 hex will be left in all three registers. From DEBUG we write:

```
-a 100
0FB2:0100 mov ax,0
0FB2:0103 sub ax,123
0FB2:0106 mov bx,-123
0FB2:0109 mov cx,123
0FB2:010C neg cx
0FB2:010E nop
0FB2:010F
```

The program is run starting at offset 100. We obtain the result.

```
-g=100 10e

AX=FEDD   BX=FEDD   CX=FEDD   DX=0000
SP=FFEE   BP=0000   SI=0000   DI=0000
DS=0FB2   ES=0FB2   SS=0FB2   CS=0FB2
IP=010E      NV UP EI NG NZ AC PE CY
FB2:010E 90                  NOP

-q
```

The hex number FEDD is left in the three registers. Expanding to a binary representation, we can convert to two's complement and obtain

hex	FEDD			
binary	1111	1110	1101	1101
complement	0000	0001	0010	0010
add one				+1
two's complement	0000	0001	0010	0011
back to hex	0123			

The internal storage of negative numbers in the PC, like most computers, is by two's complement representation. The advantage is that normal arithmetic can be used; the disadvantage is that magnitudes of the numbers are not immediately recognizable as any value except a negative one (marked by the 1 in the left bit position).

5.6 DOS INTERRUPTS

The PC can be interrupted in its operation by devices outside the 8088 microprocessor and also by software. When an interrupt occurs a (1-byte) number between 0 and 255 is provided by the device or program wanting attention, and control is passed to an address that is contained in low memory (at address = 4 times the interrupt number) in (4-byte) segment:offset form.

Interrupts can also be triggered by software through the use of an interrupt instruction INT. For example, if interrupt number 21 hex occurs, say by executing the instruction INT21, control is passed to the address located at 4 [×] 21 hex, 0000:0084. The multiplier 4 corresponds to the four bytes per interrupt number that must be stored for loading into the cs and ip registers so that control will transfer. A program for handling the interrupt is placed at the transfer address.

We can use DEBUG to see what address is stored for interrupt 21 hex. First, we dump the contents of the four bytes starting with address 0000:0084. It is important to note the specification of the four bytes by length: L4. In response to the input we obtain the screen

```
-d 0000:84 L4
0000:0080           E4 12 6E 01
```

The section of memory where this is stored is shown in Figure 5.4.

The address of the program that handles interrupt 21 hex is therefore 016E:12E4. This illustrates the way numbers are stored with the 8088 microprocessor. The combination of offset and segment is called an interrupt vector. This interrupt is the most important of several DOS interrupts. It provides a variety of services such as reading files and writing to the terminal. The method for access to these services is described in the DOS technical reference manual,

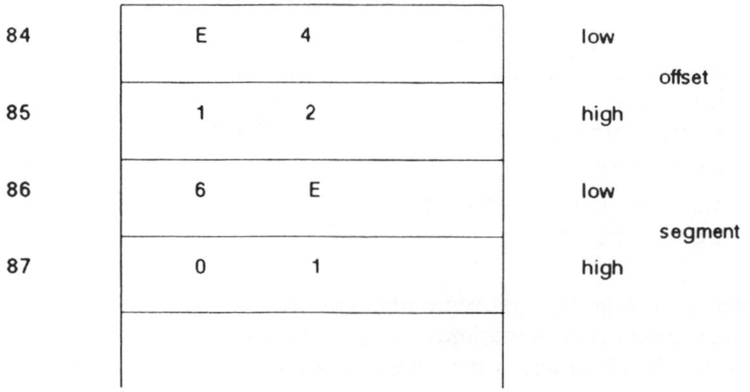

84	E	4	low
			offset
85	1	2	high
86	6	E	low
			segment
87	0	1	high

FIGURE 5.4 Section of memory.

and requires placement of control values or addresses in one or more of the registers followed by INT 21. For example, here is a program that writes a character to the terminal using this service:

```
-a 100
0FB2:0100 mov ah,2
0FB2:0102 mov dl,58
0FB2:0104 int 21
0FB2:0106 nop
0FB2:0107
```

Here, service number 2 (the value in register ah) writes the ASCII character in the low end of register dx to the screen (in this case capital X):

```
-g=100 106
X
AX=0258  BX=0000  CX=0000  DX=0058
SP=FFEE  BP=0000  SI=0000  DI=0000
DS=0FB2  ES=0FB2  SS=0FB2  CS=0FB2
IP=0106    NV UP EI PL NZ NA PO NC
0FB2:0106 90                NOP
```

The X is seen in the line following g. If we step through the program using the t for trace command, the step after INT21 transfers control to the vector address we found above:

```
-t=100 3

AX=0200  BX=0000  CX=0000  DX=0058
SP=FFEE  BP=0000  SI=0000  DI=0000
DS=0FB2  ES=0FB2  SS=0FB2  CS=0FB2
IP=0102    NV UP EI PL NZ NA PO NC
0FB2:0102 B258            MOV  DL,58

AX=0200  BX=0000  CX=0000  DX=0058
SP=FFEE  BP=0000  SI=0000  DI=0000
DS=0FB2  ES=0FB2  SS=0FB2  CS=0FB2
IP=0104    NV UP EI PL NZ NA PO NC
0FB2:0104 CD21            INT  21

AX=0258  BX=0000  CX=0000  DX=0058
SP=FFE8  BP=0000  SI=0000  DI=0000
DS=0FB2  ES=0FB2  SS=0FB2  CS=016E
IP=12E4    NV UP DI PL NZ NA PO NC
016E:12E4 2E              CS:
```

```
016E:12E5 3A26EE0D CMP  AH,[0DEE]
CS:0DEE=63
```

The control has been transferred to another program. At the interrupt the 8088 placed the address location 0000:0084 in the CS and IP registers. Continuing to use the t instruction leads us into the program that handles INT 21, which may not be what we want. The trace can be restricted to our own program, bypassing the DOS steps, by using the command p for proceed, instead of t for trace:

```
-p=100 3
```

5.7 BIOS SERVICES

We discussed BIOS in the last chapter. BIOS (basic input/output system) is an assembly-language program stored in several ROM (read-only memory) chips. The program is listed in full in the technical manual.[6] The program exists to provide services via interrupts. The BIOS routines interact directly with the hardware, whereas DOS uses the BIOS to control the hardware. This is why one DOS version can control a PC, XT, or AT, each of which has different hardware and BIOS, but common BIOS functions. Using BIOS for an operation will generally result in a faster execution than if the equivalent function is performed in DOS. However, this usually requires much more programming effort and cost to achieve this result.

It is not necessary to use either DOS or BIOS to access the computer hardware. Unless we do, we run the risk that other software will not work with software that exercises hardware directly. In our example of writing the X to the screen we used neither. Screen handling is the only exception to the rule that direct access to the hardware should be avoided, and BIOS or DOS used as a standard interface. The reason for the exception is the need for speed in dealing with the screen. However, for many applications, BIOS is fast enough.

The video (or screen) services are reached via interrupt 10 (hex). Here is the dialog with DEBUG to put X on the screen via BIOS. The X is on the line after g.

```
-a
3920:0100 mov  ah,e
3920:0102 mov  al,58
3920:0104 int  10
3920:0106 nop
3920:0107
-g=100 106
```

---

[6]Another reference for both DOS and BIOS utilities is R. Duncan, *Advanced MS DOS*, Microsoft Press, Redmond, Washington, 1986.

```
X
AX=0E58  BX=0000  CX=0000  DX=0000
SP=FFEE  BP=0000  SI=0000  DI=0000
DS=3920  ES=3920  SS=3920  CS=3920
IP=0106    NV UP EI PL NZ NA PO NC
3920:0106 90                NOP
-q
```

The BIOS screen-writing utility requires the presence of hex O E in register a h, and the ASCII code for the character to be written to the screen in register a l. Then interrupt 10 does the rest and allows the task to be accomplished.

5.8   WRITING A .COM PROGRAM

If a program doesn't exceed 64K bytes, such that it can be stored within a single 8 bit segment, and is in "proper" form, it can be stored with the extension .COM (which stands for command) and executed from DOS by entering its name (without the .COM extension).

As an example of a .COM program, let us use DOS interrupt 21 (hex) as in the example in Section 5.6, but this time we send the ASCII character BEL (code 7), which causes the terminal to beep:

```
-a 100
0FB2:0100 mov ah,2
0FB2:0102 mov dl,7
0FB2:0104 int 21
0FB2:0106 nop
0FB2:0107
```

which can be checked from DEBUG by typing:

```
-g=100 106
```

To turn this into a program which can be run by itself outside DEBUG, we need to add a way to terminate the program. DOS provides one way using the 21 hex interrupt number 4C hex. Adding this termination request to our program, we obtain:

```
-a 100
0FB2:0100 mov ah,2
0FB2:0102 mov dl,7
0FB2:0104 int 21
0FB2:0106 mov ah,4c
0FB2:0108 int 21
0FB2:010A
```

The address of the last line tells us that the size of the program is 0100 − 010A = A bytes. We give the program the name beep.com, using −n for name. The size is placed in the cx register using r for register. Use of the command −w to enable a disk write stores the program on a disk—with the assigned name. The resulting screen display is

```
-n beep.com
-r cx
CX 0000
:a
-w
Writing 000A bytes
-q
```

After return from DEBUG, the directory contains the 10-byte program BEEP.COM. If we use the internal operating system command DIR BEEP. COM, we obtain on the screen:

```
BEEP        COM        10    2-08-87    2:03p
```

To run the program from DOS we type beep on the keyboard and the speaker in the computer goes B E E P.

5.9 CONCLUSION

In this chapter we have examined some basic assembly language programming operations. We do not intend this to be a definitive presentation that will provide a detailed knowledge of this topic. It is not at all central to our intended purpose. It could even be argued that extensive coding in assembly language will inhibit software productivity! Nevertheless there must be some, at least modest, amount of assembly language programming that needs to be accomplished to initiate development of operating systems and high level programming languages. Thus the topic is of some importance for our efforts to come.

PROBLEMS

5.1   Use DEBUG to find the answer to the hex subtraction problem:

```
  678
-359
```

5.2   Check the results of your solution to problem 5.1 by hand.

5.3 Use DEBUG to find the time. Note: DOS interrupt 21H with 2c in ah will return these values:

```
ch:   hour
cl:   minute
dh:   seconds
dl:   hundredths of seconds
```

5.4 Write a .COM file which prints the hour on the screen. (Hint: be sure to convert the hour to ASCII.)

5.5 Here is a program which prints a message to the screen using DOS interrupt 21H. Analyze the program to deduce how int 21H with 9 in ah works, and modify it to print "this is a test."

```
mov  ah,9
mov  dx,10c
int  21
mov  ax,4c00
int  21
db   'hello, world$'
```

5.6 In the PC, the memory location 0000:0417 contains a byte whose bits are set by keyboard conditions such as shift lock being on. Explain what the following program does, and run it to determine which bit shows the shift lock status.

```
mov  ax,0
mov  es,ax
mov  bx,417
es:
mov  ax,[bx]
nop
```

(Hint: you can run this program from DEBUG by typing g=10010b.)

5.7 Verify the results of problem 1.11 with DEBUG.

5.8 Add hex FFF and EEE on DEBUG.

5.9 Find the ASCII representation for GMU using DEBUG.

5.10 Try using the instruction MUL to get the value for the products below (use the ax and bx registers; MUL puts the answer in dx:ax combination:

(a) FF * EE, and

(b) FFFF * EE.

6

PROCESSOR OPERATIONS

6.0 INTRODUCTION

In our last chapter we illustrated how instructions were written for the PC as assembly language programs. The instructions introduced, like **MOV**, were chosen from a set of hundreds to illustrate some simple operations. We now return to a more general discussion of computer design and processor operations. In this chapter we continue to move away from the hardware aspects of the computer and its associated equipment and examine how computer designers facilitate program execution. Thus we move one step closer in our transition from computer hardware to computer software.

6.1 COMPUTER INSTRUCTION SETS

The principal *hardware architecture* decisions associated with computer design have to do with the numbers and interconnection of registers, ALUs, memory, and I/O attachments. The principal *logical* design decisions, however, have to do with the *design of an instruction set*. The instruction set is the list of all *instructions*, which may alternatively be called *commands*, which the processor is able to perform. There may be tens, hundreds, or even thousands of distinguishable instructions. This number depends upon what one defines as an instruction. Even in small computers, builders may wish to boast enormous instruction set sizes, and may, therefore, seek a definition that allows this. To this end, every combination of source and/or destination register which might be used in a given operation may be described as comprising a distinct instruction. Indeed, if this same dramatic approach were extended to instructions containing a memory address, there might be said to be millions of possible instructions. What is important to the programmer and/or user, however, is not the precise numerical count but more importantly, a measure of the *different functions* that the computer is able to perform on *different* types of data.

Why should someone who is *unlikely* to become a programmer who writes in elementary *machine language* bother to learn about instruction sets? One reason is that we are then able to better appreciate the differences between different computer configurations at a level that has a great deal to do with limits to computer performance.

The *number of register or memory locations* which are referred to in a single instruction is a fundamental aspect of processor architecture. For example, it is not sufficient to assume in an addition that there are three addresses to be dealt with: those of the numbers to be added and that of the sum. Although three-address instructions were found in some early computer architectures, they make for excessively lengthy instructions. The designer of a computer with a 16-bit word length would prefer that as many instructions as possible be limited in length to a single word or a byte.

But how can this be done, since the address of a byte (or a word) in memory requires all 16 bits? One answer is *variable instruction length*, a property of almost all present-day computers. Instructions which must contain a memory address will have an extra word added to them to hold that address. This raises the need for instructions to be limited to one word. This need is satisfied through the use of general-purpose registers. A computer having, say, 16 different general-purpose registers (GPRs) can *address* any one of them with only *four* bits of an instruction. A second GPR can be addressed with another four bits. Three registers could be addressed with only 12 bits. In a 16-bit-word computer, however, this would leave only four bits left to describe the instruction operation. For this reason, we are most likely to find 16-bit-word length computers designed as *two-address machines*, with at least one address that of a register.

Let us examine how this works in the case of addition. Many microprocessors, such as the Intel 8088 and its family, have a convention that the first addressed register contains one of the numbers to be summed. A schematic of the Intel 8088 alterable register is shown in Figure 6.1. That register contains the sum of the two numbers after execution of the operation. In the last chapter, for example, we saw that the hex number 3 D had been added to whatever was in register a x after execution of the statement a d d a x , 3 D.

The same principle is applied to all operations that involve combining or relating two pieces of data. For example, if we AND A and B, the result is placed where A was initially located. This implies that, prior to execution of the instruction, we must move a *copy* of the data value from memory to the "A Register." Alternately, we must move data from another register to the A register if the data was in such a register as a result of a previous step. This means that in addition to the arithmetic and logic instructions, generous use must be made of instructions which move data between memory and register locations prior to and fol-

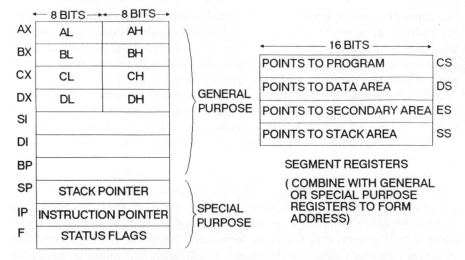

FIGURE 6.1   The INTEL 8088 alterable register. The alterable registers are those that can have contents changed by the program.

lowing many arithmetic or logical instructions. The instruction mo v that we used in our last chapter is one procedure which accomplishes this.

6.2   ADDRESSING

Single-address computers contain only a single memory or register address in any single instruction. These elementary machines contain one register, usually called the *accumulator*, which plays a unique role that enables operations to be carried out. The accumulator is the implied source or destination for all instructions which move or combine data. To add two numbers in a single-address machine, we might first *transfer* one number from memory, or from another register if present, to the accumulator. Then we would *add* the second number into the accumulator with a second instruction. Finally, we would *transfer* the sum to a register or memory destination with a third instruction. If all the data was in memory at the start of the operation and the sum must be in memory at the end, the same number of instructions is required for the one- and two-address instruction sets. The following chart illustrates the sequence of operations for these two types of addressing schemes.

		Single-address		Two-address
(load)	A	mem -> accum		mem -> Reg 1
(add)	B	mem -> accum		mem -> Reg 1
(load)	S	accum-> mem		Reg 1-> mem

The advantage of the two-address scheme appears only when intermediate values in a calculation are left in registers that are to be combined with further numbers. Of course, addition of three or more numbers is a common requirement. Thus, a two address scheme is generally quite efficient.

To more fully appreciate the possible variations in addressing within an instruction set, let us consider ways the 8088 microprocessor can refer to data in memory or a register. We recall that the 8088 can have two addresses in an instruction, only one of which may be a memory location. Among these are:

1. *Direct Register Addressing.* The address selected determines which GPR is to be used as the source or destination.

2. *Direct Memory Addressing.* The address[1] in the instruction determines at what memory location the data referred to begins.[2]

3. *Indirect Memory Addressing.* The memory address placed in the instruction is that of a memory word containing the (offset portion of the) *address* of the data required.

4. *Memory Addressing Using a Register As Pointer.* A GPR contains the memory address of the data required. We used this in the last chapter by means of the instruction mo v [b x] , a x in which the square brackets indicated indirect addressing.

5. *Indexed Addressing.* One register contains a memory address while a second contains an index to be added to the contents of the other to determine the memory address of the required data.

Two- and three-address concepts are shown in Figures 6.2 and 6.3, respectively. Some of the reasons for all of these different forms of address are:

1. The use of a GPR to hold a memory address means that later instructions referring to that address can be shorter than if the complete address had to be placed in each instruction.

2. *Indexing* allows a data structure, such as an array of numbers or string of characters, to be addressed in terms of its fixed starting address, which is held in one register, and a variable *index*, which measures position in the array. Indirect addressing allows an address, whose actual location is not known at the time the program is written but is established only when the program is executed, to be specified.

---

[1]The address in the instruction is the 16-bit offset address, always combined automatically with the 16-bit segment address to form a 20-bit memory location, as explained earlier.

[2]In every case a memory address will locate the start, or lowest address of, the actual data. If the instruction deals with a single byte, only that byte will be fetched from memory; some instructions may deal with a string of bytes, starting at the address specified.

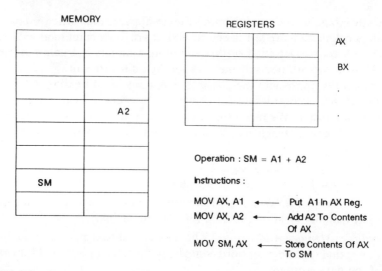

FIGURE 6.2 A two-address concept. This is the same operation as in Figure 6.3, as it might be carried out in a two-address computer in which one of the two addresses is that of a general-purpose register and the other a memory location. For 64K words (or bytes) of memory, each instruction would require 16 + 4 + ?. (Four bits will allow addressing up to 16 general-purpose registers, and the number of bits for instruction code depends on how many different instructions must be distinguished.)

MEMORY

1	2
2 A 1	4
5	6
7	8 A 2
9	10
11 SM	12

Steps In Execution
1. Fetch A1 To One Input Of ALU
2. Fetch A2 To Second Input Of ALU
3. Store Output Of ALU To SM

Operation SM = A1 + A2

Instruction (Mnemonic Form) "Add SM, A1, A2 "

Destination   Addend & Augend
For Sum

Note:
If 64K words of memory were used, instruction would be
3 * 16 + ? bits in length. (? for instruction code)

FIGURE 6.3 A three-address concept.

3. Some microprocessors have large numbers of addressing modes that are constructed by combining the elementary principles of
   (a) storing a memory address in a register,
      (b) adding two (or more) register values to establish the actual address, and
      (c) storing an address in memory as a pointer to the location of the actual data.

In the Data General 16-bit minicomputer architecture, for example, indirect addressing can be extended indefinitely. Actual addresses may be only 15 bits in length, with the sixteenth or "high" bit denoting whether the value is an address at which the intended data is located or a pointer to a further location in a chain of pointers.

Over the years, a wide range of computer designs have exposed machine-language programmers to a variety of addressing schemes. There have been no formal proofs that much is to be gained by any one scheme, however, or by elaborate combinations of schemes. Figure 6.4 shows typical addressing modes.

6.3 GROUPS OF INSTRUCTIONS

The actual processor instructions can be divided into groups which perform particular kinds of processor functions. The first four of the six groups identified next are those that actually operate on data.

1. *Data movement instructions* merely transfer a portion of data (a byte or a word) from a memory location to a register or the converse, or from one register location to another. It may also be possible to transfer a number of bytes from one area of memory to another. When these instructions refer to variable-length strings of bytes or words, one of the GPRs be designated to contain the length of the string and others to contain pointers to the memory locations. In real programs, **data movement instructions are typically exercised more than any other group of instructions**.

MEMORY

101 A1	102 A2
103 A3	104 A4
105 B	106 C
107 D	108 E
109	10 A
10B	10C

REGISTERS

101	AX
3	BX
F	CX
G	DX

Contents of memory & registers are shown – A1,..,A4,B,C.. G represent variables stored in those locations.

Direct Register Addressing	: Operand F Is In Register CX
Direct Memory Addressing	: Memory Location 107 Contains Operand D.
Indirect Memory Addressing	Memory Location 10B Contains The Address Of Operand B
Indexed Addressing :	Register AX contains Start Of Array A1..A4 . Register BX contains a "Pointer" or Index which when added to contents of register AX yields address of array term A4.

FIGURE 6.4   A typical computer addressing modes.

2. *Arithmetic or logical instructions* may combine two data values in memory or registers, addressed in one of the ways described above, to produce a result in a register or memory location. However, some logical instructions deal with one data value only, that is, to produce its negative (minus A) or binary complement (NOT A). In the latter case, all bits of the byte or word will be complemented. Certain status bits (called *flags*) in the processor's *status* word may be altered as a result of these operations, for example, if the *result* is zero or produces a carry or a negative quantity. Compare instructions are commonly the same as subtract instructions except that the difference is never produced; only the status bits which *would have resulted* from an actual subtraction (zero, carry) are activated.[3]

3. *Rotate or shift instructions* move the bits in a byte or word to left or right; *rotate* implies that bits moved out through *one end* of the byte or word are moved into the other end. A bit moved out of the most-significant bit position may set a *carry flag*. When arithmetically significant values are *shifted* to the right in an *arithmetic shift*, the most-significant bit may remain unchanged so that negative or positive numbers treated in this way will not change their signs.

4. *Input/output instructions* transmit data or control values between registers or memory and input or output *ports*. The complex sequences required to control peripheral units must often be formed in the processor and transmitted through an output port.

The following two groups of instructions do not operate on data, but control the processor's mode of operation and sequencing.

5. *Branch, jump, or skip instructions*, which will be explained soon, are the means for altering the flow of the program from a purely sequential one to a nonsequential one. They may be nonconditional, that is, executed in the same way independent of data values. Or they may be conditional upon the values taken by the status flags that follow some arithmetic or logical operation. These instructions include the ability to first *call* a subprogram that is located elsewhere in memory, and then upon its completion to return to the instruction that follows the "call." **This group of instructions is probably the most frequently used, except for the data-movement instruction group.**

6. *Miscellaneous instructions* often include special instructions which set or reset processor modes. One of these, for example, involves the way in which the processor responds to external interrupt signals. The functional capability possible is highly dependent on the particular design options that are chosen. The n o p (no operation instruction) from the last chapter is one of these.

---

[3]This is easy to carry out in computer design. The *final step* of a subtraction instruction, in which the result from the *ALU output register* is moved to the destination register, is eliminated for the compare instruction.

Within each of the first four groups of instructions there may be instructions which operate on data one byte at a time, one word at a time, or which deal with strings of bytes representing text or perhaps numbers in special formats such as floating point or BCD representations.

To better appreciate the form an instruction takes in the actual computer, we show the binary form of a data-movement instruction of the Intel 8088 and related microprocessors. In a microprocessor each bit signifies some particular feature. We will use DEBUG to assemble what is referred to as the *mnemonic* form of the instruction mov bx,[1234]. The illustration we choose is:

```
-a
3920:0100 mov bx,[1234]
3920:0104
-u 100 100
3920:0100 8B1E3412        MOV   BX,[1234]
-q
```

The DEBUG assembler converts the mnemonic into the internal code: 8B1E3412. The last two bytes 3412 are the instruction address with the bytes in reverse order. The first part of the number, 8B1E, contains the instruction itself and is shown in binary form in Figure 6.5.

It is easy to see why the assembler has great value for this kind of translation.

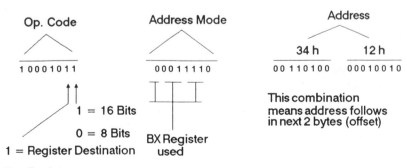

MOV BX, [1 2 3 4] Moves a word (16 Bits)
from memory location 1 2 3 4 (Hex) into the BX register.

Binary Form :

Op. Code   Address Mode   Address

                                          34 h   12 h

1 0 0 0 1 0 1 1   0 0 0 1 1 1 1 0   0 0 1 1 0 1 0 0   0 0 0 1 0 0 1 0

1 = 16 Bits   This combination
                                         means address follows
0 = 8 Bits   BX Register   in next 2 bytes (offset)
              used
1 = Register Destination

0 = Register source
    Note: The mnemonic form has meaning only
          when interpreted by an assembled diagram.

FIGURE 6.5   Binary and mnemonic forms of an 8088 microprocessor.

It is work quite unsuited for humans, who easily make mistakes at this sort of trivial task. This is ideal work for a computer however.

In the earliest computers the programmer had to specify the actual binary memory addresses for the program and data, as well as the binary value of the instruction code. The mnemonic program form is considerably easier to use than the pure binary machine language interpreted by the processor itself. As we shall see later, higher-level languages retain the mnemonic references to locations in the program and further relieve the programmer of the task of defining each individual processor instruction.

6.4 CONTROLLING PROGRAM FLOW

A *normal* operation for a conventional computer is to fetch instructions *in sequence*. When directing that the next instruction in a sequence be fetched, it is desirable that the control unit learn

(1) how long the instruction is and
(2) if it needs data from memory.

Therefore, the first byte or word of the instruction (8B hex in the example in Section 6.2) must contain the instruction *code* that identifies the instruction. The remaining parts of the instruction and the data required from memory, if any, can be scheduled for fetching from either memory or from registers.

There are several reasons for departing from a simple instruction sequence. One reason is to invoke a *subprogram* which is located elsewhere in memory. For this purpose, a *subroutine call* instruction is executed. The only data associated with this instruction is the address of the *subroutine* in memory. However, since the computer will continue executing from another location, some means of returning to the initial location must be provided. The simplest method to achieve this is through the use of a *stack*, a concept that we have discussed earlier. If the stack concept is part of the processor architecture, and it is in the 8088, the internal process activities associated with *calling* a subroutine is:

1. Determine the address of the instruction following the call instruction in sequence.
2. Push that address on the stack.
3. Put the called routine's address in the instruction pointer (IP) register and proceed.

The called subroutine is ended with a return (RET) instruction which:

1. pops the top word off the stack, and
2. puts that top word in the instruction pointer register and proceeds. Figure 6.6 shows how a stack is used to handle a subroutine call.

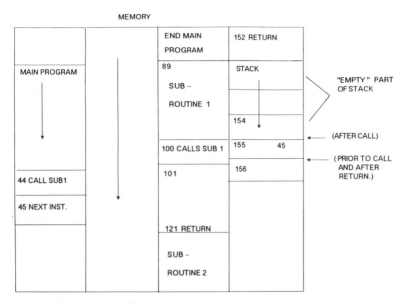

FIGURE 6.6 Use of stack to handle subroutine calls. A call to subroutine 1 at word 44 (in main program) causes address of next instruction (at word 45) to be placed on stack. Stack pointer is changed from 156 t 155 to indicate its "top." At word 121, when subroutine is complete, return causes word at address 155 to be placed in instruction counter and stack pointer is incremented to 156. If Sub 1 had called Sub 2 at Address 100, then 101 would be placed in stack location 154. Hence the stack provides a "trail" back to the main program.

If the processor did not have the ability to support stack operations, it would have to put the return address somewhere. It might be arranged to do this in memory near the start of the subroutine. This implies, however, that the part of memory containing the subroutine *cannot* be ROM. For this reason most, if not all, currently designed processor architectures support a stack.

Jumps, branches, and skips all have the same intent. They enable program transfer to another instruction location without the intention of returning to the original sequence. In a simple jump, the address of the start of the new program sequence, which may be part of the instruction or may have already been stored in a GPR, is merely transferred to the instruction counter and the processor proceeds. A branch is a term sometimes used for such a transfer to another instruction sequence. When the jump or branch is conditional upon settings of status "flag" bits, *failure to satisfy* the condition stated in the instruction simply causes the program to continue execution at the instruction following the conditional jump or branch.

Thus, there is indeed an alternate branch and the term is appropriately used. In some computers, a number of different conditions can control the outcome of a conditional jump, as shown in Figure 6.7. Almost always, the conditions present determine whether the result of the most recent arithmetic, logical, or

CONDITION :	JUMPS (BRANCHES) IF LAST ARITHMETIC OR LOGICAL OPERATION :
JUMP IF CARRY	– PRODUCED A CARRY AT ITS MOST SIGNIFICANT BIT.
JUMP ON ZERO	– PRODUCED ZERO RESULT
JUMP ON SIGN	– PRODUCED A 1 IN MOST SIGNIFICANT BIT (SIGNED INTEGER REPRESENTATION)
JUMP ON NO CARRY	– DID NOT PRODUCE A CARRY
etc.	

FIGURE 6.7 Conditional jumps. Conditional jumps respond to status bits changed by the most recent arithmetic or logical operation.

rotate/shift instruction resulted in zero or in a carry bit being produced. In addition, some processors will set a flag if the result has the most significant bit set to 1. This is potentially quite useful since it can be an indication, in signed-integer arithmetic, that a result was *negative*. In the 8088 and its family of microprocessors, a compare (C M P) operation has the effect of subtracting the second operand from the first, yet not storing the difference as we noted earlier. Hence the same status flags, zero or carry, may be set as on an actual subtract. The conditional jump instructions will permit selecting a range of optional conditions. The following sequence is typical.

Assume A and B are the two operands, each of the same length, a byte or a word; the instruction in effect *subtracts* B from A. Hence if B exceeds A, the result will generate a carry (or "borrow," as it may be referred to in subtraction). If B equals A, there would be no carry, although a zero results from the subtraction. If A is greater than B, there will be no carry and the result is not zero.

Accordingly, if the jump occurs only if the zero flag is set, it is a "jump on equal." When carry only is set, it is a " j ump i f A < B" or " j ump i f below;" when carry or zero is set, it is a " j ump i f A <= B" or " j ump i f below or equal," and so forth. The assembler recognizes mnemonics for these conditions, so J E would be used for " j ump on equal," and so on.

A *skip* differs slightly from the conditional jump. In machines using this form of sequence-changing process, when any specified conditions are met, the instruction following the skip instruction is *skipped* and execution continues from the next following instruction. This can be converted into a conditional branch by placing an unconditional branch in the instruction to follow. If the conditions of the skip instruction are not met, the program will branch to a new sequence at the jump address. Otherwise, it will continue. The skip can also be used to insert another instruction which might, for example, increment some register or memory value if not skipped.

6.5 INTERRUPTS

Interrupts also represent control changes. Often they are not specified within the program sequence. They occur as a result of some activity (input, output, or signaling) that is outside the processor itself. When an interrupt occurs, and the mode of the processor is such that the interrupt is allowed and not masked, the same basic event occurs here as a result of a subroutine call. When the currently executing instruction is completed, the address of the start of the interrupt routine is supplied as part of the interrupt process. The next instruction in the normal sequence is then pushed on the stack, and finally *the status register* (with zero flag, carry flag, etc.) is also pushed on the stack. At completion of the interrupt routine, which usually does the housekeeping needed to update memory associated with the cause of the interrupt, a variant of the subroutine return is executed. This results in return of the next instruction to the instruction counter, and return of the status information to the status register.[4] Since changes that might be made in GPRs by the interrupt routine could damage the program operation, the programmer of the interrupt routine must first save, again on the stack, the original values of any registers used by the interrupt routine. Then the program must return them to their original values prior to continuing on with other operations.

It is entirely possible that two interrupts might arrive, at almost the same time, from two different external devices. Once an interrupt has been initiated, the ability to have further interrupts is disabled, generally by an instruction which is the first one executed in the interrupt routine, to avoid the pandemonium which might occur. When it is safe to allow another interrupt, the ability to interrupt is then turned on again. An example of the use of interrupts that permit special programs to be always available is shown in Figure 6.8.

Some processors, the 8088 among them, recognize software interrupts, which are nothing more than subroutine calls that are disguised as interrupts. The stored address for which the interrupt routine is saved in memory at an address which is pointed to by an interrupt number. This interrupt number is part of the instruction called a *software interrupt*. Other processors, using the identical scheme, may call this a *system call*. It is through this scheme that the programmer of an application gets access to *system programs* which can handle input or output, find the time of day, create data files, and other operations. We saw examples of these with the DOS int 21 calls and BIOS calls in our last chapter.

Special control instructions are often included to allow the program to enable or disable (mask) interrupts from certain sources. For example, it may be possible to prevent certain I/O devices from calling for interrupt services when other (slower) devices are calling for an interrupt. Many computers include a HALT instruction, which simply stops the processor, in their instruction set. There

---

[4]Preserving the status register is essential because an interrupt may occur after any instruction unpredictably.

MAIN MEMORY

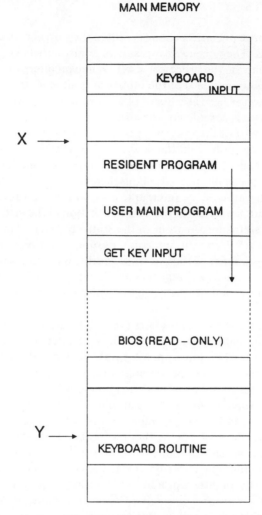

FIGURE 6.8 Use of interrupt handling addresses to allow special programs to be resident (always available). Normally, the BIOS input routine Y is stored in the memory address table for interrupt, but the address X was substituted when the resident program was first loaded into memory. Each time the user program gets keyboard input, the resident program "intercepts" the request and will begin execution if certain key combinations are sensed. Otherwise, it passes control back to the BIOS routine.

must also be an interrupt to start it again. The processor will start executing *again only when a hardware interrupt is received*. After the interrupt is handled, or serviced, it will begin normal execution. This will begin just after the next instruction following the HALT. This makes it unnecessary to put the processor into a loop that has been associated with completion of the interrupt. Of course, the processor is idle while awaiting an interrupt.

6.6 BOOTSTRAPPING

An important control operation is associated with the initial start-up that occurs when power is first applied to the computer. Various processor designs treat this event somewhat differently. In all cases, however, the first instruction to be executed on start-up is obtained from a particular memory location. In some cases this is from memory address zero, in others, from alternative locations which are characteristic of the designs.

6.7 ARITHMETIC OPERATIONS

Almost all computers can add two *word-length* numbers, subtract them, and perform logical combinations (AND, OR) of *corresponding bits* in two words. However, many processors have a much larger set of arithmetic and logical instructions.

An increasingly important facility in many modern processors is the ability to perform these operations with either 8-, 16-, or 32-bit operands.[5] This ability is important since various applications may use numerical data of different bit lengths. There will usually be *different arithmetic and logical instructions* for each length of the operand. It is the responsibility of the programmer working at a machine-language level to keep these straight. In general, it is best if the application program is able to use the full power of the ALU in arithmetic operations, rather than the less efficient process of breaking up a long number into smaller chunks.

Often an application requires a combination of numbers *larger than* the processor's word length. If no instructions are provided, the machine-language programmer must prepare a program which will add the low-order parts of the operands, save any carry produced in that process, and add it to one of the next-higher order parts of the two numbers, until the full sum is produced. For example, the instruction set may contain only primitive instructions which combine 8-bit pairs of BCD decimal digits when BCD numbers are combined for precise financial calculations. Again, it is the machine level programmer's responsibility to sequence the complete operation and to keep track of all of the many necessary details that enable this. Mainframe computers often implement more capable BCD arithmetic instructions. These operate on long strings of bytes, each containing two BCD digits, and interpret certain BCD combinations as negative-sign or end-of-number markers.

Usually, only the larger processors contain *floating-point* instructions within their normal instruction sets. Most of these will microprogram their way through the complex sequences of steps to enable floating-point arithmetic. Personal computer floating-point instructions are often executed *in a separate chip* termed a *coprocessor*. The Intel 8087 coprocessor can be teamed with the 8088 processor, for example, or the 80287 with the 80286. Certain instructions, which

---

[5]The last of these is usually found only in processors with a 32-bit wide ALU.

are not in the normal instruction set, are recognized as being floating-point instructions and directed to the coprocessor when it is present in the computer. A coprocessor fetches needed data, executes the instruction, and can store the result of an instruction in main memory. Special programs must be written to invoke the coprocessor. Some arithmetic-intensive commercially available programs are designed to exercise the coprocessor if one is installed, or otherwise to call on logically equivalent (though much slower) software floating-point routines. Other software is less sophisticated and will not use a coprocessor even if one is available.

Floating-point operations require both a *mantissa* (the fractional part) and an *exponent* (the power of 2, or more often of 16, by which the mantissa is multiplied) for each operand. A 32-bit word or combination of two 16-bit words may be used to store as a unit, a 24-bit mantissa and 8-bit exponent.

The mantissa is stored as the largest possible *fraction*, in the form of a signed integer with the highest bit equal to one for negative numbers. Hence, if only a 5-bit mantissa were used, 00111 would represent 7/16 and 01111, 15/16, while 10000 would represent -1. The reader may wish to refer to Chapter 1 for further discussion of this point. There is an implied binary point between the first and second binary digits -00111 implies 0.0111, and so on. Similarly, the exponent may represent the power of 16^6 by which the fraction is to be multiplied, using the same signed integer notation.[6] Hence, if the exponent is 8 bits in length, the mantissa 01111 with exponent 00000001 would represent 15/16 *times 16 to the first power*, or simply the value 15. To represent the number 1.0 in this same notation, we would need to use *1/16 times 16 to the first power*, which with a 24-bit mantissa would have the values

Exponent	Mantissa
0000 0001	0000 1000 0000 0000 0000 0000

We note that the bits to the right of the 1 in the mantissa would not all be zeros for a real number between 1 and 2. Although this *base-16* floating-point format permits very large or very small numbers (in the range 16^{-128} to 16^{127}) to be represented, the number of significant (binary) digits in the mantissa will be between 20 (as above) and 24. Hence the *precision* of a floating result can be only between 6 and 7 decimal digits. Accordingly, for exacting scientific calculations, *double precision* numbers of 64 bit total length or floating-point representations of 72 or 80 bits may be used.

Round-off is a term denoting adjustment of the low-order digit that occurs after an arithmetic operation in which lower-order digits must be dropped. It, or else the cruder alternative of simply lopping off low-order bits, is usually a neces-

---

[6]It would make little sense to use the power of 10 in the exponent together with binary digits in the mantissa. By using the base 16 for the exponent, the smaller of two numbers which are to be added can be shifted right 4 bits at a time, each time adding one to the exponent, until its exponent is the same as that of the larger number or all mantissa digits are shifted off the right end.

sity in digital computers. Multiplication or repeated addition can produce a result which exceeds the number of bits set aside for storage of a number. Round-off is simple for binary numbers. We simply add the value of the first bit discarded to the last bit retained. Thus 1111.101 would round up to 1111+1 = 10000. The error produced by round-off is known as *round-off error* and is of the order of 1/2 the value represented by the low-order digit of the rounded result. It can be much larger however. Suppose, for example, that we are subtracting the floating-point numbers:

Exponent	Mantissa
0000 1000	0111 1110 0011 1001 1101 0111
−0000 1000	0111 1110 0001 1111 1111 1111
=0000 1000	0000 0000 0001 1001 1101 1000

The mantissa is automatically adjusted, after subtraction, to bring the most significant digit to the left by $4 + 4 = 8$ bits, and the exponent consequently reduced by 2. The result is:

0000 0110   0001 1001 1101 1000 0000 0000

and only ten significant bits are left in the mantissa! Where accuracy is important, programs must be laid out in such a way that floating-point operations are not required to subtract numbers which are nearly identical. Increasing the length of the floating-point number representation helps, although it cannot overcome the problem. This problem is less severe in the much slower variable-length BCD arithmetic. Even here, however, a lack of care can result in unacceptable errors creeping into lengthy calculation sequences.

6.8   THE INSTRUCTION SET AND PROGRAM OPERATION

In a particular processor, instructions of a given type will require the same time for execution. For example, instructions which move data from one GPR to another will require the same time, independent of which two specific registers are involved. Instructions which must write or read one word to, or from, memory will all take the same time.

However, the execution times of some instructions depend on data values. One group of such instructions are those that operate on strings of characters of BCD information. In general, the longer the string is, the longer the execution time will be. In a given program, if the actual length of the strings is known, execution time may be calculated.

All logical, and most arithmetic, instructions which operate on fixed-length data are executed in predictable times. By its nature, however, a divide instruction's execution time will be unpredictable. This is easily seen. Consider that the division process consists of successive subtraction and shifting. The values of the data at execution time will determine the length of time required to complete the division. If by accident or otherwise the denominator is zero, well-behaved computers will sense that problem and will abort the program if not otherwise directed.

Comparative execution times for the same program or for a theoretical mix of instruction types are often used as a means of establishing a *processor speed*. This may be important in the selection of a processor for a particular application. Once the processor is installed, however, the principal interest in speed may be in its ability to carry out certain time-critical tasks sufficiently fast. When time-critical input must be handled, short portions of a program may need to execute within the length of time between successive input byte arrivals. Inability of the program to operate successfully may require study of the possibility of eliminating or replacing certain instruction sequences. Usually, this type of "fine tuning" is only applicable to the small processors that are often used in real-time systems. This may demand that certain parts of the program be rewritten in machine language so that timing is optimized. Even here, software productivity concerns will generally suggest that only a minimum amount of coding be done in basic machine language. We often write the program in a high-level language and then identify those portions of the program that are exercised often under critical-time constraints only. Those parts of the program would be rewritten in machine language.

This chapter has dealt with processor operations at the basic machine instruction level. Few programmers, and even fewer end users will control the computer at this level, though BASIC programs having brief forays into machine-level via **PEEK** and **POKE** commands are not uncommon. Most information systems engineers will be performing tasks such as integrating programs written by others to perform certain tasks, or writing programs in a high-level or very high-level language.

The question frequently arises: Is there some relationship between the instructions at the machine level and those used in higher-level languages? What is often implied by the question is *whether a given processor instruction set maps easily into a given higher-level language*. Generally, a single instruction in a high-level language will correspond to several machine language instructions. For the most part, designers of computer instruction sets attempt to include a large repertoire of instructions. Special instructions which deal with scanning of character strings, for example, would appear to be very effective for dealing with languages in which this sort of process was attacked directly by specific commands. It is possible that there would be a good "match" between the way the command in the high-level language was intended to operate and that of the processor instructions. However, if slightly different concepts of measuring location in a character string were adopted by the two languages, additional instructions might be required to make the machine language sequence produce the expected result. What follows is an illustration of an equivalency between a particular C (language) statement and corresponding instructions at the assembly language level in MSD DOS computers, including the IBM-PC.

```
C:              sum = part1 + part2;

Assembler:      mov  ax,part1
                add  ax,part2
                mov  sum,ax
```

Many programs or parts of programs are still prepared in the machine language of a particular computer. The usual argument for doing so is the minimization of program memory and execution time. In the hands of a programmer who is expert in the machine's operation and in the application area itself, there is little question that such a program *can be* near-optimum in efficiency. However, there are several important limitations to programs written in machine language. They cannot be transported (the term *ported* is sometimes used) to a different computer. They cannot be readily modified except by another machine language expert or the original author. They may be obsoleted by minor changes in the system operating environment. Thus machine-language programming and software productivity are somewhat, but not entirely, mutually exclusive terms.

The *penalties* in memory space and execution time imposed by use of higher-level languages also depend to a considerable extent on programmer experience in using them. A skilled programmer can produce more efficient programs, albeit at higher cost, than a novice. Without any sort of program optimization, memory requirements and execution time for programs written in a high-level or very high-level language may range from perhaps 10% greater than those of a machine-language program, to as much as 10 times greater.

To the question—"Should this program be written in machine language?"—there cannot be an unqualified "no" as the answer. Languages such as C are now available which provide almost as much flexibility as machine language, but with much greater portability. Critics hasten to point out that C is nearly as complex and difficult for a human to understand as is a typical machine language. A current characterization of the common point of view is as follows. *Only if* concerns about execution speed and memory requirements strongly dominate over program adaptability and programming cost, *and only if* the program will be executed on one type of processor, should a complex program generally be written entirely in machine language (assembly language).

We will meet the C language in the next chapter.

PROBLEMS

6.1 For a 16-bit computer whose instructions may refer to a maximum of one memory location and a register, or two registers, and which is to manipulate 8- or 16-bit data quantities, lay out

  (a) The set of arithmetic and data manipulations which you would like to be able to perform.

(b) A *separate* list of the possible source and destination combinations. (For the latter, consider that there are some operations which are by nature single-operand, such as inverting all bits in a byte or word. Also consider that there must be 8- and 16-bit registers depending on whether the instruction deals with 8- or 16-bit data.)

(c) For each operation, count the number of source and destination combinations which make sense, then count the number of instructions in your hypothetical instruction set. How many bits will be required to be able to assign a distinct instruction code to each? (Consider only the type of source, register or memory, and of destination, not the additional bits required to define a particular register or memory location.)

6.2 Instructions moving data from a specific register to another should require no more than 16 bits total as instruction code (4 bits for each register designation plus 8 bits additional). Instructions referencing memory in a 16-bit-address computer will require at least 24 bits (3 bytes).

(a) Why should we have at least a few instructions which include memory addresses in them?

(b) If the instruction set contains a single register-to-memory transfer instruction and a complementary memory-to-register transfer, with all arithmetic instructions using only 16-bit registers as source and destination, make a simple list of the series of instruction steps which would be required to add *two register-length* data values located in memory and then put the sum back into memory.

If each instruction referring to a register and a memory location requires 32 bits and each instruction referring to registers only requires 16 bytes, add the number of 16-bit transfers to or from memory which are required to complete the addition operation, including the reading of instruction words.

6.3 Repeat Problem 4.2b for a case in which an add instruction is provided which will add a data value stored in memory to the contents of a register.

6.4 Using the two concepts of (1) addressing memory by storing a memory address in a register and (2) indexing in which the contents of two registers are added to produce a new memory address, describe how a series of successive bytes can be brought into a register for comparison with the byte value stored in another register.

6.5 **(a)** Show the use of the zero and carry status bits in comparing two operands by a subtraction for all cases of relative value of the input operands.

(b) What use can be made of a status bit which indicates the value of the most significeant bit in the result of an arithmetic operation in the ALU?

6.6 In an interrupt (among other steps) we push the contents of the register holding status bits onto the stack prior to branching to the interrupt routine and pop it off the stack on returning. In subroutine calls we do not do this. Why?

6.7 In floating point arithmetic instructions, the mantissa and exponent are handled separately for arithmetic. In addition and subtraction, the exponents are adjusted to be the same prior to combination, while in multiplication and division this is not necessary, as you can easily convince yourself.

(a) Using for simplicity a decimal floating-point representation, show the steps which would be carried out in adding, subtracting, multiplying, and dividing the normalized data values 0.52345 E 23 and 0.32987 E 21, and producing a similarly normalized result. (The notation E 23 means times 10 to the twenty-third power, and the normalized mantissa is maintained between 0.1 and 1.0.)

(b) In floating point addition or subtraction, justify an argument that the operation can often be shortened if the exponents are examined before combining the mantissas.

6.8 Analysis of a particular class of program results in statistics which show that the percent of each of a set of classes of instructions appearing in a program will be as below (the instruction "mix"):

Class	1	2	3	4	5	6	7	8
Percent occurrence	22	10	3	18	7	14	13	13

For a given machine under study for an application, an instruction in each class requires the following execution times in microseconds:

Class	1	2	3	4	5	6	7	8
Time	.5	.8	3.4	1.0	2.0	1.2	.3	.7

For the given instruction mix, determine the calculated performance of the processor, in MIPS, by determining the length of time required to process some *fixed* number of instructions, in the *proportions* given by the mix.

7

C: A HIGH-LEVEL LANGUAGE

7.0 INTRODUCTION

In this chapter we provide an introduction to C, a high-level language. We depart from the more conventional practice of using Basic or Pascal as the introductory high-level language because of our belief that C is not much more difficult to learn, and is often a more suitable language than either Basic or Pascal for software development. We have discussed this rationale earlier and will not repeat it in detail here. We do provide appendices to many of our chapters that discuss equivalent Pascal code for many of the C programs that we develop here.

7.1 WHY USE A HIGH LEVEL LANGUAGE?

In Chapter 5 we saw how a simple assembly-language program could be written using mnemonics like MOV and ADD. Some large application programs are written in assembly language today, as are almost all operating system utilities. As we observed at the end of the last chapter, such programs usually execute faster than programs written in the more human-oriented high-level languages. Most high-level languages are more like English and hence easier to write and follow than assembly language. The source code for a given application is usually much more compact in a high-level language than an assembly-language source code. On the other hand, the size of the executable code and its execution time are smaller for assembly language code than for code written in a higher-level language. This particular advantage to assembly language code is rapidly disappearing as optimizing compiler designs, that result in very efficient executable codes, are perfected.

Some high-level languages have been in existence since the very early days of computers. Source code that has been written in one high-level language can easily be made to run, generally with only minor changes, on a completely different machine for a number of languages for which relatively tight standards exist.

The high-level language we have chosen is C. It has an advantage over some earlier languages of a *block-structured organization*, which makes programs written in C relatively easy to create and to understand. It also has an advantage over some newer languages in *simplicity*. It has a simple vocabulary and is never far, in concept or implementation, from the machine itself. Sadly, this latter fact necessarily leads to some austerity in cryptic notations that renders C less of a human oriented high-level language than others such as Basic and Pascal.

7.2   GETTING STARTED WITH COMPUTER SOFTWARE

The best way to learn about computers is to use one. This is true whether the learning has to do with applications software, such as system design packages or word processors; or with the fundamentals of the machine itself, as when we used **D E B U G** to illustrate some features of machine architecture. A high-level language helps in the communication process, and our intent here is to introduce such a language now and to use it first as a tool to aid in understanding the machine. Later, the same language will be used to develop some elementary applications. Every one of these applications and languages is a *program* which runs on the machine to do a particular job.

The process of writing and running a program begins with an *editor* that processes the text that represents source code, which is entered at the keyboard by a programmer. There are many editors available. This book, for example, was written on several editors, or word processors, with elaborate text formatting capabilities (Microsoft Word, Wordstar 2000, Wordstar Classic, and Multimate). There is a very simple one-line-at-a-time editor in PC-DOS called *Edlin*. *Edlin* is a line editor, as contrasted with a text editor. It is so primitive that it is a little difficult to use, even for simple program text editing. Most program writing is done on editors which fall between these extremes, and which use the full terminal screen to display the work progress.

The best editors for program writing by professional programmers allow multiple programs to reside in memory. Comparisons and copying back and forth from program to program are quick and simple operations. Many modern word processors and programming text editors have this capability.

There are other high-level languages which are widely used for instruction. Pascal is among these. We will end each of the next few chapters with a section or appendix showing how the C programs we develop could be written in Pascal. The two languages are somewhat similar, so the translation from one language construct to the other is often not difficult. Readers may wish to skip these Pascal sections, or may want to try out the alternate language. At the end of this chapter there will be a short introduction to becoming multilingual (in a computer sense). We will also discuss numerical analysis algorithm implementation using both Pascal and C.

7.3 THE C LANGUAGE

The C programming language is defined in a book titled *The C Programming Language* by Brian Kernighan and Dennis Ritchie (universally referred to as K&R) which was first published in 1978. The C language was created with sophisticated commercial software development in mind. It was the basic high-level language for the UNIX operating system, which was actually written in C through the use of a bootstrapping procedure. It is a language which has power and capability well beyond those of the student language Pascal. C is a loosely defined and undisciplined language, close in many ways to assembly language, and it has been justifiably criticized for this. It has been widely adopted, however, and is used in a variety of commercial products. Its wide adoption has enabled a path to C language portability, a term which means the adaptation of a single program to a variety of machines.

All the C programs in this book have been run on the compiler in the **Borland Turbo C** package on a MS-DOS personal computer. Almost all of them have also been run on Microsoft Quick C. As long as we use only the K&R defined conventions, programs are fully portable from one compiler to the other. The conventions used are similar to those in UNIX, so that the programs will run under that operating system also. The reader should obtain a copy of **Turbo C, Quick C,** or some other C development compiler,[1] and try out the programs given here in the text.

An excellent way to learn a language is to make changes to working programs. Just, reading about programming is not an effective way to learn about it. This is also true for flying an airplane, riding a bicycle, playing tennis, or solving differential equations.

The first simple C program we use is:

```
main()
{
        printf("\nhello, world");
}
```

This can be typed using the editor furnished with *Turbo C*, and other editors as well. The details of using the editor and the other features of Turbo C are contained in the manuals which come with the software.

---

[1]Many are available. The most complete for the PC environment are probably Microsoft C and Lattice C.

We start the program with

```
A:> tc hello.C
```

from the DOS prompt. This program was given a convenient name, as in the K&R text, with the .C extension. This extension is not required by the Turbo C compiler, but it is standard practice to use this to enable easy identification of the program as a C language program. The program can be run by typing <alt r>, that is, hold down the Alt key and press r. To avoid possible confusion, we will describe Turbo C conventions in our discussions.

The program hello.c and hello.exe will be in your directory after you leave the editor (by typing <Alt f> and then <q> from the pull-down menu). The executable file hello.exe will run from the DOS prompt if its name is typed: hello. The greeting will appear on the screen.

Let us examine the hello program again. The first word we note in this program is main. Every C program has a block called main, and this is the starting place for the code to follow. The block structure is marked by curly brackets or braces: { and }. The (built-in) library function printf causes everything inside the double quotes to appear on the screen. The \n (backslash-n) is a *newline* character, and is printed as a carriage-return-line-feed combination. It is treated as a single symbol, even though two symbols are used in the PC-DOS and MS-DOS operating system.

The printf function is the subject of the next section. It is the primary means in the C language for sending data to the screen of a terminal. This function is widely used for report formatting; it is also a primary debugging tool for C. It will be used in the next section to illustrate some of the points about the hex number system that we discussed in Section 1.3.

The C language itself does not formally include functions like printf. This input/output package is not considered part of the C language. This makes the language vocabulary especially simple, but requires the presence of functions like *printf* in a library where programs can use them. We will introduce many functions as we go along, and later present an inventory of functions. C is more dependent, we believe, on an effective and sizable library than other programming languages. C is a cumbersome language in which to program without an effective and sizable library. This is also due, as we have noted, to its strong similarity to assembly language.

7.4 THE PRINTF FUNCTION

Let us write a program in C which prints the values of the variables x and y and their sum on the screen. In C, all variables must be *declared* before they are used. The statement

```
int x, y;
```

does this and sets aside storage in the machine for the numbers with those names. The int part of the declaration means that x and y will be stored in 2-byte (16-bit) memory locations since we are using a 16-bit machine. The declaration symbol *int* is a mnemonic for "integer." (This is not to be confused with the use of int from our earlier discussions of machine language calls.)

A program which accomplishes this printing function is

```
main()
{   int x,y;

    x = 4289;
    y = 41;

    printf("\n%d + %d = %d", x, y, x + y);
    printf("\n%d in hex is %x", x, x);
}
```

When this program runs, it prints the following expressions on the screen:

```
4289 + 41 = 4330
4289 in hex is 10c1
```

In the program the statement x = 4289 is called *assignment* of the number 4289 to the variable x. C uses the equals sign for assignment.[2]

The printf statement now shows the two parts of its normal argument:

1. a part in double quotes which contains matter to be printed, together with format information about the variables; and
2. a list of variables that follows the second double quote.

Inside the quotes, text is printed verbatim except for the format information, which is signaled by the percent sign %. Each percent sign stands for one of the variables in the variable list. In this example, the format is indicated in the first printf statement by the letter d, which is used to indicate *decimal integer* format. Remember that the \n is treated as a single symbol meaning newline.

In the second printf statement, the variable x is to be printed both as an integer, with the %d format, and as a hex number, specified by %x.

We will be saying more about the printf function in later chapters. It is an important function and is often used as a principal means for diagnostic testing.

---

[2]Pascal and Ada use :=.

7.5 NEGATIVE NUMBERS

As an example of the kind of probing that simple programs can accomplish relative to the insides of our computer, we look at the way negative numbers are stored. This subject was introduced in Section 1.4, and it is convenient to return to it here.

Here is a C program that prints the internal storage form of ‾1 on the screen:

```
main()
{   int x;
    x = -1;
    printf("\n%d is stored internally as %x
      hex", x,x);
}
```

When the program is run, this is printed:

```
-1 is stored internally as ffff hex
```

Notice that the p r i n t f line in the source program has been now split into two lines to fit on the page. C pays no attention to newlines, or for that matter to indentations or other arrangements that make text more readable. These are really intended only for the human eye and as aids in visualizing the program structure.

The result that ‾1 is stored as hex F F F F suggests to us that integers are stored in a 16 bit world as 2 bytes or 16 bits. Knowing this, it is easy to verify, using the description in Section 1.4 that two's complement is indeed used on this machine.

7.6 FLOATING-POINT NUMBERS

Another example will show how nonintegers are handled. The objective is to print a table of inches and centimeters, given that 1 in. is 2.54 cm. Here is the program:

```
#define CPI   2.54      /* CPI is cm per inch */

main()
{
    int inches;
    float centimeters;
```

```
for (inches = 0; inches <= 12; inches++)
{
   centimeters = inches * CPI;
   printf("\n%4d %6.2f",inches,centimeters);
}
}
```

The C program makes use of what is called the *preprocessor* in order to give a value to the constant C P I that is specified by the #de f i ne statement. Before the beginning of compilation, the C P I in the program is replaced by the defined value: 2.54. A comment, which is ignored by the compiler, is enclosed in / * . . * / . These comments are intended to enhance the ability of humans to understand the code.

There is a loop here which is implemented by the f o r construction. It specifies the starting condition (i n c h e s = 0), the ending test (inches less than or equal to 12), and the changes that are to be made each time the loop is executed (increment inches). The loop itself is contained inside the curly bracket following the f o r.

The f o r construction is very useful and is often seen in C programs. The incrementing operator + + is also often seen and is our first occurrence of one of the special C notations that cause complaints from critics of the language.

The p r i n t f statement contains a new format: f for floating. The space allowance numbers following % provide for a field containing room for six characters, two of which are decimal places. The program is run by typing <A l t r> from the *Turbo C* editor. The following is then printed to the screen:

```
 0     0.00
 1     2.54
 2     5.08
 3     7.62
 4    10.16
 5    12.70
 6    15.24
 7    17.78
 8    20.32
 9    22.86
10    25.40
11    27.94
12    30.48
```

There is much new here, and the reader is urged to type this program into the **Turbo C** editor and experiment with it until its features and performance are well understood.

7.7 APPENDIX: NOTES ON PASCAL

Pascal, like C, is a member of a group of modern programming languages called *block-structured* languages. With block structure, the development of applications can proceed in an especially orderly way. The two languages are enough alike to make learning them together relatively easy. They are part of the common language of computing, and knowing them opens communications paths to much contemporary activity in modern computing.

Pascal was invented by Niklaus Wirth in Switzerland in the early 1970s. It was meant to be a teaching language, and many of its features reflect academic rather than commercial goals. However, its design was so attractive that it was soon used in commercial software products.

The usual way to introduce a language is to show how it can be used to connect the computer to the world around it via a message on the screen. Here is such a program:

```
program hello(output);
     begin
           writeln('hello, world');
end.
```

Every Pascal program begins with the word program followed by the name of the program, in this case hello. The word output is an indication to the compiler that the program when it is run will write something to the screen of the terminal or to some other output device.

The block structure of Pascal can be seen in the begin-end construction. In a larger program this structure isolates parts of the program in sections which can be checked out independently, separate from the rest of the program. While it is not apparent here in this simple example, the block device is an important contribution to the creation of efficient software.

The built-in function writeln causes the expression within single quotes to be printed on the screen; a carriage-return-line-feed combination (a newline) is appended by writeln itself.

The reader should type in this program, and run it using *Turbo Pascal* or another Pascal package, to see the greeting on the screen.

If you use *Turbo Pascal*, choose the e for Edit option from the menu, give the program a name, and type in the text you want. Certain keys or combinations of keys are used for moving about the screen and adding and subtracting text.[3] When you are through press ∧k (to get control-k, the control key is held down like a shift key while k is pressed) and then d. This combination terminates the edit session and returns you to the menu.

---

[3]As we have noted, both Turbo Pascal and Turbo C use editors whose commands are largely derived from Wordstar, a most successful general PC word-processing program that has been continuously revised and updated.

After leaving the editor, do not save the program yet; simply type r for Run. The program will be compiled, if it has no errors, and the resulting object program will then be executed.

After observing the greeting on the screen, type s for Save, and if you provide the name `hello`, the program `hello.pas` will be written to a diskette. The `.pas` term, called the extension, is added automatically by *Turbo Pascal*, which assumes that was your intention.

Next, in order to do some manipulation of numbers, we introduce the idea of a variable in a simple Pascal program. Let us consider

```
program vari (output);
var
    x, y: integer;
begin
  x := 4289;
  y := 41;
  writeln(x, ' + ', y, ' = ', x + y);
end.
```

In this program the variables x and y have been declared to be integers. Pascal is a "strongly typed" language, which means that the *nature* of all objects (data, etc.) occurring in a program must be declared to the compiler. This declaration was accomplished here by the statement that *x* and *y* are variables. C is more relaxed about declarations, but all variables must be declared before use, or the compiler will complain. In general, these complaints are for our protection.

The symbol `:=` is used by Pascal for assignment, and the first statement could be read "set x equal to 4289." The `writeln` statement this time is a mixture of text in single quotes and variables which are printed to the screen in their own format. If we try running this program, it writes to the screen:

```
4289 + 41 = 4330
```

Here, the plus and equal signs are provided as text in the single quotes of the `writeln` argument.

Our final example in this chapter will show how nonintegers are handled by Pascal. The objective is to print a table of inches and centimeters, given that 1 in. is 2.54 cm. Here is the Pascal version of the program:

```
program itoc (output);
const
  cpi = 2.54; (* centimeters per inch *)
var
  inches: integer;
  centimeters: real;
```

```
begin
  for inches := 0 to 12 do
    begin
      centimeters := inches * cpi;
      writeln(inches:6,centimeters:8:2);
    end
end.
```

This program has an added category at the beginning: c o n s t, which contains the values of numbers which are unchanged during the running of the program. The declaration of 2.54 as r e a l is implicit from its decimal format. The variable c e n t i m e t e r s is declared to be r e a l in the v a r section. A comment is enclosed in (* and *) and the symbols mean that the enclosed expression or remarks will be ignored by the compiler. Pascal allows the use of curly brackets for comments too, but we will use (* to avoid confusion with C's use of braces in order to enclose collections of statements or blocks.

This program contains a loop controlled by the f o r . . . t o . . . d o construction. The variable i n c h e s is started at 0 and incremented to 12; the block inside the loop is executed each time through. The w r i t e l n statement contains the limited format control provided by Pascal. The colons set aside the positions to be occupied by the variables, and in the case of the r e a l, the number of decimal places. When it is run, it produces the same output as its C counterpart at the end of Section 7.6.

PROBLEMS

7.1 Write a C program which prints a table of squares and cubes of integers from 0 to 20.

7.2 Write a C program which prints a conversion table for decimal integers to hex; the decimals should go from 0 to 128, and the table should have 7 columns.

7.3 Print a table of ASCII characters corresponding to the decimal integers from 33 to 126. Also show the hex values of the decimal integers. The table should have five columns. (Hint: the p r i n t f format for characters is % c.)

8

DATA STORAGE AND POINTERS

8.0 INTRODUCTION

In this chapter we continue with our discussions of C through the introduction of some very simple concepts concerning data structures and data pointers. We will return to these concepts often, especially when we examine some basic features of database and information systems.

8.1 HOW VARIABLES AND CONSTANTS ARE STORED

The data stored in computer memory requires memory space that is proportional to the bit size of the data and to the representation format that is used. Integers generally require less space than a floating-point-number representation of the same integer, for example. We have already met the declarations for these C-language types of variables and constants. They are:

	Type	Bytes
integer	int	2
real	float	4

C provides extra precision through the following declarations:

double integer	long	4
double decimal	double	8

110

The storage size required by C programs in bytes (a byte is 8 bits, as we know from several previous discussions) is shown in the last column. This byte size may vary from machine to machine. Those just given are the numbers for the IBM-PC and the *Turbo C* compiler, and are valid for most C-compiler PC combinations.

There is also a 1-byte variable which is used mainly to store the internal codes for characters. The declaration for this variable is

character   char   1

The c h a r type is the subject of our next section.

8.2 CHARACTERS AS VARIABLES

Because the alphabetic characters are given numerical codes (for example, 'a' = 97 or 61 hex), text and graphic symbols, as well as numbers, can be stored and manipulated by the computer. The PC uses the ASCII code for the upper- and lowercase alphabet, as well as a variety of other symbols, including simple graphics. In addition, 31 nonprinting characters are also available. The ASCII code 13 (decimal) produces a carriage return, for example, and 10 produces a line feed.

The C program next shown prints a table of the lowercase alphabetic characters and their ASCII codes on the screen. We have arranged the table in two columns of 13 lines each.

```
/* print a table of ASCII values */

main()
{
   int i;
   for (i = 'a'; i <= 'a' + 12; i++)
   {
     printf("%c%5d%4c%5d\n",
       i, i, i + 13, i + 13);
   }
}
```

A new feature is present in this program; it is represented by the % c format notation in the p r i n t f statement. This feature allows printing of a character together with the ASCII code that corresponds to it. Another new feature is represented by the use of single quotes to represent the ASCII value of a single character (e.g., 'a').

Because the format part of the p r i n t f argument is transferred to the screen verbatim, except for the % parts and special symbols like \n, careful examination is sometimes needed to unscramble the resulting congestion of symbols. In the foregoing example, the format, now spread out for legibility, is:

```
%c    %5d    %4c    %5d
```

In words, we are representing the following: a character; 5 spaces with an integer, right justified; 4 spaces with a character, right justified; and so on.

The for loop begins with the variable i set to the code of a. There are some extra terms in our printf expression. We have inserted these in order to get the answer to print out in two columns. Programs which loop often pose unfortunate problems related to the end points of ranges, as we easily discover upon writing some simple programs. In this example, we might question whether we should add 12 or 13 to the variable? Often, trial and error is the shortest practical way to determine a correct number for the end point of a range, or for the correction of other errors.

The result shown on the screen after compiling and executing this program is:

```
a    97      n   110
b    98      o   111
c    99      p   112
d   100      q   113
e   101      r   114
f   102      s   115
g   103      t   116
h   104      u   117
i   105      v   118
j   106      w   119
k   107      x   120
l   108      y   121
m   109      z   122
```

Some of the nonprinting characters, like the carriage return, are represented by special backslash combinations in C. These are sometimes called *escape sequences*. We have already met the expression \n, which is used to represent newline. Other useful escape sequences include:

```
carriage return      \r
line feed            \n    (printed as a newline)
tab                  \t
backspace            \b
formfeed             \f
backslash            \\
single quote         \'
null (binary 0)      \0
```

We note the use of \, also called the *escape* character. It is used to represent itself and the single quote and illustrates how to represent a single quote inside single quotes. The *null* character, represented by 8 bits of all zeros, is \0. Turbo C has some other escape sequences, such as \a for the IBM PC beep.

8.3 ARRAYS

The simplest arrangement of multiple objects in a program is called an *array*. An array is somewhat like mail boxes in a post office. Numbers or characters can be placed in the boxes of an array such that they can later be retrieved by an *index* which is related to position. The index is the position, numbered from a zeroth box. C always starts numbering at zero; some other languages, such as Pascal, start at one.

Arrays can have more than one dimension, but we will only consider one-dimensional arrays for the time being. We next present a program which puts the letters of the alphabet in an array and then prints a message by referring to their positions. The program is:

```
main()
  {
  int i:
  char letter[26];
  static int message[5] = {7, 4, 11, 11, 14};

 for  (i = 0; i <= 26; i++)
    letter[i] = 'a' + i;

  for (i = 0; i < 5; i++)
    printf("%c",letter[message[i]]);

  printf("\n\n");
}
```

The array letter is declared to have 26 elements of type char. In C, arrays always start counting or numbering at 0, as we have just noted. In this program a second array message contains the array positions for the letters of hello. This second array is declared to be of storage class static so that it can be *initialized*. We will return to a more complete discussion of storage classes and their properties later.

The first for loop fills the array letter with the letters of the alphabet. The next one prints the contents of the array message by using its members to pick out letters from the first array. The actual object printed is a nesting of the two arrays: letter[message[i]]. It sounds a little complicated, but studying it by stepping carefully through the first few cycles by hand may help in understanding.

The result is:

```
hello
```

8.4 STRINGS

A *string* is a special kind of character array. For reasons to be described, strings are character arrays in C, with the last character an ASCII null. Strings are the basis for all applications which handle text and are therefore very important.

To be meaningful, a string often needs to be handled as a unit. In this way it can be moved, copied, compared, and so on. This requires that its *end* be marked in some way, either by storing the length somewhere or by putting some special marking in the last position of the array. The array letter in the foregoing example contains characters—the letters of the alphabet—but it is not a string because its length is not marked.

C has adopted the convention that all strings end with a byte of binary zero, the \0 special character which stands for the binary number 0000. A C program that stores and retrieves strings is now given:

```
char greeting[] = "hello, world";

main()
{
   int i;

   printf("\n%s\n", greeting);

   for (i = 0; greeting[i] != '\0'; i++)
    printf("\n%4c%4d",greeting[i],
      greeting[i]);
}
```

When this program is run, it writes to the screen:

```
hello, world

   h 104
   e 101
   l 108
   l 108
   o 111
   , 44
```

```
   32
w 119
o 111
r 114
l 108
d 100
```

The string is defined in the first declaration, which is placed outside the main block in order to make initialization possible.[1] The program prints the string "hello, world," and then prints a table of its characters and their decimal internal ASCII storage codes. In this program the declaration includes an assignment which initializes the array g r e e t i ng with the string in double quotes. In C all double quoted expressions are strings. They must be properly terminated with a null.

A new format, %s for string, has been introduced in this program. The variable reference in the p r i nt f list is the *name* of the string (which, as we shall see in the next section, is a *pointer* to the first member of the array holding the string). The p r i nt f statement prints the whole string under this format.

In this program the f o r loop runs until the null at the end of the string is reached. As a result, we print out the characters one at a time, together with their internal storage codes. The expression != means not-equal-to.

8.5 POINTERS

Pointers are simply the memory addresses of the objects that are pointed to. If we think of the task of sorting personnel records containing name, address, age, and so forth, the idea of sorting *pointers to the records*, rather than the bulky records themselves, is appealing. Pointers are the key to efficient management of data. For this reason, they are very important, and efficient and effective use of pointers is vital to success in the development of software.

In the C language any variable can have a pointer associated with it by using the operator &, which means *address of*. The inverse operator is *, which means *contents of*. The process is called *indirection*.

If a variable x is declared in a C program,

```
int x;
```

then & x is the address of, or the pointer to, the variable x. The pointer is the physical offset address of the memory location where the variable x is stored in the majority of personal computers.

---

[1]Turbo C will initialize arrays inside the block, but some other compilers will not. The Turbo C initialization is in accordance with Kernighan and Ritchie's book *The C Language*.

The contents of the storage location are obtained by using the operator ∗. If y is declared to be a pointer to an integer, and is then assigned the value of the pointer to x, such as in the program

```
int *y; /* this is how a pointer is declared */
         y = &x;
```

then ∗y will be the contents of the address of x, or x itself in this C program.

Here is a C program which illustrates the use of address and indirection (*contents of*) operators:

```
main()
  { int number, *ptr;
             ptr = &number;
             number = 5;
             printf("\nnumber = %d address of
                number = %x",
              *ptr, ptr);
  }
```

The program prints this:

```
number = 5   address of number = ffda
```

The variable ptr is declared to point at an int, and the address of number is assigned to it. The contents of ptr are printed together with the address itself in hex. The address is the offset part of the physical address of the place where number is stored.

8.6 POINTER AND ARRAYS

We now return to arrays. The name of an array is a pointer to the first member of the array. Here is a version of the "hello, world" array program that we have used so often which illustrates this:

```
main()
  { char greeting[] = "hello, world";
  printf("\n%s\n", greeting);
  printf("\nthe 1st character of greeting is
    %c", *greeting);
  printf("\n...and the second is %c",
    *(greeting + 1));
  }
```

This program prints:

```
hello world the 1st character of greeting is h
...and the second is e
```

The contents of the name `greeting` is the first character of the array. Pointers can be incremented, and the amount of the increment will be that needed to reach the next character (or member) of the array, in this case the letter `e`.

Here is another short program which illustrates the relation between pointers and arrays:

```
main()
  { stat  int arry[5] = {1,2,3,4,5};
  int *ptr;

  ptr = arry;

  printf("\nptr[2] = %d", *(ptr + 2));
}
```

The result of compiling and executing this program is a display on the monitor of

```
ptr[2] = 3.
```

There is a fundamental relation between an array and the pointer to the array. It is that `array[n]` is the same as `*(array + n)`.

We will return to the subject of pointers again. Here we have used pointers to characters and integers. But pointers can be associated with any object in C. Thus they are extremely useful.

8.7 CONVERSION AMONG TYPES

The C language allows mixing of types in expressions if the mixing *makes sense*. For example, `2*2.5` should be `5.0` even though a `float` is multiplied by an integer. The rules are complicated, and the reader is referred to the K&R text for details. Generally, it is most productive to write a code that seems to make sense and then let the compiler, or tests performed after the program is written, do the checking.[2] In the UNIX environment a program called *lint* checks C programs for potential problems such as unused variables or mismatched data types. There are versions of this program that run under MS-DOS.

The C language has a mechanism for forcing or coercing a change in

---

[2]This is not an invitation for carelessness: simple tests may not always exercise all possible data combinations, and an error may not show itself until the program is in use.

type. It is called a *type cast*, or *cast* for short. In using this mechanism, the variable is written with the desired type in parentheses ahead of it to produce the result.

As an example, here is a program which tries to print an integer as a floating point number:

```
main()
   { int i = 55;
   printf("\ni = %f", i);
}
```

The *Turbo C* compiler complains about this program and refuses to compile the program. The inconsistency can be corrected with a *type cast*, such as in the program

```
main()
   { int i = 55;
   printf("\ni = %f", (float)i);
}
```

which, when compiled and executed gives the correct result:

```
I = 55.000000
```

8.8   APPENDIX: PASCAL DATA STORAGE AND POINTERS

In writing a Pascal program that will print the ASCII table, the more limited writeln statement means that the conversion from internal code to character must be provided by a library function. Turbo Pascal has a pair of functions, chr and ord, which decode and encode characters. A program to print the alphabet is given below, modified to give the codes for uppercase letters:

```
program asc ( output);
     var
              start, i: integer;
     begin
              start := ord('A');
              for i := start to start + 12 do
                   begin
                        writeln(i:3, chr(i):5,
                             (i + 13):8,
                        chr(i + 13):5);
                        end
     end.
```

The o r d function is used to find the starting place (the internal code for ' A ').
The c h r function is used to decode the variable i in the loop. The result is:

65	A	78	N
66	B	79	O
67	C	80	P
68	D	81	Q
69	E	82	R
70	F	83	S
71	G	84	T
72	H	85	U
73	I	86	V
74	J	87	W
75	K	88	X
76	L	89	Y
77	M	90	Z

Here is a Pascal program which puts the letters of the alphabet in an array
and then prints a message:

```
program arr (output);
var
   i: integer;
   letter: array [0..25] of char;
begin
   for i := 0 to 25 do   (* fill the boxes *)
      begin
         letter[i] := chr(ord('a') + i);
      end;
   writeln(letter[7],letter[4],letter[11],
           letter[11],letter[14]);
end.
```

In this program l e t t e r is declared to be an a r r a y with 26 positions,
numbered from 0 to 25; each space is to contain a c h a r a c t e r. The program fills the array with the lowercase letters of the alphabet, beginning with
c h r (o r d (' a ')), which is a itself. The message is written out by picking
letters by their positions in the array. The result is

```
hello.
```

This program uses the a r r a y letter as a *buffer*—a place to put data. The
standard Pascal definition is casual about strings and leaves the details of their
management up to the programmer. *Turbo Pascal* has added a s t r i n g type,
but it requires specification of the length *before* use. Strings are not a strong

point of the Pascal language. The treatment of strings by C is much more convenient we believe.

In this Pascal program the "hello, world" message is sent. However, the program is somewhat more complicated than its C counterpart:

```
program str (output);
     const
             greeting = 'hello, world';
     var
             arry: array [1..12] of char;
             i: integer;
     begin
             arry := greeting;
             writeln(arry);
             writeln;

             for i:= 1 to 12 do
           begin
               writeln(arry[i]:4,ord
                  (arry[i]):4);
           end
        end.
```

With Pascal it is possible to define a text constant with single quotes. Because we want to examine letters in the text, the array variable arry is filled with the constant text by assignment. (This is not possible with C, where uninitialized arrays must be filled one element at a time.)

Pascal provides a limited pointer capability which we will initially illustrate in the following program. The program has two blocks or *procedures*. Each is named in a line with the word procedure. The main part of the program invokes the procedures by naming them. We will discuss the subject of procedures more thoroughly in the appendix to Chapter 10.

```
program ptr (output);
var
  number: integer;
  ptr1, ptr2: ^integer;
procedure show;
  begin
    writeln('ptr1^ = ',ptr1^,'
       ptr2^ = ',ptr2^);
  end;
procedure test;  begin
    if ptr1 = nil then
      writeln('ptr1 points to nothing')
```

```
    else
      writeln('ptr1 points to ',ptr1^)
  end;
begin  (* main part of program *)
  number := 5;
  ptr1 := nil;

  test;

  new(ptr1);
  new(ptr2);
  ptr1^ := number;

  test;

  ptr2^ := 3;

  show;

  ptr2 := ptr1;

  show;

  release(ptr1);
end.
```

The program prints:

```
ptr1 points to nothing
ptr1 points to 5
ptr1^ = 5    ptr2^ = 3
ptr1^ = 5    ptr2^ = 5
```

In this program two pointers, ptr1 and ptr2, are declared as pointers to integers by means of the circumflex: ^. The program has two procedures which print information about the variables.

In Pascal the declaration of pointers does not create the object pointed to; this must be done by the function new. Pointers can be assigned to variables of the same type. We start by assigning nil to ptr1, which means that ptr1 points to nothing. Then we test.

Next, we create places to point to with new. The contents of the places just created are filled with integers by assignment, using the ^ at the *right* side of the name to indicate "contents of." At that point the variables can be shown graphically like this:

```
ptr1 -----> 5
ptr2 -----> 3
```

ptr1 is then assigned to ptr2 so that the picture is

```
ptr1 ------> 5 <------ ptr2
             3
```

Finally, the space allocated for storage of whatever was pointed to by ptr1 is returned to memory with the release function. This is done for illustration, and is not really needed here, since all allocated memory is returned at the termination of the program.

In Pascal pointers are much more limited than in C, where any pointer to any object can be obtained with the & operator. It is also quite evident from the example presented that using pointers in Pascal is more complicated than in C.

PROBLEMS

8.1 Write a C program to print the ASCII value of a question mark.

8.2 Use a type cast to convert a character to an integer.

8.3 Write a C program that uses a pointer to print the contents of an array with "hello, world" in it.

8.4 Write a program that fills a 4 × 4 two-dimensional array with the numbers from 0 to 15 and then prints it in hex. (Hint: the two-dimensional array x is declared int x[4][4]; .)

9

COMPUTER DECISIONS AND LOGIC

9.0 INTRODUCTION

One of the fundamental operations of a computer, that enables it to perform many functions, is making elementary decisions based on simple logic calculations. We recall that there were adding machines and mechanical calculators in widespread use before the days of the stored-program electronic digital computer. Those who had an opportunity to see inside one of these early calculators found sets of wheels, each of which advanced the next wheel to the right or left by one gear-tooth for each of its own full revolutions. The operations of these machines were *fixed*. They could add or subtract, and the more complex ones could also multiply and divide (at a cost of more than $1000, in the 1940's!). But they were incapable of being programmed or of performing elementary logic operations. Most importantly, they could usually not be made to perform sequences of connected computations. Further, they lacked the ability to *change* the sequence of the operations that they performed in response to the values of data fed into them.

Logic capability is the special feature of computers which permits them to perform variable sequences of complex operations in response to data values. To understand this more fully, we will need to examine how the binary numbers or data in a computer can be manipulated. In the binary system, with such a very limited number of possible digit values (zero and one), the primitive operations are limited and rather simple.

9.1   COMPUTER LOGIC

Binary logic had its early origins in philosophy and *rules of logic*. It evolved into *mathematical logic* or *Boolean*[1] *algebra or logic*, before stored program digital computers were imagined. Instead of using zeros and ones, this early work used *true* (1) or *false* (0) as the symbols to be manipulated.

To demonstrate the principles of binary logic, we first limit ourselves to combination of only *two* bits. The most basic operations are AND and OR. An AND operation on two input bits produces a 1 output *only* if *both* input bits are 1s. An OR operation, on the other hand, produces a 1 output if *either* or *both* inputs are 1s. This is also sometimes referred to as an *inclusive* OR, to distinguish it from yet another two-bit operation, the *exclusive* OR, whose output is 1 if either but not both inputs are 1s. Often, but not exclusively, the symbol + is used for inclusive OR and the symbol for exclusive OR is XOR. In early electrical implementations of logic functions, switches and/or relays were used. If we have two switches A and B, or two normally open relay contacts that are closed through energizing of relays A and B, then the AND operation is obtained by connecting the switches or contacts in series, as shown in Figure 9.1.

If we represent a closed switch by A = 1 (or B = 1), then we easily see that the *transmission* function of this network is T = AB. On the other hand, if we connect the switches in parallel, the transmission function B is T = A + B.

It is useful to represent these binary logic operations or functions in tabular form, with the values of the output for each combination of input shown as in Figure 9.2.

This representation is usually referred to as a *truth table*, in which case the ones are referred to as representing true and the zeros as representing false. A little thought will convince the reader that the transmission functions noted above are indeed correct for the given assignments of true and false to 1 and 0. We will verify this soon, when we examine some essentials of Boolean algebra.

With two binary input variables, there are 2^4 (sixteen) *different* tables possible. This allows us to define several other functions. It turns out that several of these are trivial. We have no interest, for example, in tables filled with four zeros or four ones, since the output does not depend on the input. We can generate

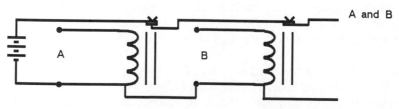

FIGURE 9.1   Result of energizing relays A and B.

---

[1]The nineteenth-century work of the Englishman George Boole resulted in logic foundations for the computer field.

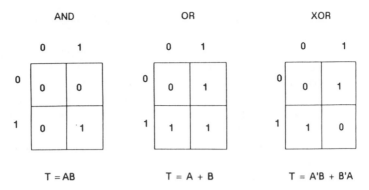

FIGURE 9.2 Binary logic operations.

other needed combinations by making use of the inversion or NOT function. A *NOT* function is a Boolean function with one input, which simply reverses the input to the *NOT* function from a zero to a one or the converse. If, for example, we wanted a function like the *AND*, but inverted in every one of the four cases, it is simpler to merely invert the output with a *NOT* function following the *AND*. This is sometimes called a *NAND* function. If we have T = AB, then T ' = (AB) ' = A' + B'.

9.2 BOOLEAN ALGEBRA

Let us now examine Boolean algebra in a more formal way. Boolean mathematical relations can be written to describe complex binary logic functions. The result *C* of *AND*ing *A* and *B* would be expressed as

C = A AND B,

or more simply

C = AB

and spoken "*C* equals *A* and *B*" or "*C* equals *A B*." The result, *D*, of *OR*ing *A* and *B* would be written

D = A OR B

or

D = A + B

and spoken "*D* equals *A* or *B*."

If a Boolean variable E is the inverse of A, we would write

$$E = A'$$

and say "*E* equals *not A*." One notation for the inverse of a Boolean variable is to put a bar *over* the variable. There are other notations in common usage—one is the apostrophe, such that not A is written A'. This is a simpler notation to use, especially when we wish to write the inverse of a complicated expression. We will use this notation from this point forward. The *manipulation* of binary logic forms is usually referred to as *Boolean algebra*. This algebra can be used to re-duce a complex expression to one which is more easily recognized. For example, Boolean expressions can be factored. We see that since $B' + B = 1$,

$$AB' + AB = A(B' + B) = A$$

The factoring used in the foregoing expression follows the same rule as ordinary algebra, with the AND expression treated analogously to a product and the OR expression treated analogously to a sum. The final step is observed if we note that the term within the parentheses is 1 if B is 0, and it is also 1 if B is 1. Thus it does not depend on B at all and can simply be replaced by 1. To obtain this "proof" we have made use of the fact that, for Boolean logic, $AB = AB + AB$ and have employed some simple factoring. Venn diagrams provide an easy way to visualize these operations. We can use Boolean algebra to verify each of the fundamental logic expressions shown in our table. For the OR relation we have

$$T = A'B + B'A + AB = A'B + B'A + AB + AB = B(A' + A) + A(B + B') = A + B$$

9.3 VENN DIAGRAMS

An alternate form of logic expression, widely useful even outside the computer world, is the *Venn diagram*. Here a closed area on the paper is used to represent the "part of the universe" in which A is one (or true). Also needed is a representation for the universe. As shown in Figure 9.3, the universe is just $A + A'$.

We can also represent other variables as closed areas, as shown in Figure 9.4, in which case we see that the *intersection*[2] of A and B in the diagram is AB, and the union is $A + B$.

There is some need here to explain what might appear as a double counting possibility. The union of A and B is formally:

$$A + B = A(B + B') + B(A + A') = AB + AB' + A'B$$

---

[2]Intersection and union are terms common in set theory and logic. The intersection of two sets is the set of points which the two sets have in common, while the union is the set of points which belong to either set or to both sets.

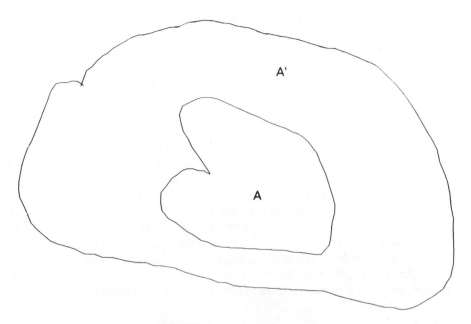

FIGURE 9.3   Venn diagram.

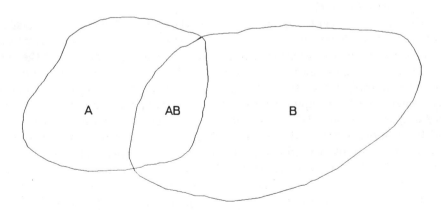

FIGURE 9.4   Venn diagram of the intersection of A and B.

where we make use of the fact that $A(B + B') + B(A + A') = AB + AB' + A'B$ and $AB = AB + AB$. We are dealing with logic statements and not with arithmetic operations.

The relation at the end of Section 9.2

$$AB' + AB = A$$

could be proven in a geometric way, using a Venn diagram, by noting that (A) AND (NOTB), or AB', is the area of A which does *not* lie within B; while (A) AND (B), or AB, is the area of A which lies *within* B. The ORing of these two (i.e., the total area of the two parts) is simply the area A.

It is not at all difficult to envision how this Boolean algebra finds a place in computer programming and usage. Logic is very important in the design of computers, as well as in the design of programs. Often, in a computer circuit, a number of wires will carry binary signals that indicate states of particular parts of the computer. A particular action may need to be taken whenever a certain combination of states occurs. For example, one bit might be used to indicate that a disk drive has finished transferring data and a second bit to indicate that the processor may be interrupted because it has finished performing an instruction. The ANDing of these two bits, known as an "AND gate" in a circuit realization, provides a signal which actually causes the interruption to take place.

9.4   LOGIC DESIGN

Digital computer circuits can be described schematically as we now show. Let us consider the gates shown in Figure 9.5. We also indicate the transmission function performed by each circuit.

Figure 9.5 shows one notation used for AND gates, OR gates, and *inverters*. An inverter is seldom referred to as a NOT gate. In practice, most electronic circuits have a voltage-sense reversal, or inversion characteristic, in that the output voltage is high when the input voltage is low. Thus inversion of inputs or outputs naturally occurs. In a particular gate representation, this may be shown as a small circle at the input or output of the gate. On passing this circle an input (or output) A becomes NOTA. In the examples described above we have dealt with *two-input* ANDs and ORs only. These particular functions easily lend themselves to simple definition when there are more than two inputs. Thus an N-input AND will produce a one output, if and only if ALL inputs are ones. Likewise, an N-input OR will produce an output if any (or all!) inputs are ones.

Two other gates are shown in the foregoing figure, each with a built-in inversion. In electronic computers, because of the inversion which is natural to the transistor circuits actually used, the primitive building blocks are most often "NAND gates," whose output is simply the inverse of the AND of its inputs and "NOR gates," the output of which is the inverse of the Boolean sum of the inputs. It is also common, in actually talking about the signals in the computer

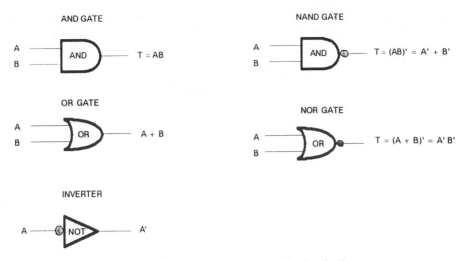

FIGURE 9.5   Notation as used in logic-circuit diagrams.

circuits, to replace 1 and 0 with "high" and "low," referring to whether the voltage at the particular point is near the power supply voltage or nearer to ground voltage.[3]

It should be noted that 1 and 0, or true and false, are not absolute definitions. A particular binary signal which is referred to, for example, as *Data Terminal Ready* may be defined, in a particular equipment, as being *true when low*. This means that when the voltage representing that variable is near ground-voltage, the condition it represents is *valid*. This uncertainty in mapping of voltage to Boolean *truth* usually causes no problems, since it is never necessary to deal with expressions connecting *all* of the states and voltages in a computer. What is important is that the circuits *generating* a certain signal and those *interpreting* it are designed such that they understand the values of that signal *in the same sense*.

9.5   COMPUTER ARITHMETIC—THE HALF ADDER

In practice, the simple computer logic introduced in our previous section is extended to produce all of the functions that are required to enable the computer to manipulate and access data, and to control various operating sequences. A simple example which illustrates this process is the basic building block for arithmetic operation called the half adder. This name is appropriate since the two *halfs* of addition, summation and carry, are each obtained, but there is no provision for an input carry from a lower order bit.

---

[3]Modern computers are invariably driven by a central clock and the associated clock pulses. In this case, 1 and 0 are used to refer to "pulse present" and "pulse not present" at some particular point.

Let us examine what is required for the addition of two binary digits. There are two things to be calculated: the *sum* and the *carry*. The sum must be one, if one of the two added bits is one, or zero, if neither or both of the input bits are one. A half adder is shown in Figure 9.6.

In the half-adder we see that the sum function requirement is satisfied directly by the exclusive-OR. Sometimes an exclusive-OR circuit is referred to as a *modulo-two* adder, that is, an adder whose output is the proper binary sum, but which does not generate carries.

The carry for the half-adder will be a one only if both of the bits to be summed are also one. This may be realized by the use of an AND gate. Hence all the circuitry required can be constructed from elementary gates according to the expressions at the output of the boxes in the foregoing figure.

The reason for the half-adder terminology is that this representation makes no provision for combining a carry from the summing of previous bits. Thus while it would suffice for the least significant bit of a parallel binary adding circuit, for all other bit positions there must be *three* inputs: two bits to be summed and a carry bit from the previous stage of addition.

A *full* adder accomplishes this somewhat more complex function. Let us examine what we need if two sum bits A and B are combined with a carry bit C. *The sum bit S will be one if any single input (A, B, or C) is a one, or if all three inputs are ones. The new carry C'* will be a one if two or more (of *A, B, and C*) are ones. We could write this in expanded form as

$$S = A\ B'C' + A'B\ C' + A'B'C + A\ B\ C$$
$$C' = A\ B\ C' + A\ B'C + A'B\ C + A\ B\ C$$

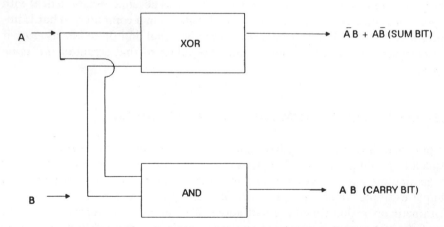

FIGURE 9.6   A half-adder. A half-adder combines two bits to form a sum bit and a carry bit. If AND and XOR gates are available, it can be implemented using only one of each.

One way to implement it would be merely to combine, for the sum bit S, a four-input OR (to collect the major terms) circuit which obtains its inputs from four three-input AND gates. It would also be necessary to utilize inverters preceding two inputs on each of the AND gates. Though this is simple to accomplish, the design realization of logic circuits is obtained as an integrated circuit on a single chip. These functions are realized in this way, rather than by using discrete components.

In the early years of computer design, the ability to *design logic circuits* was probably the principal skill of the computer designer. Each two-input AND gate required at least one electron tube or a discrete transistor. Consequently, minimization of the number of tubes or transistors was an important economic consideration. The *control* portion of a computer was, in those early days, a complex of discrete logic circuits.

Today, in the era of very-large-scale semiconductor integrated circuits (VLSI), chip designers are the principal individuals concerned with logic-circuit minimization. The most important minimization is that propagation of *time delay* between circuit elements, as this directly influences computer performance speed. In this respect, the main consideration may be to keep the *maximum number of gates* through which a signal must pass on its way from input to output to a minimum.

9.6 OPERATIONS ON VARIABLES

We now return to the matter of the implementation of operations performed on numbers or symbols that have been stored in memory. The logic design is fixed in the 8088 chip for the IBM PC, and we are viewing data manipulation as provided by the tools of the C language.

The arithmetic and logical operations defined for the C language, along with examples for each operation symbol, are listed in Figure 9.7.

We notice that division of integers is rounded down to the nearest integer answer. The remainder can be recovered with the modulo operator. We will now discuss the latter four operations, which are not among the usual familiar operations.

The logical operations &&, || and ! are applied to variables which are either false or true (either zero or not zero). In C, the number 0 is false and anything else is true. When asked, C will usually provide the value 1 for !0. These operations are usually applied to expressions which are true or false.

We have already met expressions as the second argument of a *for* statement. In the *for* statement of the program below, i 8 is an expression which is true for all values of i up to and including 7, but false otherwise. The value of such an expression is zero when false, and not zero otherwise. Thus, if i were 9 (i 8) would evaluate to 0. We will cover other notions associated with expressions in the next chapter.

	SYMBOL	EXAMPLES
Add	+	2 + 3 = 5
Subtract	–	5 – 3 = 2
Multiply	ˣ	2 ˣ 3 = 6
Divide	/	21.0 / 4.0 = 5.25
Integer Division	/	21 / 4 = 5
Modulo	%	21 % 4 = 1
Logical AND	&&	1 && 2 = 1
Logical OR	I I	1 I I 2 = 1
Logical NOT	I	I 1 = 0

FIGURE 9.7 Arithmetic and logical operations for C language.

9.7 BITWISE OPERATORS ON BINARY VARIABLES

C has *bitwise* operators which operate on numbers at the binary level. For example, the hex number f (binary 1111) is transformed to 0 (binary 0000) by the bitwise negation ˜f, which changes each one to a zero. The bitwise operators in C are shown next,[4] with binary numbers used for illustrative examples in Figure 9.8. Both the logical operators like && and the bitwise operations like & are defined by the truth tables at the beginning of this chapter.

For illustration let us write a C program and use the hex numbers 9A and B7 (1001 1010 and 1011 0111 in binary). We can print the results of bitwise operations on the numbers with the program

```
main ()
{
   int a = 0x9a;
   int b = 0xb7;
```

[4]The reader should not confuse these binary operators with the AND, OR, and NOT gates described earlier. Many are involved in steering the data bits of the actual operands into the computer's ALU to perform the logical operations.

```
printf("\n%x & %x = %x",a, b, a & b);
printf("\n%x | %x = %x",a, b, a | b);
printf("\n%x ^ %x = %x",a, b, a ^ b);
printf("\n~%x = %x   ~%x = %x",a, ~a, b, ~b);
printf("\n\n%x << 2 = %x",a, a << 2);
}
```

Here, the values of a and b are initialized at the beginning of the program; the notation for hex constants is the leading 0x. The result of running the program is

```
9a & b7 = 92
9a | b7 = bf
9a ^ b7 = 2d
~9a = ff65 ~b7 = ff48
9a << 2 = 268
```

The results can be verified by expanding the hex numbers into binary simply through the use of pencil and paper operations. The line with ~9a (NOT 9a hex) reflects the internal storage of integers as 4-byte numbers: 0x9a is really 0x009a.

The last two bitwise operators shift the bits to the right or left, thereby filling in the vacant spaces with zeros. 0x9a shifted left by two places would be written 0x9a<<2 and would produce from 0000000010011010 the shifted result 0000001001101000 or hex 0268. Please see the last line of the

	SYMBOL	EXAMPLES
AND	&	1111 & 1010 = 1010
OR	|	0110 | 1010 = 1010
NOT	~	~0110 = 1001
Exclusive OR	^	0110 ^ 1010 = 1100
Shift right	> >	0110 > > 2 = 0001
Shift left	< <	0110 < < 2 = 1000

FIGURE 9.8   Bitwise operators in C.

foregoing program and the associated results for the computer monitor representations associated with this discussion.

Let us now check the formulae for the full adder. These are

```
S = A  B'C'+ A'B  C'+ A'B'C + A  B  C
C'= A  B  C'+ A  B'C + A'B  C + A  B  C
```

We will use the C program:

```
main()
{
   int a, b, c, i;
   int s, cprime;

   printf("\nA  B  C  S  C'\n");   /* table
     header *?
   for (i = 0; i < 8; i++)
   {
     a = 0x1 & i;
     b = (0x2 & i) >> 1;
     c = (0x4 & i) >> 2;

     s = (a & ~b & ~c) | (~a & b & ~c) |
         (~a & ~b & c) | (a & b & c);
     cprime = (a & b & ~c) | (a & ~b & c) |
              (~a & b & c) | (a & b & c);
     printf("\n%d %d %d   %d  %d", a, b, c,
       s, cprime);
   }
}
```

The program prints:

```
A B C   S  C'
0 0 0   0  0
1 0 0   1  0
0 1 0   1  0
1 1 0   0  1
0 0 1   1  0
1 0 1   0  1
0 1 1   0  1
1 1 1   1  1
```

The logic for the adder produces the right outputs for the sum and carry. For example, with the input 1 0 1, that is, one input and a carry, the sum is zero with a carry, as it should be.

This program checks the logic by using the bitwise operators in C. The inputs a, b, and c are generated from a count of i from 0 to 7, with the variables set to the value of the individual bits. This is done by picking out the bit of interest (e.g., the second one for b) and shifting it to the right until it is in the first position.

For example, take the statement

```
b = (0x2 & i) >> 1;
```

Before the shift, the contents of the parentheses looks like the following when i is 6:

```
0x2:        0000 0000 0000 0010
i:          0000 0000 0000 0011

(0x2 & i):0000 0000 0000 0010
```

and after shifting to the right:

```
0000 0000 0000 0001
```

the value of b is 1 when the middle bit of i is 1 and zero otherwise.

The loop sets a, b and c to the binary value of i and computes the sum and carry from the formulas. It would be appropriate to step through this program by hand in order to appreciate the operations that are performed by the computer.

9.8   APPENDIX: OPERATORS FOR PASCAL

The arithmetic and logical operations defined for Pascal and C are listed in Figure 9.9. The logical operators are applied in Pascal to Boolean variables which can have the values *true* and *false*. In C the int 0 is false and anything else is true.

Turbo Pascal has a number of extensions not found in the standard version of Pascal. For example, there is an *xor* (exclusive or) logical operator. This is also not found even in Turbo C. As long as portability to other versions of Pascal is not planned these extensions are ok, but some caution is advised. There are no bitwise operators in Turbo Pascal.

	PASCAL	C
Add	+	+
Subtract	–	–
Multiply	×	×
Divide	/	/
Divide integer	div	/
Modulo	mod	%
Logical and	and	&&
Logical or	or	||
Logical not	not	!

FIGURE 9.9   Arithmetic and logical operations in Pascal and C.

PROBLEMS

9.1   Draw a *truth table* for the 3-input logic function
F = A (B'C).
Hint: draw *two* 2 × 2 boxes, one for A = 0 and the other for A = 1, and
show B = 0,1 and C = 0,1 on each.

9.2   Using a *Venn diagram*, and intersecting circles for A, B, and C, show the
region in the diagram which is defined in the relation F above.

9.3   Using binary two-input logic gate schematic notation for the inputs A, B,
C, and D, draw a logic circuit whose output is
D (C + (A D + B'C'))

9.4   What is the value in the C language of the following?
(a) !0
(b) 1 && 1
(c) !5
(d) ~0
(e) 1 2
(f) 5 % 4

(g) 5 / 4

(h) 5.0 / 4

(i) 1 ^ 2

9.5   What is the value in C of each of the following?

(a) 1001 & 0111

(b) 0xAB & (˜9)

(c) 75 & 21

(d) !55

(e) !(2 * 3)

(f) 1001 |0111

(g) 0xA |0xB

(h) 75 && 21

(i) !0xa

(j) 0x33 & 25

PART II

ELEMENTARY DATA OPERATIONS AND PROGRAMMING

10

APPLICATION OF ELEMENTARY COMPUTER DECISIONS AND LOGIC TO EXPRESSIONS AND FLOW CONTROL

10.0 INTRODUCTION

Computers perform arithmetic and logical manipulations on numbers and symbols. In addition, they may also change activities to be followed and make decisions concerning which program path to follow on the basis of the results of the computations themselves. The process which determines what is to be done is called *flow control*. The decisions that lead to change are made by examining what are generally called *expressions*.

The flow of the computations in a program may be repetitive and may involve one or more loops. There may be many opportunities to branch to other parts of a program that perform very different types of computations, and for entirely different purposes, from those initially performed when the program is initiated. The logical relational operator is shown in Figure 10.1, while proper nesting of loops is shown in Figure 10.2. In this chapter we will examine the mechanisms provided by the C programming language for looping, branching, and other forms of flow control.

10.1 EXPRESSIONS

We have already used the f o r construction. In this construct, a loop based computation continues as long as an expression in the f o r construction is true. In Section 7.6 we used the statement:

```
for (inches = 0; inches < = 12; inches++)
```

Operator	Symbol
And	&&
Or	| |
Not	|

FIGURE 10.1   Logical relational operator.

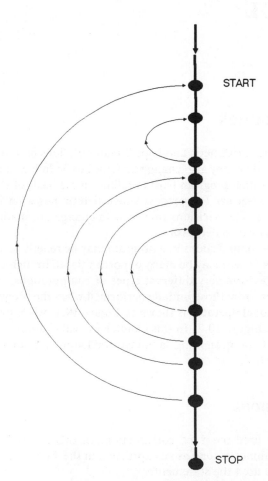

FIGURE 10.2   Proper nesting structure for program loops.

in which the controlling expression is

```
inches <= 12
```

In this case, the loop continues as long as inches does not exceed 12; that is while the expression inches <= 12 is *true*. Expressions like this one have a value 0 if they are false, and 1 or another non-zero integer value if they are true. To illustrate this concept in an actual program, we present a short C program which prints the value of the foregoing expression for a range of values of the inches variable:

```
main()
{
        int inches;
        printf(" inches   (inches <= 12)\n");
        for (inches = 10; inches  < 16;
        inches++)
    {
        printf("\n %2d %2d", inches,
        (inches <= 12));
    }
}
```

We notice that the calculated expression evaluates as 1 until inches exceeds 12; at that point it then returns 0 or false. Our display monitor should indicate

```
inches   (inches <= 12)
  10            1
  11            1
  12            1
  13            0
  14            0
  15            0
```

for this simple example, after we have compiled and executed the given program. One example of a loop-controlling expression from Chapter 8, Section 8.2, is

```
i <= 'a' + 12
```

Another, from Section 8.3, is

```
i <= 26
```

A final example comes from Section 8.4:

```
greeting[i] != '\0'
```

These expressions, as they stand, will result in values of 1 for true and 0 for false in C language programs. There are, of course, many other possible illustrations of flow control expressions.

10.2   RELATIONAL OPERATORS

Each of the flow control expressions we used in the previous section contains a relational operator. Some of the relational operators used in expressions in C are shown in Figure 10.3.

It is important to note that C uses the == expression for the relational equal. This is another of its special and uncommon notations. It is important to distinguish between the relationship of being equal, where we use the symbol ==, and the use of the single = expression for assigning a value to a variable or for *requesting* the computer to perform the computation that follows the equals sign.

We could potentially use either == or = without obtaining a syntax error in the same expression, potentially for example, through use of the statements

```
if (x = 1)
    printf ("unity");
```

Operator	Symbol
Equal	==
Not Equal	!=
Greater than	>
Less than	<
Less than or equal	<=
Greater than or equal	>=

FIGURE 10.3   Relational operators in C.

What was probably intended here is the program with the relational operator:

```
if (x == 1)
    printf("unity");
```

which will test x and print unity only if x is 1. In the first example x is changed; in the second it is not.

The *Turbo C* compiler will question the first program as being not well formed, but not the second. Other compilers may not complain about the first given program statement; so, be careful!

10.3 THE IF...ELSE STATEMENT

The basic program flow device in the C programming language is the if...else construction. This is a very similar construction to the if construction. Whereas the if statement results in the following statement being potentially executed, the if...else construction allows one of two expressions to be exercised. An example of this usage is:

```
main()
{
   int number = 3;
   if (number > 2)
     printf("\nnumber > 2");
   else if (number < 2)
     printf("\nnumber < 2");
   else
     printf("\nnumber = 2");
}
```

The program, when compiled and executed, results in the display:

```
number > 2
```

The succession of

```
if..else if..else if...else
```

statements is a natural one that can continue through as many mutually exclusive choices as required in order to obtain the desired logic flow control. The use of the else prevents further evaluation of choices once the choice preceding the final else statement is made. On the other hand, a succession of *if* statements would all be evaluated, even if a given evaluation is unnecessary.

Another point should be made about the if...else statement. The else clause goes with the nearest if which has no else of its own, that is, the nearest unaccompanied if. It should always be remembered that the C compiler does not recognize indentation. Paragraph indentation is a device for making the programmer's intention clearer, both to the programmer and to others. Therefore, we must be sure that if..else clauses are correctly placed without regard to format.

The intention of the programmer can be made clear both to the compiler and in the printed copy of the source code by putting in curly brackets. For example, the short programs

```
if (cond A)
   if (cond B)
      C;
   else
      D;
and
if (cond A)
   if (cond B)
      C;
else
   D;
```

do exactly the same thing. The paragraph or tabular indentation for the first program version is correct, since the else goes with the unaccmpanied if above it. The confusion can be removed by using curly brackets, such that the program statement becomes

```
if (cond A)
{
   if (cond B)
   C;
else
   D;
}
```

This program form will group the program and execution logic according to the braces no matter how the indentations are arranged.

10.4 THE ? OPERATOR

There are relational operators other than the ones we have discussed thus far. C has a special conditional operator with symbol ?. An example of correct usage of this relational operator is

```
x > 1000 ? puts("large") : puts("small");
```

If the expression before the ? is true, the first statement after it is executed. If the expression is not true, the second statement is executed.

10.5 LOGICAL OPERATORS

Expressions can easily be combined with the logical relational operators shown in Figure 10.1 that are available in C. The result of these combinations is determined by the use of truth tables shown in Figure 10.4.

C does not provide the exclusive OR function X O R as an operator. This can be created from the others. We have as the definition of the X O R the operator

```
A XOR B = (A AND B') OR (A' AND B)
```

A short C program that generates the XOR function from the logical operators that C provides is:

```
main()
{
  int a, b;

  printf("\nA   B    A XOR B\n");
  for (a = 0; a <= 1; a++)
    for (b = 0; b <= 1; b++)
      printf("\n%d   %d        %d",
             a, b, (a && !b) || (!a && b));
}
```

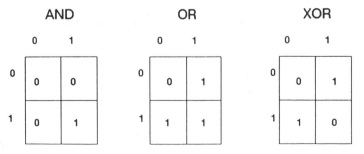

FIGURE 10.4   Input/output relations for truth tables.

Notice that we have used two nested f o r statements to generate the values for a and b. Since a and b are either 0 or 1, (i.e., true or false), the logical operators are appropriate here. The printed output is a truth table for X O R as shown in Figure 10.5.

We have noted before that C is a very cryptic language. This enables us to write programs that others may have great difficulty in understanding. This can easily lead to programming errors and difficulties in such important software systems engineering efforts as software maintenance.

For example, let us consider the following C program using logical operator expressions:

```
main()
{ int  number = 2;

  if ((number >= 2) && (number <= 2))
    printf("\nnumber = 2");
  else
    printf("\nnumber not = 2");
}
```

which executes as

```
number = 2
```

A warning about these combinations is in order. It is very easy to write compound expressions using the operators & & , ‖ , and ! , which are difficult to understand and which may mean something quite different from what was intended. It is often better to use extra parentheses or compound i f clauses to make the meaning clear. Let us now turn our attention to some of these important details.

A	B	A XOR B
0	0	0
0	1	1
1	0	1
1	1	0

FIGURE 10.5   Truth table for XOR.

10.6   PUNCTUATION

We now expand on the proper use of *punctuation*. C uses the semicolon as a *terminator*. **There must be one terminator at the end of each statement.** Unfortunately, it is not always clear what a statement is. However, proper use of semicolons generally comes easily and naturally with practice. Most of the time, punctuation errors are caught by the compiler. Omitted semicolons are very common errors for beginning C (and Pascal) programmers,[1] and these will generally always be caught.

There are cases where the addition or deletion of a semicolon is correct syntactically; but the action of the resulting program is not what was intended. This kind of bug[2] may be very difficult to find and correct. We will return to this subject later.

10.7   CONDITIONAL LOOPS

As we have seen, the middle part of the f o r construction contains an expression which must be true for the loop to continue. F O R is a "reserved" word in C. It can only be used for the purpose described here. Good nesting style is where inner loops are always completely enclosed by the next larger outer loop, as shown in Figure 10.2. A prototypical example of use of the f o r statement is:

```
for ([initial conditions] ; [expression] ;
   [changes])
```

The f o r loop and f o r expression is used more than any other relational operator in C programs. However, there are alternates. C also has a w h i l e loop construction. A program that counts and prints from 1 to 10, and which uses this flow expression, is:

```
main()
{
   int i;

   i = 1;
   while (i <= 10)
      printf("%3d", i++);
   printf("\n");
}
```

---

[1]Recall that the semicolon in assembly language indicates that what follows, to the end of the line, is a comment.

[2]A *bug* is a program error. Historically, *bug* is a very relevant term in computing. It first came to be used when switching circuit-based computers at Harvard did not work because a dead bug caught between a contact prevented the relay contact from closing.

The **while** statement in C results in a continuation of looping back to the initial use of the while statement so long as the condition in the parentheses associated with the while statement is true.

The **++** operator increments the variable **i** after it is used by **printf**. If the line had been written with **++i** instead of **i++**, the incrementing would have been done before use of the expression by **printf** instead of after. We note that *decrementing* can be done with the **--** operator in a manner similar to incrementing with the **H** operator.

The **while** statement tests the associated parenthetic statement before it starts, so the contents of the loop following a while statement *may* be skipped entirely. Thus it is possible to have a while loop that is never exercised. It would also be possible for a variable in a loop to never change.

Another loop construction is available which executes the program statements in the "loop" following it at least once, and makes the test at the end of this loop. The C language uses the **do...while** statement to do this.

A simple illustration of the use of this important relational operator is

```
main()
{
   int i;
   i = 1;
   do                        /* start do */
      printf("%3d", i++);
   while (i < 11);           /* end do */
   printf("\n");
}
```

We note that the final **while** is followed by a semicolon, and that the **do...while** construction takes into account the final incrementing of **i** after 10 is printed. The results of using this simple program is, again, printing of the numbers from 1 to 10. On the other hand, substitution of the statement

```
Printf("%3d", ++i);
```

would cause printing of the numbers 2 through 11. The symbol **i++** causes incrementing of i after printing, whereas the **++i** statement causes incrementing before printing.

One of the most common and most troublesome programming bugs that can occur in a C program occurs in connection with the use of while loops. A program with such a bug is:

```
main()
{
   int i;
   i = 1;
```

```
while (i <= 10);
    printf("%3d", i++);
  printf("\n");
}
```

This program is the same as the **w h i l e** program at the beginning of this section, but with one important difference that is easily overlooked when writing or reading the program. There is a semicolon at the end of the **w h i l e** line. *Do not* try running this program: if you do, it will produce no output, the system will crash and you will have to reboot the machine to regain control. The reason can be seen from a rewritten version of the changed line

```
while (i <= 10)
    ;
```

The semicolon has been moved to the next line (but remember, the new lines are ignored by the compiler so the line is really the same). The semicolon standing by itself is a line which does nothing (we will have uses for this later). In this case, since i is always less than 10, the expression in the **w h i l e** statement is true and the loop continues doing nothing forever or until we turn off the machine. The problem here is that the semicolon forces a return to the beginning of the loop as it denotes an end to a particular block or set of commands. All of this occurs before the statement has a chance to up increment i. Thus the i variable is never incremented. Since most C lines end in a semicolon, this is an easy mistake to make, but a hard one to find. The semicolon is a very small symbol and can easily be missed when reading a program.

10.8   SORTING

Sorting is the activity of putting objects in order. The objects can be numbers. Or, if the codes for other objects like letters form an order themselves (as they occur in ASCII), objects such as names and addresses can be sorted also. To illustrate ideas of looping and program control we will soon write a program to sort letters in a string. Let us first look at some more general issues.

There are whole books written on methods of sorting, and much computer time is spent on sorting activities. Transactions processing and information systems make intensive use of sorting approaches. Our purpose here is to illustrate the use of the C language in applications such as this, so a simple *sorting algorithm*[3] will initially be used.

We may sense the variety of procedures available for solution of a sorting problem by examining the procedures for sorting a set of 3 in. by 5 in. index cards with book titles on them. What scheme do we use? Do we first group all the

---

[3]Knuth, D.E. *The Art of Computer Programming*, Vol. 3, Reading, MA: Addison-Wesley, 1973.

books by the first word in the title such that we have all the A's together, all the B's together, and so on, and then sort each of these groups? Or do we insert each card sequentially into a deck in the proper position such that all cards in the deck are sorted?

A simple, and often inefficient, method of sorting using a computer is called the bubble sort. The name comes from the way the larger values in the list to be sorted "bubble to the top" during the process. We will first write a program which shows the central features of the bubble sort algorithm.

First, we state the algorithm. The objective of putting members of an array in order is simple enough, so why an algorithm? The answer is that we need to be systematic in our thought process. If we do not have a statement of requirements for a problem solution, then we have little to compare the actual code against in order to validate its performance. One result of attempting to convert the requirements specifications to system specification is the emergence of an algorithm to (presumably) resolve the initially stated problem.

Given an array `message[bound]` containing `bound` members to be sorted, the algorithm for the bubble sort is:

1. Set `t = 0`, and `j = 0` (t keeps track of how many swaps of members have already been made).
   Perform step 2 for `j = 0, 1, 2, ..., b - 1`.
   Go to step 3.
2. Compare members of the `j`th and `(j + 1)`th member of `message`, and swap them if they are out of order.
   Each time there is a swap, set `t = j`.
3. If `t` is zero, stop; otherwise set `b = t` and return to step 1.

In step 3 of the algorithm, the `bound` is set equal to `t`, which keeps us from testing pairs that have already been swapped. Figure 10.6 presents a flow chart for this algorithm for bubble sort. A program that implements the bubble sort algorithm is:

```
main()
{
    char message[] = "hello, world";
    char temp;
    int bound;
    int t = 11;
    int i, j;

    printf("\n\n%s", message);
    do
    {
```

```
bound = t;
t = 0;
for (j = 0; j <= bound -1; j++)
{
   if (message[j] > message[j+1])
   {
      temp = message[j];
      message[j] = message[j + 1];
      message[j + 1] = temp;
      t = j;
   }
}
if (t > 0)
   printf("\n%s", message);
}
while (t > 0);
}
```

The program prints step 2 each time through. The bubbling of the largest value to the right can be seen from the output:

```
hello, world
ehll, oorldw
ehl, looldrw
eh, lloldorw
e, hllldoorw
, ehlldloorw
,ehldlloorw
,ehdllloorw
,edhlllloorw
,dehllloorw
```

In the flow diagram for a bubble sort shown in Figure 10.6, we note that the space finally ends on the left with the comma, because they have lower ASCII codes than do the letters. Of course, this result is "silly" in that the appearance of the sorted letters makes no sense at all to us, whereas the initial phrase "hello world" did make sense. Sense is, however, relative and context dependent. The characters are properly sorted. There was no requirement in the problem statement for the resulting sorted string to denote meaningful English-language words. Generally, we would be more interested in sorting on words rather than letters. We will return to a much more detailed discussion of sorting soon.

A program of the size just presented has reached the stage where the introduction of structured blocks begins to make writing it and reading it easier. So we pause to define *functions* as a vehicle to allow this. We will rewrite this program in a better form when we have the appropriate tools to enable this.

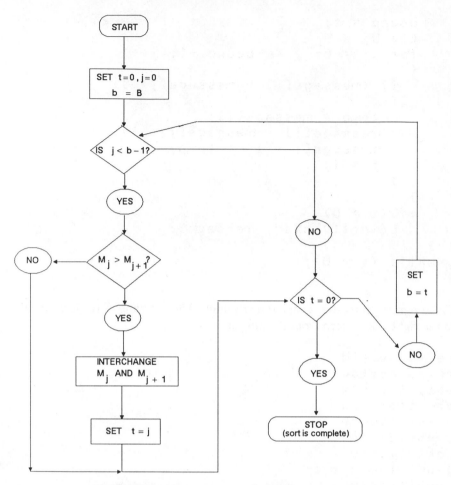

FIGURE 10.6   Flow diagram for simple bubble sort.

10.9   FUNCTIONS

If you have previously used a high-level programming language, particularly BASIC or FORTRAN, you may be familiar with use of the GOTO statement. In our discussions of C thus far, there has been no use of a GOTO statement. In programming languages, movement about the program in loops and branches is often accomplished by jumping to a new part of the program using a GOTO statement in which the destination is a program line number or label. C provides a GOTO statement, and there are valid uses for it, especially in response to errors. We will generally not use it at all in this book. Instead, we will use blocks or functions to accomplish the same thing. The use of many GOTO statements may destroy the simplicity and utility of the block structure, and may lead to programs that cannot be reliably tested because of the absolute addresses.

The use of the GOTO statement allows branching from loops that have not been completed. For example, the statement

```
main ( )
  {
    int i;
    for (i=1; i; i++)
    printf ("%3d", i)
    if (i=3)
    goto (   );
  }
```

will force branching out of the loop as soon as i = 4. The program statements are syntactically correct, but not logically consistent. This is surely our fault, and not that of the GOTO statement. Nevertheless, many feel that GOTO statements encourage logical inconsistencies.

A C *function* is a self-contained block of program with a name, parentheses, and a body enclosed in curly brackets. We have already met one function— main()—in every program we have written thus far.

The parentheses have been empty in main() so far, but values can be passed from a *calling* program to the function by their appearance there.

A function in mathematics might be, for example, $f(A, B) = A^2 + B^2$. We might say that this function *returns* $A^2 + B^2$, where the key word here is *RE-TURNS*. C functions always return *something*. The number returned is assumed to be an integer if it is not explicitly declared otherwise. It will be declared to be *garbage* if it is not explicitly defined inside the function. We need not make use of what is returned, however.

The order of appearance of a function in a program is NOT important. It is common to place the functions in a list after main. Here is a program which illustrates the idea:

```
main()
{int i , j;

   i = 5;
   j = dbl(i);
   printf("\ntwice %d is %d", i, j);
}

dbl(k)
   int k;
{
   k = 2*k;
   return k;
}
```

The function db l (), which is defined in this program as a doubling function by the statement k = 2 ∗ k, is invoked by assigning its name to j; j will then receive the return value. The function itself is written below ma i n. The formal parameter k is declared in the line following the function's name, but is known only inside the function. The value of the function is returned via the return statement. In this case, the returned value is an integer; so db l () need not be declared in ma i n.

In C data is passed to functions by value.[4] In the foregoing example, this means that a copy of i is passed and, therefore, anything done to it by the function has no effect on i itself. In this case doubling the value of i left the original, as printed out, unchanged:

```
twice 5 is 10
```

Now let us rewrite our initial bubble sort program in C using functions. We obtain:

```
main()
{
    char message[] = "hello, world";
    int bound;
    int t = 11;
    int j;
    do
    {
      bound = t;
      t = 0;
      for (j = 0; j <= bound -1; j++)
      {
        if (compare(message[j], message[j+1]))
          {
            swap(&message[j], &message[j + 1]);
            t = j;
          }
      }
      if (t > 0)
        printf("\n%s", message);
    }
    while (t > 0);
```

[4]Some languages, like FORTRAN, pass the variable itself to functions (which are called subroutines in FORTRAN). In that case, changes to the variable in the function remain after return to the calling program. In C a copy of the variable is sent to the function and the original is unchanged by whatever happens there.

```
}
compare (x, y)
  char x, y;
{
  if (x > y)
    return 1;
  else
    return 0;
}
swap (x, y)
  char *x, *y;
{
  char temp; /* local variable */
  temp = *x;
  *x = *y;
  *y = temp;
}
```

In this program, the function receives the values of two members of the array being sorted and the comparison is made. Nothing is done to the members themselves. On the other hand, to the function swap is passed the addresses of the variables to be swapped. If we had passed the variables themselves, nothing would have happened, because all function passing in C is by value.

Another point to note is the use of the value 1 as true. The line

```
if (compare(message[j], message[j+1]))
```

uses the returned value of the function compare as the expression; a returned value of 1 is true, 0 is false.

10.10   APPENDIX: FLOW CONTROL IN PASCAL

So far the loops in our Pascal programs have been controlled by a predetermined number of cycles specified in the for...to...do structure, such as the one that we used in Chapter 7. The typical usage is:

```
for inches := 0 to 12 do
```

Pascal has other control structures, each of which is based on expressions, as in C. The expressions used in the Pascal while and until loop constructions have values of true and false and are of type boolean. These are the counterparts of the C while and do loops. The relational operators used in expressions in C and Pascal are summarized in Figure 10.7 and their logical relational operators in Figure 10.8.

Operator	C	Pascal
Equal	= =	=
Not Equal	! =	< >
Greater than	>	>
Less than	<	<
Less than or equal	< =	< =
Greater than or equal	> =	> =

FIGURE 10.7   Relational operators in C and Pascal.

Operator	C	Pascal
And	&&	And
Or	||	Or
Not	!	Not

FIGURE 10.8   Logical relational operators in C and Pascal.

In Pascal, expressions can be assigned to variables of type boolean, and the variables will print their true or false values in writeln statements. The following statements are typical of program construction:

```
program exp (output);
var
  cond: boolean;
  number: integer;
```

```
begin
  number := 3;
  cond := number > 2;
  writeln('(number > 2) is ', cond);
end.
```

This program, when compiled and executed, prints to the screen:

```
(number > 2) is true
```

In Pascal the keyword t h e n is used with i f as in the following small program:

```
program exp1 (output);
var
  number: integer;
  cond: boolean;
begin
  number := 3;
  cond := number > 2;

  if cond = true then
    writeln('number > 2')
  else if number  2 then
    writeln('number < 2')
  else
    writeln('number = 2')
end.
```

Pascal uses the semicolon to separate statements. This is very unlike the usage of the semicolon in C, where it denotes the equivalent of a return statement. Thus there are no semicolons after the first i f in the foregoing Pascal program. Note also that the final e n d in a Pascal program is followed by a period. This is very necessary and a Pascal program will not compile without this period.

The f o r . . . t o . . . d o construction in Pascal controls a programming loop, but fixes the number of times it executes at the beginning. Incidentally, the loop can also be written f o r . . . d o w n t o . . . d o in cases where the index is to be decremented each time the program executes through the loop.

```
program count (output);
var
  i: integer;
begin
  i := 1;
  while i <= 10 do
```

```
        begin
          write(i:3);
          i := i + 1;
        end;
        writeln;
end.
```

We have used **write** instead of the usual **writeln**. **Writeln** always adds a newline, and in the program output for Turbo Pascal the numbers print horizontally:

1   2   3   4   5   6   7   8   9 10

The final **writeln** simply adds the newline at the end. This same program with the **repeat...until** structure may be written as:

```
program count1 (output);
var
  i: integer;
begin
  i := 1;
  repeat
    write(i:3);
    i := i + 1;
  until i = 11;
  writeln
end.
```

The repeat construction does not require a **begin...end** block; as everything is included in the repetition, which continues until the **until** is reached.

A Pascal program that implements the bubble sort algorithm discussed earlier is presented next. This program sorts the characters in **message**:

```
program bsort  (output);
const
  message = 'hello, world';
var
  arry: array [1..12] of char;
  temp: char;
  bound: integer;
  t: integer;
  i, j: integer;
begin
  arry := message;
  t := 12;
```

```
  writeln(message);
  repeat
    bound := t;
    t := 0;
    for j := 1 to bound - 1 do
      begin
        if arry[j] > arry[j + 1] then
          begin    (* swap *)
            temp := arry[j];
            arry[j] := arry[j + 1];
            arry[j + 1] := temp;
            t := j;
          end;
      end;
    if t > 0 then
    begin
      for i := 1 to 12 do  (* write step 2 *)
        write(arry[i]);
    end;
    writeln;
  until t = 0;
end.
```

Pascal allows the definition of blocks in the list at the beginning of the program. The bsort program has been rewritten next to include these block structures:

```
program bsort (output);
const
  message = 'hello, world';
type
  line = array [1..12] of char;
var
  arry: line;
  bound: integer;
  t: integer;
  i, j: integer;
procedure ascii;
  begin
    writeln;
    for i:= 1 to 12 do
      write(ord(arry[i]):4);
    writeln; writeln;
  end;
```

```
function compare(x, y: char):boolean;
begin
   if x > y then
     compare := true;
   end;
procedure swap(var x, y: char);
   var
     temp: char;
   begin
     temp := x;
     x := y;
     y := temp;
   end;
procedure result(x: line);
   begin
     for i := 1 to 12 do
       write(x[i]);
     writeln;
   end;
begin (* main *)
   arry := message;
   t := 12;
   writeln(message);
   repeat
     bound := t;
     t := 0;
     for j := 1 to bound - 1 do
       if compare(arry[j], arry[j + 1]) =
         true then
         begin
           swap(arry[j],arry[j + 1]);
           t := j;
         end;
     if t > 0 then
       result(arry);
   until t = 0;
end.
```

Several of the functions performed by parts of the program above have been rewritten as blocks above the (* main *) part of the program and so labelled to help identify it from among the other blocks. Each of the blocks has the same general arrangement as the basic block we have used until now. The heading includes const, type (a new one), and var. Standard Pascal, but not Turbo Pascal, requires that they be listed in that order. Following these headings, there can be procedure and function blocks, each reflecting the same structure. There can even be structures nested within structures. This construction is not allowed in C.

The first block in the foregoing program is a function block with the terms: function compare. This is different from a procedure in that it returns a value, in this case a boolean variable. It is passed values when it is called in the main part of the program; actually, it is passed copies of the variables arry[j] and arry[j + 1]. If the function or procedure which receives values in this way changes them, it makes no difference to the original variables, since we are dealing only with copies. Sometimes these copies are called *dummy variables*. C always passes by value. Pascal has an alternate approach, as we shall see shortly.

The next procedure swaps the members of the array. The variables themselves are *passed by reference* by use of the word var. Changes are made to the original variables, as well as the dummy variables x and y. In C the same can be accomplished by passing the address of a variable, that is, a pointer variable.

The variable temp in procedure swap is a local variable; it is known[5] only inside the procedure. The variables declared at the beginning of the program, like bound, are global variables, known throughout. Local variables are unavailable outside their own block, and the same name can be used locally in another procedure block without interference.

The last procedure prints the contents of the array at each step. The array itself is passed by value. Pascal requires that the declaration in a function or procedure be a predefined type, and we have introduced the type statement at the top for this purpose.

The procedures are invoked in the main part of the program by mention of their names; functions are called by use of their returned values as variables. Pascal requires that the names so invoked be defined before use; hence the listing of procedures and functions in the upper part of the program. The rules about order can be circumvented by using the forward statement, but we will stick by the rules.

---

[5]Outside the procedure, or in a subordinate procedure, another variable of the same name could be defined without objection from the compiler. This is not good practice because of the likelihood of the programmer becoming confused.

PROBLEMS

10.1   What does this poorly written C program print:

```
main()
{
    int i, j;

    for (i = 0; i < 26; i++)
    {
        while (i > 26);
        j = 'A' + i;
        printf("%c", j);
    }
    printf("\n");
}
```

10.2   In Problem 10.1, what is the effect of changing the line `while (i > 26);` to `while(i < 26);`

10.3   Write a C program to print a table of meters and feet.

10.4   Write a C program to bubble sort an array of integers.

10.5   Write a C program to test the line illustrating the construction in Section 10.4.

10.6   Please rewrite the program in Problem 10.1 in a more acceptable form.

11

COMPUTER PERIPHERALS

11.0 INTRODUCTION

We momentarily interrupt our discussion of the C language to discuss some of the peripheral equipment, or peripherals, that are usually connected to the computer. It is useful to have some understanding of these input/output devices and how to access them. Thus our efforts here are not at all a digression from our central purposes in this text.

11.1 INPUT/OUTPUT—PERIPHERAL HARDWARE

One legacy from early computer days, when central processors were very large physical hulks, is the reference to that equipment which is *not* part of the central processor or its memory as peripheral. In the early days, about a decade or two ago, much of the machinery which provided input, output, and large-capacity information storage for a processor was physically peripheral, that is to say, located in the computer room or an adjacent area. Since the late 1960s, there has been a growing emphasis on truly physical locations for *remote* input/output equipment. Oftentimes this equipment is located thousands of miles from the processor and is connected to it by cable, microwave radio-relay, or satellite data links. And now we see the hub of the problem. We can speak of peripheral equipment and use peripheral to infer either physical separation or equipment that is not an integral part of the functioning of the primary processor. In this chapter we will discuss primarily peripheral storage devices. There are many others, such as printers and local area networks, that we will not discuss.

11.2 MAGNETIC STORAGE

Between about 1955 and 1970 most computers used magnetic devices for their *main memory*. The magnetic elements themselves were most often tiny dough-nut-shaped pieces of magnetic ceramic materials which were called *cores*. The smaller cores were only 15-thousands of an inch in outside diameter and could sustain *magnetic flux flow* in either of the two circular directions *around* the IR ring. By threading (usually three) tiny electrical conductors through the hole in the core, simultaneous electric currents in two of the wires[1] could switch the direction of the magnetic flux. The third wire served as the output and produced a small but detectable voltage pulse when the core *switched* its magnetic direc-tion. Although the magnetic sense of each core remained fixed after power was removed and then reapplied,[2] data was destroyed by each *readout* and had to be restored by a separate operation, requiring additional time.

These magnetic core memories could be used as primary or secondary mem-ory devices. A prototypical example of a primary storage device is the *random access memory* (RAM) that is part of the computer system itself. Here we are concerned with secondary memories, or secondary storage, or auxiliary storage. Notice that we have added another set of descriptor terms to our lexicon. We could also describe secondary storage as being either direct access storage or sequential access storage. Direct access secondary storage systems need to have rapid access as they are used when on-line, perhaps even interactive, response is needed. Magnetic disks, to be discussed soon, represent one form of this type of secondary storage. Cassette tape systems represent one form of off-line sequen-tial access storage. Retrieval time for tape devices is bound to be slow and so this sort of storage is best for infrequently accessed data. A prototypical use might be to back up programs and data such that we are insured against loss of these when other more rapid access storage in a computer system fails.

In the early days, primary storage could not be included as part of a periph-eral device. If we view peripherals from the perspective of physical location, then primary storage could certainly be in a remote location, especially if we are con-cerned with a distributed computing environment with active workstations at remote locations. However, the primary memory at a remote location would have to be associated with a CPU at that location. So we see that the notion of com-puter peripherals is perhaps a bit antiquated today. Nevertheless, it is the orga-nization that we will use here, in part for historical reasons.

---

[1]When a current flows in only one of the wires, it does not produce enough magnetic force to switch the magnetization. Accordingly, a single core in a planar x-y array could be selected by passing current through one x wire and one y wire. Each such array contains a particular bit of all memory words.

[2]A memory which can retain its data after power has been removed is said to be *non volatile*. Though most computers today use volatile semiconductor memory, there are forms of semiconductor mem-ory which will retain data after power is removed. However, they are not suitable for very large memories and are often not very fast by contemporary standards.

There are four attributes of primary importance relative to evaluation of various forms of storage, either primary or secondary, technology. These are:

1. *Retrieval speed* or *access time*, which represents the time that it takes, after a program instruction has been interpreted, to locate and retrieve data
2. *Costs per byte of capacity*
3. *Storage capacity*, which represents the maximum capability of the system to retain data and
4. *Reliability*, which infers both short-term dependability of the disk in terms of being able to correctly access individual bits of data and the long-term reliability of large segments, and perhaps all, of the system.

Clearly, low values are desirable for the first two attributes and large values for the other two attributes. There are tradeoffs involved among these four attributes. The precise needs for these depends upon whether the storage technology is being used for primary storage, direct on-line access secondary storage, or sequential off-line secondary storage.

Magnetic bubble memory or storage devices are semiconductor chips that retain their stored contents even after the excitation power is removed. They were first introduced a decade ago, in the late 1970s, with the hope that they would replace the magnetic disk systems that had been used for secondary storage. Disk storage costs have fallen very rapidly over the last decade, while reliability factors have improved. Bubble memory storage costs have never declined to meet the initial expectations regarding this. Today they find only very special applications, such as in robots in hazardous environments and in the military. Some portable computers use them. Their storage capacity is quite large.

Magnetic core memory is of little interest today for either primary or secondary storage, except in a few strategic military applications where the resistance of a magnetic memory core to data loss during nuclear weapon attack is important. The same magnetic ceramic materials, in the form of fine powders densely suspended in a plastic film, are a common medium for high-density, low-cost digital storage in computers as well as in audio and video applications. It is found in the form of tapes of various widths and lengths. Commonly used computer tape is 0.5 in. wide and perhaps 2400 ft. long. It can store 1600 or 6250 bytes to the lineal inch. There are other standard formats in the form of 1/4 in. digital tape cartridges. The now-ubiquitous floppy diskette, which is either 3.25, 3.50, or 5.25 in. in diameter and can store from 90 kbytes to over 1 megabyte of digital information.

The same magnetic ceramic powder, in its plastic binder, is also deposited on the surfaces of rigid metal disks for even higher-density computer storage. The most recent high-density disk surfaces may be coated with even magnetically more dense magnetic-metal alloys. This results in a hard disk that contains more magnetic material for a given thickness than possible in earlier disks. It can be used in thinner films which store bits at a higher surface density (i.e., bits/ square inch) than formerly was possible.

Magnetic surface recording, as practiced today in most digital storage devices, uses the same physical principal as that used in audio or video tape recording. A schematic diagram for a magnetic recording head is shown in Figure 11.1. Magnetic fields from a nonmagnetic *gap* in a moving *read/write head* are imposed on the magnetic material, thereby leaving it magnetized in a direction parallel to the surface. Minute magnetic fields extend out of the surface and their presence, can, therefore, be detected by the same read/write head. Of course, a given head can only be used for either write or read purposes at a particular instant in time. For the write operation, current is passed through an electrical coil in the head. For read, the same coil serves as a magnetic flux-sensor. As the head moves over the surface, some of the magnetic fields emanating from the previously written surface pass through the moving head. This produces a voltage in the coil which depends on the rate of change of the magnetic flux. The voltage, which may be only a few thousandths of a volt, is amplified and shaped electronically to represent the data originally *written* to the coil.

In writing to a magnetic surface, the magnetic field is switched from one po-

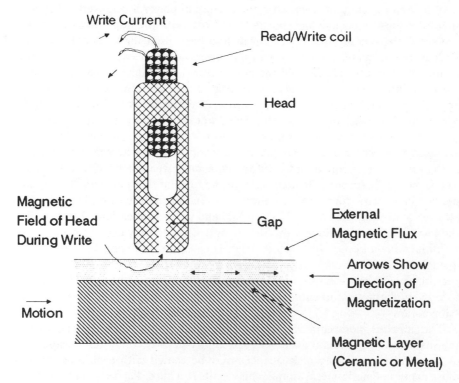

FIGURE 11.1 Magnetic surface recording.

larity to the other to signify data. Therefore, writing over a previously recorded area effectively erases its earlier contents. The head is narrow, as little as a few thousandths of an inch wide, in the direction normal to the head-surface relative motion. It magnetizes or senses magnetization only in a narrow strip, referred to as a *track*.

The ultimate limits to the density of storage depend on (a) how narrow the head can be made and (b) the size of the short magnetized regions it can produce and sense. The nonmagnetic gap in the head, in reading the stored magnetization, is the critical element. The width of this gap effectively determines the shortest section whose magnetization can be sensed. (This can be as little as 1/10,000 in.). When high densities of recording are achieved, however, it is essential that the spacing between the head and the medium (i.e., the magnetic film) be no more than the head gap length. Ensuring a very small head-surface spacing is essential for high recording densities. With magnetic tape, the tape is pulled across the surface of the head with some pressure applied to keep the tape surface *close* to the head. With magnetic disks, the head is pressed against the disk. In either case, the relative motion is such that, in effect, the magnetic medium moves and the head remains stationary. This causes entrapment of air between the head and the recording surface. This is the ultimate determiner of head-surface spacing and, in addition, provides a form of needed lubrication.

Because of the critical nature of the head-surface spacing, the highest-density magnetic storage devices are hermetically sealed. This is done to prevent entry of dust particles that would interfere with achieving the desired small spacing and which could also abrase the head or recording surface. In their earliest form magnetic rigid disks were not hermetically sealed. They could easily be removed from the disk drive. The majority of modern high-density rigid-disk drives use a hermetically sealed structure. Often they are referred to as "Winchester drives" after the internal IBM code name for an early development of this type of system.

Despite the precautions taken, it is nonetheless not unusual for a particle of abrasive material or some part of the head or surface to appear in a sealed disk drive. This causes the magnetic surface to be scored and results in errors when attempting to read or write that portion of the disk. In most high-quality modern storage devices, a spring lifts the head from the magnetic surface when power is removed from the system. Mechanical problems or abrasive intruding material will occasionally cause the magnetic surface to be gouged. In early disk drives, this kind of damage was often caused by the read/write head bouncing against the surface. This was called a *head crash*. The term crash has been adopted in the computer world for any event which causes a computer system to fail. Often head crash is used to denote hard disk failure even though there may be other reasons for the hard disk to become imperfect than the read/write head crashing into the disk.

In a magnetic reel or cartridge tape system, access to a particular piece of data requires the tape to be moved bodily such that the tape position with the data stored on it is within proper distance of the read head. In a disk system the head assembly is moved radially to the proper track and the system waits until the required block of data on the rotating disk appears under the head. Hence disk systems are much faster than tape systems in which the head position is fixed and only the long tape moves from spindle to spindle.

The terminology used for disk drives and depicted in Figure 11.2 is as follows:

Track—a narrow circular strip on a disk surface. A track is completely passed over by the read/write head when the disk rotates 360 degrees

Block, sector, or segment—a portion of a track containing the minimum-size data unit which can be written and read at one time, usually a few hundred to a few thousand bytes (512 bytes in the PC)

Surface—one side of one disk (there may be several disks, each with one or two surfaces and read/write heads)

Head assembly—a mechanism which contains one head per surface and which moves radially

Cylinder—the combination of tracks read by one read/write head, as the head moves from one extreme head position to the other extreme position.

In disk drives with very narrow tracks, the optimum position of the head is sometimes determined dynamically, that is, it is roughly prepositioned near the center track and then adjusted to obtain near optimum minimum access time output from the recorded data.

It is necessary to initialize, calibrate, or format a hard disk such that it is prepared to receive data. Most magnetic disk surfaces are first written to with header data including both track and block numbers on every block. The data storage portion of the block is then filled with simulated data, most often a single repeated character. This process of *formatting* the disk is a necessary precursor

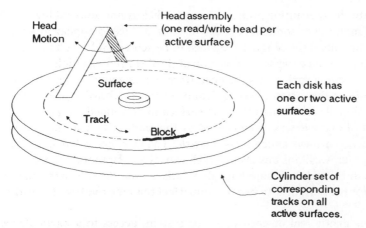

FIGURE 11.2   Disk storage terminology. Tracks and blocks are not visible, but created only by positioning of head assembly.

to writing or reading data onto particular blocks on particular tracks. It is required for both floppy disks and rigid disks. A starting point for each track is defined by an index. In floppy disks, this takes the form of a hole whose position is sensed by a lamp and photoelectric cell as the disk turns to expose the hole.

No formatting process is applied to some tapes, or drives, if altering selected data within the *written* region of a tape is not allowed. Additional data is then written following previously recorded regions, and the entire tape is erased before rewriting. A tape may be selectively read by the process of skipping data blocks until the desired block appears under the head. Other more sophisticated tape systems do use any of several formatting systems that serve the same purpose as formatting a disk. While there are standards for hard and floppy disk formats, there are no standards for tape formats. This leads to major incompatibility problems across the producers of different tape drives.

Both tape and disk storage formats are logically structured so that some part of the recording contains a *directory* or *file allocation table* which indicates the allocation of data blocks to particular named files. The importance of this is easily seen. If there were no file allocation table (FAT), the only way to discover contents of a particular disk or tape would be to read the entire surface. The size and location of directory information is structured by the computer operating system program, not by the manufacturer or the formatting process. It has been found that the directory information is the most likely part of the recording to be damaged, simply because it is the region which is most often read or written to. Some systems set up duplicate recording areas for this information, to avoid its accidental loss. In DOS the directory is in two parts. One of these stores file names and other data and the location of the first sector of the file. A file allocation table, of which two copies are stored, provides information leading to the next sector. In operation the FAT is brought into memory and only written out if files are extended in length. In formatting a DOS floppy disk, the entire disk is formatted. Hard disk formatting is done in two stages. In the first stage, the entire disk is scanned and the contents of each entry reset. In the second stage, only the contents of the FAT are reset. Generally the *format* command for DOS only resets the FAT. A *prepare* command is first used to reset the entries.

The reader should be aware that, unlike the computer itself, magnetic storage devices are complex mechanical systems. The operation of these, especially as it effects hard disk reliability, has been highly refined and dramatically improved by continued developments. At the same time, storage capacity has been increased and price reduced. In 1981 a 5-megabyte hard disk cost about $5000. Now a 40 megabyte hard disk costs as little as $350.

11.3   MANAGING EXTERNAL STORAGE AND OTHER PERIPHERALS

From the central processor's point of view, peripherals are systems which operate asynchronously with respect to the carefully timed clock cadences of the CPU. Because peripherals are mechanically or human-input limited, they are often much slower than the CPU. Consider, for example, a relatively high-speed computer printer which can print 1100 *lines*, of 132 characters each, per minute. Even if we neglect short lines which contain fewer than 132 characters, this blazing speed corresponds to 145,200 characters per minute, or 2420 per second. This amounts to about 400 usec per character, in which time most microprocessors can execute 400 instructions. Many printers are much slower than this. For this reason, it is not uncommon to use a *print spooler* into which printer data is stored by the CPU. The CPU then is time shared between transferring data from the spooler to the printer and performing other computations.

This is not to say that all peripherals are glacial in speed compared to the processor. High-speed disk storage units may read or write *bits* (in extended sequences) at a rate approaching ten million per second, or slightly more than one byte per microsecond. Telephone lines used for digital input and output usually transmit no more than 9600 bits per second (1200 bytes per second at most). Human-operated keyboards will transmit from zero to as much as 15 characters per second. Hence, if anything characterizes computer input/output, it is variety both with respect to types of devices and data rates.

11.4 MEMORIES BASED ON OPTICAL TECHNOLOGY

We have limited most of our discussion thus far to magnetic storage technologies. Computer storage can be based on light, as well as on magnetism. For several years now, optical laser-based compact disks have been available in the video and audio markets. The operating principal of these is relatively simple. Very tiny, microscopic sized pits are pressed or burned onto a thin coating of an appropriate metal or other material that is in the form of a disk. The pattern used for these pits represents some codification of the digital data streams that represent images and/or sound. A beam of laser light is used to sense these patterns and to convey them into the video and audio signals that are needed to produce television pictures or audio sounds. As this discussion suggests, the signals that are stored on the disk cannot be (easily) erased and so the disks cannot be used to rerecord new video or audio sounds.

This suggests several important innovations relative to computing. First, we could control the placement of the read head on a video or audio laser record through use of the computer and therefore use these optical devices to provide video and audio components for applications such as computer based training. In addition, we could use the same technology to store, and later retrieve, digital data.

This has recently happened. The same 4.7-in. (often called 5) compact disk (CD) technology used for high quality audio has been adapted to develop what is generally called compact disk, read only memory (CD-ROM) technology. Current technology includes so-called WORM drives (write once read many) and the coming general availability of read/write CD-ROM systems. The storage density of these disks is truly immense. The storage cost per byte of storage is very low, and the access time is quite fast. One 5-in. CD-ROM disk can store about 570 million alphanumeric characters, or 550 megabytes. This is the equivalent of about 14 hard disks, each with 20 megabytes of storage, or 1250 floppy disks that have been formatted to hold 360K bytes of data. It represents about 225,000 pages of double spaced manuscript pages, each of which holds about 2K bytes of storage.

Several manufacturers now produce CD-ROM drives, some of them selling for about $650. Clearly, the future for this technology is very bright, especially for the production of electronic encyclopedias, enormous catalogs of parts, and perhaps even a world telephone directory! This latter statement is actually slightly frivolous. If we need to allocate 22.5 bytes per entry, which is a generous amount, one CD-ROM disk could only hold 20 million entries. Thus we would really need two of them to hold only a telephone directory for the United States. But then, the technology will probably improve! But will our typing speed improve to meet the needs of this technology? A very fast typist might produce 100 words/minute, or about 500 bytes/minute if words average 5 bytes each. It will take that typist almost 2 yr. to type the material for one CD-ROM disk if he or she works 8 h./day and 250 days/year.

11.5   INPUT/OUTPUT FOR HIGH-SPEED MAGNETIC STORAGE

As discussed in the foregoing, it is not possible to merely change a few bytes of data on a magnetic storage device. Instead, an entire *block* must be read into memory, the necessary bytes altered, and the block written back to the disk surface at its original location. This location consists of (a) a particular block (rotational position), (b) on a particular cylinder (head on, radially from the axis of the disk), and (c) a particular surface (particular side of particular disk). The needed result of these three operations is that data is moved between memory and the disk surface. This requires three steps, two of which involve mechanical movement. In personal computers executing only a single program, the computer will simply await completion of these relatively slow steps before proceeding with anything else. In large computers, or any multiprogrammed computer, they are carried out concurrently with other processing tasks. Depending on the sophistication of the disk controller unit, which is external to the central processor, all three steps may be assigned as a single control-unit task. Alternately, the central processor may assign each in turn to a simple controller.

When the task assigned to the control unit is completed, it interrupts the processor. Once the desired data block has been located, data transfer is carried out between the disk and the main memory using DMA with the time-critical disk transfers of one memory word at a time taking precedence over the task. Normally, the CPU is performing prior to the interrupt. For this and other reasons, one of the most critical parameters of a high-speed computer is its I/O bandwidth. This is usually defined as the number of bits, or bytes, per second which can be moved in and out of the main memory of the CPU. A larger I/O bandwidth allows more simultaneous transfers of data to or from high-speed disk drives. Also, program execution is faster.

11.6   INPUT/OUTPUT FOR BYTE-ORIENTED DEVICES

Magnetic disk or tape storage is, because of its physical nature, block-oriented, as we have just noted. Most other I/O is byte oriented. This includes such peripherals as printers, paper tape readers and punches, and remote systems connected by telephone lines. The byte-transfer rates of these devices are far slower than those that magnetic storage can attain. However, a large number of such devices may be connected to a single computer. Hundreds of remote terminals for data entry or handling of queries are not at all uncommon.

The simplest computer systems transfer this *slow* I/O directly, one byte at a time. It is one byte at a time because the data is almost always in the form of single characters. When the external device is *ready* to send or receive a byte, it interrupts the processor. The processor, under control of software, first accepts the byte from an input port or transmits it to an output port. Then it updates a count of bytes transferred and disposes of an input byte somewhere in memory. Finally, it proceeds with any other concurrent tasks.

If there is relatively little such byte-movement activity, only a small fraction of the processor's time is taken up with it. With hundreds of terminal keyboards receiving input from a busy operator, byte-interrupt processing activity could begin to dominate the activity of the processor. In this case, a separate I/O processor of relatively modest performance may be installed as an interface between the main processor and the terminals. The I/O processor will usually operate as a direct memory access device, and will *steal* memory read-write cycles to move data between the processor's main memory and the terminal I/O devices. It will also interrupt the main processor, though only when an operator has completed a line of typed input with a "carriage return." Accordingly, the main processor now deals with the terminals on a message basis, rather than for each byte.

Such slow output devices as printers or paper tape punches, which are inherently mechanically limited, may be equipped with internal memory buffers. These make it possible for the processor to transmit bytes at a rate faster than the device can operate continuously. Such devices, if equipped with input buffers, can usually accept data at computer-memory-like speed until the buffer is filled. At that point they signal a refusal to accept more data to the CPU. This is accomplished either by activating a single signaling line used only for that purpose or, if they are using serial transfer, by transmitting an **XOFF** (ASCII **dc1**) character. Depending on the computer program operations, it is possible that the output device's buffer would never be completely filled. Although it is necessary that the processor check *availability* of the device before sending another byte, it is seldom the case in practice that the buffer is filled.

11.7   SERIAL AND PARALLEL I/O; POLLING VS INTERRUPT CONTROL

Input and output data exchanges may be carried out using parallel wires to transmit or receive many bits (usually one byte) simultaneously. *Serial* (two-wire) connections, which convert the bits of a byte into a series of pulses which follow one another in time, may alternately be used. These connections may be *synchronous,* transmitting *idle* bytes when there is no actual data to be sent, or *asynchronous* in which case each byte is transmitted separately, being preceded by a *start bit* and followed by a *stop bit*. Serial/parallel data conversion is the responsibility of a receiver-transmitter system which is external to the CPU, except in some very simple low-cost data terminals which use a microprocessor for both this and all other terminal functions.

Parallel input/output operations require, in addition to the actual data bits, transmission of signal bits which verify that the parallel interface has received an n byte or is ready for the next output byte. Once such serially transmitted information is in parallel form, it is handled just like parallel I/O. The conversion device develops status information which may be tested by the processor to determine if an input byte is ready or if the previous output byte has been transmitted. In the case of external serial output devices using **XOFF** and **XON** characters to signal readiness, these characters must be treated like data until the processor determines that they are in fact control signals.

Polling is an alternative to interrupt-controlled input/output. This may be used when *slow I/O* tasks are the processor's main or only job. Instead of waiting for the I/O interface to interrupt it, the processor *periodically* scans each active input/output port, thereby determining its status. When it discovers a port with a ready input byte, this byte is transferred to memory. When an output port is found ready to receive, the processor transmits any data that is then awaiting the chance to be output. Polling can be more *predictable* than interrupt control. If many input interrupts happen to arrive in a short period of time, an input byte may be *lost*, or not accepted prior to another byte being received. Polling can guarantee sufficiently frequent scanning of each input port. However, it consumes more processor time than does interrupt-controlled I/O.

11.8   THE PROCESSOR I/O INTERFACE

Because of the great variety of input/output devices, processor designers usually are content to provide a very simple input/output interface and to leave the details either to (1) external hardware or (2) software implementation. With processors implementing large numbers of arithmetic, logic, and control operations, it is sometimes surprising to find that the input/output instruction repertoire of many processors consists of a single input instruction and a single output instruction, which are used to transfer a byte or a word to a specified I/O address. The same simple I/O instructions can be used to determine the status of the I/O interface or device. It does this by addressing a separate input port, which selects input of status information rather than the actual input data. Likewise, a separate port address can provide a way to send control signals which are not actual output, but which change the state or mode of the I/O device.

At the complete computer system level, one finds a wide range of I/O implementations. For example, IBM mainframes always perform input and output using *channels*, which are themselves programmed and which can read their programs from locations in the main computer memory. A channel program in this system may cause some control operation at the level of a I/O device. Alternately, it may transfer bytes, individually or as a block, between the main memory and I/O devices.

Over the history of the IBM System/360 and its descendants, three different channels have been defined. A *selector* channel is used to communicate with slow I/O devices which transfer a byte at a time. *Multiplexer* and *block multiplexer* channels are intended for interfacing to magnetic storage devices. The *channel program* can be carried out concurrently with the operation of the CPU, with the channel using interrupts to signal its termination. Completion status information is loaded into main memory such that the processor can examine it and either take necessary corrective actions or proceed with the next steps in program execution.

In some lower-performance models of the IBM System/360 and later machines, I/O channel functions were actually carried out by the main processor hardware. This was accomplished in a time-sharing fashion, such that the primary programs running on the computer were unaware of these operations. Since the same hardware performed both functions, the result was a less expensive, though slightly slower, processor. This is an excellent example of architectural *flexibility*: the *System/360 Architectural Definition*[3] emphasizes the instructions which the members of the computer *family*, and the I/O channels, are to execute and the results they should obtain when doing so. It is silent as to the arrangement of *hardware* for carrying this out.

This computer family was the first which was designed "top down;" most earlier families of software-compatible computers evolved from a single first design into other machines, both faster and slower. Some of these other computer families could not be extended in a software-compatible manner. As a result, user programs must be converted in some way to operate on newer machines in the family, a process which for the most part has not been faced by IBM mainframe users.

Microprocessors and most minicomputers use simple input and output instructions, thereby relying on software and external hardware control devices to handle complex control sequences. Some minicomputers which can address only a limited number of different I/O ports, say 256, use additional bits in their I/O

---

[3]This is a document first developed in the early 1960s and which has since served, with some extensions, as a basis for development of a large family of software-compatible computers.

instructions to designate one of several *registers* which are supposedly located within the I/O device. These extra bits can be used, in connection with the external I/O hardware, in the same way as low-order port address bits would be used, that is, to select particular functions on the I/O device (chip).

11.9   PROGRAMMING INPUT/OUTPUT

One of the advantages of using a higher-level language such as C is that the details of handling the input/output interface are made invisible, or transparent, to the programmer. These details are incorporated into the action of library functions which read from and write to the various devices. We have already seen one such function: printf. It not only handles the details of formatting output to the terminal, but takes care of the physical interface itself, so that we need not be concerned with these details. There is a collateral benefit to the use of a high-level language to handle I/O interrupts. The resulting program is easily portable to other machines with completely different input/output hardware. If programming is to become a productive activity, burdens such as this must be reduced or eliminated entirely.

In our next chapter we will study the interface of the C language with the outside world.

PROBLEMS

11.1   The relative processor efficiencies (i.e., wasted processor time) involved in *polling* by the *processor* versus *interrupt* by the I/O unit depend on how many I/O units are being serviced and the frequency of their activities. Discuss how one might in a given situation determine the more effective process or select a combination of the two processes.

11.2   We have noted that tradeoffs must be made among various storage technologies and for various purposes. Explain this comment further and prepare a brief synopsis of the results of scoring the four storage technology performance attributes for several available storage systems.

11.3   Prepare a brief discussion of how modern information systems engineering technology could be used to improve on one or more application areas in which microfilm technology is conventionally used.

11.4   What determines the access or retrieval time for primary storage technology, direct access secondary storage technology, and sequential access secondary storage technology? Illustrate this for several available storage technologies.

12

PROGRAMMING INPUT/OUTPUT

12.0 INTRODUCTION

In our efforts thus far we have often written programs with output to the monitor or printer. In this chapter we examine more general forms of input and output. First, we will examine some approaches to inputting characters by means of the keyboard. Then we will examine some more general standard input/output situations involving the keyboard and monitor and conclude with a discussion of file inputs and outputs.

12.1 KEYBOARD INPUT

Let us begin our discussions with a rather pragmatic look at ways we might use the keyboard. A C program which requests input from the keyboard is

```
# include <stdio.h>
main()
{
   int i = 0;
   int j;
   char c, buf[10];

   printf("\nenter up to 10 characters\n");

   while ((c = getchar()) != '\n')
     buf[i++] = c;
```

```
    printf("input was: ");
    for (j = 0; j < i; j++)
      printf("%4c", buf[j]);
    printf("\n\n");
}
```

Most of the new features found in this program appear in the line

```
while ((c = getchar()) != '\n')
```

`getchar()` is one of the C library functions and is much like `printf()`, another C library function. Functions like this are not considered to be formally part of the C language. They have become standardized over the years through evolution and continued use of the C language. The basic reference for these functions is the UNIX library of C subroutines. We have already noted that C has only user defined input/output operations. Compiler designers generally do much of this for us and provide a comprehensive set of library functions.

The statement in parentheses `(c = getchar())`, defines c, and the parenthesized statement has the value of the defined term. In C the assignment beginning with `while` can be part of the conditional statement.

The `getchar()` function causes one character to be read from the keyboard. If the character is a newline, the `while` condition fails and the program continues past the loop. The function `getchar()` is defined, together with many others, in the *Turbo C Reference Guide* (page 107 in the 1988 edition). This definition tells us that the header file `stdio.h` must be included in the program statement in order to use the getchar statement. It is on the first line in our program. The `stdio.h` inclusion causes the compiler to find the file `stdio.h` and read all of its contents. Clearly, the file we call `stdio.h` must contain valid statements in the C programming language. `Stdio.h` is a mneumonic for standard input output header. The rest of this program should be familiar from our previous example programs in C.

12.2   FILES

The purpose of input/output statements in a C language program is generally to enable performance of operations on a file. Most computer applications store data on, and retrieve it from, a disk drive of some sort. The operating system takes care of the details of storage (which track, sector, etc.) and all the programming language needs to do is to invoke a small group of functions which access the storage device.

Several activities need to be performed in using a file:

1. Select it for use, and *open* it
2. Write to it

3. Read it
4. Adjust the place where reading or writing begins
5. Finish with it and *close* it.

Because file operations are so important, there are many versions of these simple operations available for use by a C language programmer. To keep things simple, we will use the set of functions which are called buffered. In a buffered function, the details of handling input and output are kept out of sight.

Two details of housekeeping are needed here. Our program must include the file st di o . h, and a file descriptor must be declared as a pointer to an object of type F I LE, which is defined and out of sight in s t d i o . h. The file descriptor will be used to refer to the newly opened file in the remainder of the program.

To show the way the file descriptor is declared, we present a simple program that does nothing except open a file:

```
#include <stdio.h>
main()
{
   FILE *fd;
   char message;

   fd = fopen("filename", "r");
}
```

Here, a file named f i l en a me is opened for reading by the r statement. It is then closed again when the program reaches its end. Files can also be opened for writing through use of w, and for both writing and reading through w +. There are also other options. The description of f o pe n in the *Turbo C Reference Guide* describes these options.

The pointer fd is used after opening in order to refer to the file. Here is a version of a program which writes as well as reads:

```
#include <stdio.h>
define BUFFSIZE 80
main()
{
   FILE *fd;
   char message[] = "hello, world";
   char buffer[BUFFSIZE];
   int n;
   fd = fopen("hello", "w+");
   n = fwrite(message, 1, strlen(message) +
      1, fd);
   printf("\n%d bytes written", n);
   rewind(fd);
```

```
n = fread(buffer, 1, BUFFSIZE, fd);
printf("\n%d bytes read: %s", n, buffer);
fclose(fd);
}
```

The message is written to a file named **message** by the statement:

```
n = fwrite(message, 1, strlen(message) +
1, fd);
```

The number of bytes actually written is returned to n. This is useful in that it can be used for error checking. The second argument, **1**, says that the size of the object to be written is **1** byte. The number of such objects is the next argument. We have used another library function, **strlen**, to return the length of the string in **message**, and added one for the null at the string's end.

After writing to this file, the start position is set back to the beginning of the file by the **rewind()** statement. We could have set the starting position to any point we desire through use of the function **fseek()**, but here the **rewind()** suffices.

Next, we read the file into **buffer**. The file will be read until its end, and the number of bytes will be returned by the function. We have used n a second time for this. Again, the size of the object to be read is **1** byte, and the number is the size of the **buffer** (only the actual contents will be read though.)

Finally, we close the file. While the file would be closed at the end of the program anyway, it is good practice to close files when we are finished with them.

When the program is run, the message

```
13 bytes written
13 bytes read: hello, world
```

is written to the screen. Before leaving this example, let us ask a question: How do we find out about functions like **strlen()**? One way is to spend some time looking through descriptions of them in a reference such as the *Turbo C Reference Guide* or the *Quick C Reference Guide*. Another way is to look at classified lists of them: the *Reference Guide* has such lists (beginning on page 10 for the *Software Version 4* guide). Of course, familiarity comes with practice, and writing programs is the best way to get that. If we have the opportunity or need to write many C programs, we will naturally expose ourselves to the need to learn many of these.

12.3 WRITING A TEXT FILE

Here is a program which opens a file called **poem**, and which also writes text to it as entered from the keyboard:.

```
/* program prep.c  write text to file poem */
# include <stdio.h>
main()
{
  FILE *fd;
  char c;

  fd = fopen("poem","w");

  while ((c = getc(stdin)) != 'ə')

    fwrite(&c, 1, 1, fd);

  fclose(fd);
}
```

As was the case with the program in the last section, the file descriptor f d is declared to be a pointer to type F I LE, which is defined in the i nc l ude file stdio.h.

This time, we have used another of the C functions, getc(), which reads a character from the file named inside the parentheses. In this case we read from the *standard input*, or keyboard; it is defined as stdin in stdio.h.

We have used the character ə to mark the end of the input data. The function fwrite sends a byte at a time to the disk memory from the buffer; in this case the buffer is a single byte variable c, whose pointer &c is provided to the fwrite function.

The poem which we will enter is attributed to Augustus de Morgan, who was one of the founders of Boolean algebra.

The poem was used for illustration by Brian Kernighan and Robert Pike in their excellent book *The UNIX Programming Environment* (1984). The poem speaks of a phenomenon which seems central to computers and programming.

The C program is named prep.c. After it is compiled and executed, we type on the keyboard the following *poem*:

```
A:>prep

Great fleas have little fleas
  upon their backs to bite 'em,
And little fleas have lesser fleas,
  and so ad infinitum.
And the great fleas themselves, in turn,
  have greater fleas to go on;
While these again have greater still,
  and greater still, and so on.
Augustus de Morgan
ə
```

whereupon a file containing the poem and named *poem* is created. The @ at the end terminates the program, but does not get written into the file (why?).

We need a program that will read the file just created. Let us consider how we might write one.

12.4   READING A FILE

A program that reads *poem* into a buffer and which prints the contents to the screen is:

```
/* program rdp.c   reads the poem file */

#include <stdio.h>
#define BUFFSIZE 512

main()
{
   FILE *fd;
   char *cptr, buffer[BUFFSIZE];
   int i, n;

   fd = fopen("poem","r");

   n = fread(buffer, 1, BUFFSIZE, fd);
   printf("\n%d bytes read:\n", n);

   cptr = buffer;
   for (i = 0; i < n; i++)
     printf("%c", *cptr++);

   fclose(fd);
}
```

This time we read the bytes into a buffer of size 512. This is more than enough space for *poem*. The constant BUFFSIZE is defined by the preprocessor via the #define construction. The number actually read is returned by fread() to the variable n. A loop prints out the n characters one at a time. Note that we have used a pointer cptr which moves from character to character in the buffer to do the printing.

```
The program prints:
284 bytes read:
Great fleas have little fleas ... etc
```

It is easy to modify the characters as they are read in a program like this. Such a modifying program is an example of a f i l t e r: a program that processes an input. We will now change the r d p program into a filter to change the poem to upper case. We use:

```
/* program rdf.c   reads the poem file */

#include <stdio.h>
define BUFFSIZE 512
main()
{
   FILE *fd;
   char *cptr, buffer[BUFFSIZE];
   int i, n;
   fd = fopen("poem","r");
   n = fread(buffer, 1, BUFFSIZE, fd);
   printf("\n%d bytes read:\n", n);
   cptr = buffer;
   for (i = 0; i < n; i++)
   {
     if (*cptr >= 'a' && *cptr <= 'z')
       *cptr -= 'a' - 'A';
     printf("%c", *cptr++);
   }
   fclose(fd);
}
```

The result of compiling and executing the program is:

```
284 bytes read:
GREAT FLEAS HAVE LITTLE FLEAS
   UPON THEIR BACKS TO BITE 'EM,
AND LITTLE FLEAS HAVE LESSER FLEAS,
   AND SO AD INFINITUM.
AND THE GREAT FLEAS THEMSELVES, IN TURN,
   HAVE GREATER FLEAS TO GO ON;
WHILE THESE AGAIN HAVE GREATER STILL,
   AND GREATER STILL, AND SO ON.
```

Only two lines have been added to our original program. They are:

```
if (*cptr >= 'a' && *cptr <= 'z')
  *cptr -= 'a' - 'A';
```

Each character is tested as it is read to see if it is a lowercase letter (greater than a and less than z.) We remember that && is a logical operator, an operator which requires that both statements about the contents of *cptr be true. For *cptr's that meet the test, a constant value, equal to the displacement between upper and lower case in the ASCII table, is added.

We have used another of C's shorthand notations here. It is:

```
c -= 'a' - 'A'   /* the same as c = c -
   ('a' - 'A') */
```

The replacement of a variable by the same value after some operation is so common that this notation is often found in C programs. It works with all the binary operators (+, *, /, ... >>, etc.). In general, we see that var1 = var1 op var2 can be replaced by var1 op= var2. For example,

```
x = x + 2:       x += 2
x = x >> 3:        x >>= 3
```

12.5   ERROR CHECKING

The input/output programs in this chapter have been written without error checking in order to keep them simple and easy to read. However, a few added lines can help find the errors that inevitably occur, either through the fault of the programmer or the user. Something as simple as a floppy disk drive door being open can be hard to find, and error checking in a program can make debugging of the program easier.

Here is another version of the C program, without the filter, that reads the poem file, and which provides for error detection:

```
# include <stdio.h>
main()
{
   FILE *fd;
   int c;

   fd = fopen("poem","r");

   do
   {
     c = getc(fd);
     printf("%c", c);
   }
   while (c != EOF);

   fclose(fd);
}
```

This program uses the function g e t c to read from the file. The g e t c returns an integer, even though what it reads is a character. The purpose of this is to allow the special code for E O F, which is defined in s t d i o . h. If only characters were returned, then one of them would be needed for the end-of-file marker, and this character would be wasted.

Most functions have provisions for error checking. Many of them are listed under *Return value* in the *Turbo C*. They can also be found in the *Quick C Reference Guide*. Our new version of the program with error checking is:

```
#include <stdio.h>
define BUFFSIZE 512

main()
{
   FILE *fd;
   char c, buffer[BUFFSIZE];
   int n, i;

   if ((fd = fopen("poem","r")) == NULL)
   {
      printf("\ncan't open \"poem\" file");
      exit(1);
   }

   if ((n = fread(buffer, 1, BUFFSIZE, fd)) ==
      0)
   {
      printf("\nread error");
      exit(1);
   }

   printf("\n%d bytes read.\n", n);
   for (i = 0; i < n; i++)
      printf("%c", buffer[i]);

   if (fclose(fd) == EOF)
   {
      printf("\ncan't close file");
      exit(1);
   }
}
```

If we rename *poem* to something else, the program above will not be able to find any file with the name "poem" and will print the statement

```
can't open "poem" file
```

on the monitor.

In the error-checked version, various returns from the functions indicate error. The constant E O F is defined in the i n c l u d e file s t d i o . h. N U L L is a pointer to nothing, and is also defined in s t d i o . h. The f r e a d ( ) function returns the number of bytes actually read, and zero indicates an error. It is important here to note that the quotes in the message need the backslash escape character in the p r i n t f format.

We have written three versions of the program to read the file *poem*. Each uses a different approach. There are usually a number of ways to obtain a desired result. The one chosen may depend on some measure of efficiency or effectiveness, or it can simply be based on selection of a familiar approach. Appropriateness and importance of the selection criterion will vary from application to application.

12.6   CURIOUS I/O BEHAVIOR

A very simple input output program is the following:

```
#include <"stdio.h">

main()
{
char c;

printf("Enter any characters, Z = halt
   program.\n");

do {
c = getchar(); /* get single character from
   keyboard */
putchar(c);       /* display character on
   monitor */
} while (c != 'Z');  /* until a Z is hit */

printf("\nEnd of program.\n");
}
```

In this simple program the single variable c is defined and we enable a message to be printed out through use of the familiar p r i n t f function. We will be in a continuous loop so long as c is not equal to Z. The two new functions within the loop are of much interest to us here, as these are functions to read a character from the keyboard and display it on the monitor one character at a time.

The function get char () reads a single character from the keyboard, the standard input device, and assigns it to the variable c. The next function, put - char (c), uses the standard output device, the screen, and outputs the character contained in the variable c. The character entered on the keyboard is output at the current cursor location on the screen and the cursor is automatically advanced one space for reception of the next character to be entered on the keyboard.

When we execute this program, a possibly strange thing occurs. When we enter characters on the keyboard, they are displayed sequentially on the screen as we type them. However, when we hit the return or enter key, the entire message repeats itself. We have generated an echo! An explanation is in order. When data is read from the keyboard, under DOS control, the characters are stored in a buffer until a carriage return is entered. At that time, the complete string of characters on the line is input to the compiled program. When the characters are being typed, the characters are also displayed one at a time on the monitor. This happens in many applications.

Let's try another simple program as an alternative to the foregoing one:

```
#include <"stdio.h">

main()
{
char c;

printf("Enter any keyboard characters, stop
   at Z\n");

do {
c = getch();            /* get a character */
putchar(c);             /* display the hit key */
} while (c != 'Z');

printf("\nEnd of Program.\n");
}
```

When we compile and execute this simple program, we discover that there is no echo of the lines when we hit the enter key, and when we enter a Z, the program stops. No carriage return is needed to get the compiler to accept the line with the Z in it, as is the case with the first program noted. But we have introduced another problem. There is no linefeed with the carriage return.

The problem here is that we are perhaps too used to typewriter type operations. On the computer the return key should cause the curser to move to the left-hand side of the screen. But what about the linefeed? Not only do we usually wish to return to the left side of the monitor, we also wish to drop down a line. The linefeed is not automatic however. We need to improve our just presented program to do this. A little thought will convince us that a simple addition of two statements that define the character codes for the linefeed (LF) and the carriage return (CR) is what we need. These codes are 10 and 13. After outputting a character, we compare it to CR, and if it is equal to CR, we also output a linefeed. All of this certainly indicates that the C programming language is very flexible. Unfortunately, this flexibility has a price. The programmer must keep a large number of elementary details in mind or things may not work quite as expected. The reader is encouraged to try these last two programs and verify this.

12.7   I/O WITH INTEGER VARIABLES

The program next shown results, when compiled and executed, in reading formatted data:

```
#include <"stdio.h">

main()
{
int valin;

printf("Input number from 0 to 32767, stop
  with 999.\n");

do {
scanf("%d",&valin);    /* read a single integer
  value in */
printf("The value is %d\n",valin);
} while (valin != 999);

printf("End of program\n");
}
```

In this simple program we define an int type variable and loop until the variable attains a value of 999. Instead of reading in a character at a time, as we did in the last two programs, we read in an entire integer value with a single call through use of the function named scanf. This special function is similar to the printf that we have often used, except that it is an input rather than an output function. The scanf function does not request the variable valin directly, but gives the address of the variable. It does this since it anticipates a value returned from the function. The function scanf causes the compiler to scan the input line until it finds the first data field. It will ignore all leading blanks and will read integer characters until it finds a blank or an invalid decimal character. At that time it will stop reading and will return a value. The occurrence of the value 999 will cause the program to stop executing, even if there are numbers following the number 999. Also, if we enter a number greater than 32,767, curious things will happen that depend upon the specific compiler and the word length of the computer. We remember that $2^{16} = 65,536$ and that half of this is 32,768, and so do expect trouble in a 16-bit machine with this number.

String variables are also of importance and the first program in this chapter has illustrated how one might read a string variable with up to 10 characters. As we now see from our more recent examples, it would perhaps have been desirable to include some statement in the program that would have caused it to terminate upon receipt of a specific character and before the 10 characters have been entered. Depending upon the specific compiler that we use, exceeding 10 characters may cause an orderly termination of the program, or perhaps a rather disorderly one. So again we see that there is a sort of treachery inherent in the freedom allowed by C. We must take care to be precise with lots of little details. So while this may allow for a very efficient and effective program, it may reduce software productivity through reliability problems.

This has led some to conclude that C is not a good language to use when there are many input/output operations. This is possibly a valid criticism, as the myriad of bookkeeping details required does slow productivity. However, there is also great flexibility associated with the C language for I/O operations. The resolution of this dilemma would appear to be the repeated use of reusable I/O modules that have been very carefully designed and documented.

12.8   FILE INPUT/OUTPUT CONSIDERATIONS

Before we can write to a file, we must open it. In effect, this says that we must tell the computer that we want to write to a file and also the name of the file. We do this with the **fopen** function, as we have already discussed. The file pointer points to the file and two arguments are required in the parentheses, the filename first, followed by the file attribute.

The file attribute can be any of three types: reading (r), writing (w), or appending (a). The letters r, w, or a must be lower case. Opening a file for reading requires that the file already exist. If it does not exist, the file pointer will be set to **NULL** and can be checked by the program. When a file is opened for writing, it will be created if it does not already exist. It will have its contents erased if it does exist, and this may have the disastrous effect of destroying data. When a file is opened for appending, it will be created if it does not already exist. In this case, it will have no initial contents. If the file does exist, the data input pointer will start at the end of the present data. In this way, new data may be added to any data that already exists in the file.

Outputting to a file is almost the same operation as sending an output to the standard output device, the monitor. The function names are different and a file pointer must be one of the function arguments however. The only real difference may be to replace `printf` by `fprintf`.

To close a file, we use the function `fclose` with the file pointer in the parentheses. Often, it is not necessary to close a file because the compiler logic is such as to automatically close all open files before returning to DOS, as we have already noted. Generally, it is good programming practice to close all files, simply because this is a forceful reminder to everyone of the files that are open at the end of a program.

The following program is worth studying as an indication of how C accomplishes a typical file operation:

```
#include <stdio.h>

main()
{
FILE *fl1;
char oneword[200],filename[50];
char *c;

printf("Enter filename - ");
scanf("%s",filename); /* read the desired
  filename */
fl1 = fopen(filename,"r");

do {
c = fgets(oneword,200,fl1); /* get one line
  from file */
if (c != NULL)
 printf("%s",oneword); /* display it on the
   monitor   */
} while (c != NULL);   /* repeat until NULL
*/

fclose(fl1);
}
```

12.9 APPENDIX: INPUT/OUTPUT WITH PASCAL

Let us briefly examine some I/O concepts using Pascal. Here is a Pascal program which reads characters from the keyboard:

```
{$g512,p512,d-}
program rd;
```

```
var
  buf: array [1..10] of char;
  i, j: integer;
begin
  i := 1;
  writeln(trm,'enter up to 10 characters:');
  while not eoln do
    begin
      read(buf[i]);
      i := i + 1;
    end;

  write('input was: ');
  for j := 1 to i - 1 do
    write(buf[j]:4);
  writeln;
end.
```

When this program is compiled and the executable program run, it asks for input from the keyboard; the screen looks like this:

```
enter up to 10 characters:
abcdef
input was:    a    b    c    d    e    f
```

There are various input/output processes through which a program interacts with the environment. The environment is different for each computer, terminal, and printer and the language must adapt to the differences. Pascal's interface with the outside world is not rigidly specified, so differences among language implementations are common in this area. Turbo Pascal for the MS-DOS operating system has features which fit the particular environment of the IBM PC and compatible. Many of these are illustrated by example in the foregoing program. We note the following:

1. The first line is a Turbo Pascal compiler directive which makes possible the use of the redirection and other features of PC/MS-DOS. The details are not important at this point; we include this line in this and subsequent programs to get access to these features.

2. We have dropped the standard Pascal practice of including input and output specifications in the program line. Writing program r d (input, output) causes conflicts with the first line, and Turbo Pascal does not require it.

3. The first w r i t e l n statement has an added term in the parentheses: the destination t rm for terminal. Normally, that destination is understood when the term is omitted, but the use of input and output buffers needed by DOS make it necessary to say so if the screen is wanted.

These items represent details which would be better hidden at this point. However, it is one of the symptoms of the incompleteness of Pascal that they are not invisible.

The Pascal file handling procedures are listed in Table 12.1.

The function r e a d has been introduced here. Reading is done from the standard input, which is the keyboard, without specification of source.

The best way to keep this all straight is to see it in examples and to use these constructs in actual programs. The following Pascal program writes keyboard input to a file:

```
{$g512,p512,d-}
program prep;
var fd: text;
    ch: char;
begin
  assign(fd,'pfile');
  rewrite(fd); (* get ready to write *)
  while not eof do
    begin
      read(ch);
      write(fd,ch);
    end;
  close (fd);
end.
```

This program uses the built-in file t e x t, which describes a file containing lines of characters terminated by newlines. The file descriptor f d is assigned to the

TABLE 12.1 Pascal File-Handling Procedure

Prepare For Use	Assign (Fd ,' Name')
	Rewrite(Fd)
	Reset (Fd)
Write	Write (Fd, Var)
Read	Read(Fd , Var)
Finish	Close (Fd)

file named p f i l e. From then on, the file descriptor is used to open (rewrite), read, write, and c l o s e the file.

When the program is run, text can be entered from the keyboard. At the end, we enter a ^Z (control Z) to mark the end of file. The contents of the file thus created can be verified by typing t y p e p f i l e from DOS.

A Pascal program which reads the file p o e m and which prints it on the screen is:

```
{$g512,p512,d-}
program rdp;
var fd: text;
    ch: char;
begin
  assign(fd,'poem');
  reset(fd); (* get ready to read *)
  while not eof(fd) do
    begin
      read(fd,ch);
      write(ch);
    end;
  close (fd);
end.
```

We note here the use of r e s e t. We used r e w r i t e in the program p r e p . p a s to open a new file or erase an existing one. The command r e s e t opens the file and puts the index pointer at the beginning.

The function e o f returns one of two Boolean responses, t r u e or f a l s e, depending on whether or not the end of file has been reached. The program writes the poem to the screen, with the ə sign in the last line. The ə can be removed by writing

```
if ch <>'ə' then
  write(ch);
```

PROBLEMS

12.1 Write a program which reads a date from the keyboard in the format 4/ 12/65 and prints it to the screen as April 12, 1965. (Hint: look up the function g e t s ( ).)

12.2 Write a C program that echoes a string that you enter to the screen.

12.3 Write a program that prints the individual words of the *poem* file to the screen, one word to a line.

12.4 Perform the same task as in Problem 12.3, but protect all the file operations with error trapping. Check the error features by renaming the file.

12.5 Write a program that indexes each word of *poem* so that you can print the nth word by entering its index number.

12.6 Write a program that replaces all punctuation in *poem* with asterisks.

12.7 Write a program that echoes each line you enter backward.

12.8 Write a program that echoes each line you enter in upper case.

12.9 Write a program that counts the characters, words, and lines of *poem*.

12.10 Write a program that replaces all the "fleas" in *poem* with "frogs." Use the string compare function.

12.11 Write a simple program that will:
(**a**) prompt for a filename for a read file;
(**b**) prompt for a filename for a write file; and
(**c**) open both as well as opening a file to the printer.
Now write expressions for a loop that will read a character and output it to the file, the printer, and the monitor. Be sure to include the ability for the program to automatically stop when the data is exhausted.

13

AN ELEMENTARY PROGRAMMING APPLICATION—MENUS

13.0 INTRODUCTION

So far our examples of use of the C language have emphasized operations of the machine itself, such as changing characters or writing to files. In this chapter we will show how the language can be used to provide ways to do one job that might be of some importance around an office or factory. In particular, we will describe approaches for menu design.

13.1 PROGRAMMING A MENU

As we have already noted several times, computers can perform two basic kinds of operations: arithmetic and decision-making. We have already seen examples of the computer's decision function for logic statements, such as the i f statement. In execution of this logic statement, such an expression is evaluated and some action is taken depending on the result of this evaluation. Now we will examine methods for making multiple branches in program logic.

At the same time, we will illustrate this by developing one method that is useful for providing both unskilled users and experts a means of relatively easy access to the computer. The idea is to give the user a *menu* showing which choice options are available, and a simple means to tell the computer which option is selected.

Here is a C program which creates a menu that gives the user a number of choices:

```c
#include <stdio.h>

main()
{
  char c;

  show menu();
  do
  {
    c = getchar();
    pick(c);
  }
  while (c != 'e');
}
show menu()
{
  printf("\nmenu\n");
  printf("\na      select a");
  printf("\nb      select b");
  printf("\nc      select c");
  printf("\ne      exit\n\n");
  printf("enter your choice: ");
}
pick(ch)
  char ch;
{
  switch(ch)
  {
    case 'a':
    case 'b':
    case 'c':  printf("you have entered
               <%c>",ch);
               show menu();
               break;
    case 'e': = printf("\nreturning to
               DOS\n");
               exit();
    case '\n': break;
    default :  printf("illegal character");
               printf("\n\nenter your
               choice: ");
  }
}
```

This C program has two functions which follow ma i n ( ). One of these, which is called s h o w _me nu, prints the menu, and the other, which is called p i c k, acts on the choice. The reading of the keyboard is done conveniently in ma i n.

The s w i t c h construction is new. It selects a variable, in this case c, and compares it with the various c a s e statements that appear within the curly brackets that follow the s w i t c h statement. The c a s e statements are labels, and execution of these starts at the label which matches the s w i t c h variable. For example, if b is chosen, execution starts at the label c a s e ' b ' : .

When a c a s e is found that matches, all the statements following the colon associated with the particular c a s e statement will be executed. Unless there is a b r e a k statement, which causes the s w i t c h to terminate, all the statements that follow the successful match will be included. The other case statements are known as *labels* and are ignored. Only one success in terms of a match is looked for, and the first success starts execution of all that follows. Hence the value of b r e a k is determined.

In C the b r e a k statement is used for immediate exit from a s w i t c h, f o r, w h i l e, or do block. Upon exit from one of these blocks, the program continues at the statement following the block. Another statement related to break is c o n t i n u e. This statement causes the loop to start again with the next iteration.

We notice that b r e a k has been placed in the switch block of the foregoing program at places of exit. Without these expressions, succeeding statements would be executed whether we wanted them or not. Also, we note that the newline \n expression, which is generated in the entry process, is ignored by simply placing a b r e a k in its c a s e. The d e f a u l t label picks up all other inputs.

When the program is run the menu is presented each time a choice is made, unless the e is picked, in which case we return to the DOS prompt.

```
menu
a        select a
b        select b
c        select c
e        exit


enter your choice: a
you have entered <a>
menu
a        select a
b        select b
c        select c
e        exit
```

```
enter your choice: c
you have entered <c>
menu
a        select a
b        select b
c        select c
e        exit

enter your choice: e

returning to DOS
```

This program keeps printing the menu on the next line, and so the display on the screen keeps scrolling down. The program works, but its physical appearance on the screen is not attractive. Let us, therefore, improve the looks of this program by better screen handling.

13.2 BETTER SCREENS: USING BIOS

To improve the appearance of the menu program, we only add two functions. One of these clears part of the screen, and the other causes movement of the cursor. Using these two functions, we can write the menu in the same location each time we need it, and the screen will not scroll.

The functions that enable this use the **BIOS** interrupt functions. We met these functions before in Section 5.7. This time we invoke the interrupt by the **geninterrupt()** function that is provided by *Turbo C*. The BIOS functions require that various quantities be placed in the PC's registers, and *Turbo C* provides *pseudovariables* (e.g., AX) for that purpose. We have included the header file **dos.h** for this. The details of the BIOS services are covered in the references;[1] those of the **geninterrupt()** function are on pages 262–263 of the 1988 edition of the *Turbo C User's Guide*.

```
#include <stdio.h>
#include <dos.h>

main()
{
   char c;

   show menu();
   do
   {
```

[1]Duncan, R., *Advanced MS-DOS*, Microsoft Press, Redmond, WA., 1986.

```
      c = getchar();
      pick(c);
   }
   while (c != 'e');
}
show menu()
{
   cls(0, 17);
   setcurs(10, 0);
   printf("\nmenu\n");
   printf("\na      select a");
   printf("\nb      select b");
   printf("\nc      select c");
   printf("\ne      exit\n\n");
   printf("enter your choice: ");
}
pick(ch)
   char ch;
{
   switch(ch)
   {
      case 'a':
      case 'b':
      case 'c':   printf("you have entered
                  <%c>",ch);
                  show menu();
                  break;
      case 'e':   printf("returning to DOS
                     \n");
                  exit();
      case '\n':  show menu();
                  break;
      default :   printf("illegal character
                     ");
                  show menu();
   }
}
cls(x, y) /* clears screen from row x to row
   y */
   int x, y;
{
   AH = 6;    /* initialize window */
   AL = 0;    /* blank it */
   BH = 7;    /* with normal attribute */
   CH = x;    /* upper left: */
```

```
   CL = 0;    /* x, 0  */
   DH = y;    /* lower right: */
   DL = 79;   /* y ,79 */
   geninterrupt(0x10);
}
setcurs(x, y) /* sets cursor to row x and
   column y */
   int x, y;
{
   AH = 2;    /* bios set cursor */
   BH = 0;    /* page 0 */
   DH = x;    /* row */
   DL = y;    /* column */
   geninterrupt(0x10);
}
```

We have made minor adjustments to the p i c k ( ) outputs in order to make the response to the various keys uniform. Otherwise, the program we have just written is nearly the same as before, except for the addition of these two new functions.

This is a good illustration of the ease with which a C program can be modified. It also shows how a little searching through manuals easily enables us to identify means to accomplish common tasks like clearing the screen.

13.3 RUNNING ONE PROGRAM FROM ANOTHER

Now we will change one of the menu choices such that it will result in the execution of another program. Here is the program, a version of h e l l o . c :

```
main()
{
   printf ("hello, world          \007");
}
```

The backslash (\) escape character is used here to include the ASCII character with code 007 (octal) in the string to be printed. Reference to the table of ASCII in Chapter 2 will confirm that this is the code for b e l which causes a beep on the IBM PC. (Actually, the b e l code caused a bell to ring on the original teletype machines as well.) When it is compiled, the program is stored as h e l l o . e x e and can be executed by typing h e l l o and then pressing the enter key.

Actually, we only needed to replace c with g for *greeting* to the menu itself, and to revise the p i c k ( ) function of the menu program to include the option of running h e l l o . e x e. The new p i c k ( ) function is:

```
include <process.h>
pick(ch)
  char ch;
{
  switch(ch)
  {
    case 'a':
    case 'b':    printf("you have entered
                 <%c>",ch);
                 show menu();
                 break;
    case 'g':    spawnl(P WAIT, "hello.exe",
                 NULL);
                 break;
    case 'e':    printf("returning to DOS
                   \n");
                 exit(0);
    case '\n':   show menu();
                 break;
    default  :   printf("illegal character
                   ");
                 show menu();
  }
}
```

The choice g causes hello.exe to be invoked via the *Turbo C* spawnl() function (which needs the header file process.h). The latter causes the program named in its argument to be executed. Upon completion, control returns to the calling program, in this case menu. The constant P WAIT tells menu to wait until the child program hello.exe is finished.

Looking forward to a time when MS-DOS or a successor operating system can run multiple programs, a P NOWAIT constant is provided for this, or other, future use.

The new version of this simple menu program will provide a greeting:

```
menu
a        select a
b        select b
g        greeting
e        exit

enter your choice: g
hello world
```

13.4 SIMPLE GRAPHICS

To further illustrate the power of the C language in applications, we will write a short program to analyze the letter frequencies of *poem*.

Our program will need to examine each letter in *poem* and to accumulate a count of each one as it occurs. We will count all the letters regardless of case. Finally, a histogram of letter frequency will be printed. This sounds like a big order, but the program to do it is really short and simple:

```c
#include <stdio.h>
#include <ctype.h>
#define BUFFSIZE 512
char buffer[BUFFSIZE];
int letters[26];

main()
{
   int i;

   i = rdpoem();
   count(i);
   hist(i);
}
max(s) /* find the maximum in array s */
   int *s;
{
   int i, m = 0;

   for (i = 0; i < 26; i++)
     if (*(s + i) > m)
       m = *(s + i);
   return m;
}
FILE *fd;
rdpoem() /* open poem, read it to buffer,
   return count */
{
   fd = fopen("poem", "r");
   return (fread(buffer, 1, BUFFSIZE, fd));
}
count(n) /* count letter freq of buffer with
   n letters */
   int n;
```

```
{
   int i;
   char c;

   for (i = 0; i < 26; i++)
     letters[i] = 0;

   for (i = 0; i < n; i++)
     if (isalpha((c = buffer[i])))
       letters[tolower(c) - 'a']++;
}
hist(n)   /* histogram for n total in letters[]
   array */
{
   int i, j;

   printf("\n        relative frequency\
   of %d letters in \"poem\"\n\n", n);

   for (i = max(letters); i >= 0; i -= 2)
     {
       for (j = 0; j < 26; j++)
       {
         if (letters[j] > i)
           printf("X "); /* replace X with \262
             for block */
         else
           printf("  ");
       }
       printf("\n");
     }
   printf("\n");
   for (i = 'a'; i <= 'z'; i++)
     printf("%c ", i);
}
```

The resulting histogram that is displayed on the screen is replicated in Figure 13.1. This figure presents a relative frequency of 285 letters in *poem*.

The program has four functions in addition to main(). We have opened and read this file into a buffer before, so there is nothing new to us in doing this here.

The frequency counting function count(n) checks each letter with the function isalpha() in order to remove white space and punctuation. It then

```
        X
        X
        X
 X      X
 X      X
 X      X
 X      X                              X
 X      X                            X X
 X      X              X             X X
 X      X              X   X         X X
 X      X      X       X   X       X X X
 X      X      X       X   X       X X X
 X      X  X X X       X   X X     X X X
 X    X X X X X X      X   X X     X X X X
 X    X X X X X X      X X X X     X X X X X
 X X  X X X X X X      X X X X     X X X X X

 a  b c d  e  f g h i  j  k  l m n  o  p q  r  s  t  u  v w x y z
```

FIGURE 13.1   Relative frequency of 285 letters in Poem. Each X represents a count of two letters; if a letter appears an odd number of times, the count is rounded down.

changes all letters to lower case for uniformity with t o l o w e r ( ). Both of these functions are defined in the header c t y p e . h. Next, the index of the array holding the count, l e t t e r s [ ], is calculated by subtracting ' a ' from the letter that is being counted. Finally, the count itself is incremented with + +.

The h i s t ( ) function starts at the maximum count, as returned by m a x ( ). It then counts down to zero by putting an X on each column, depending on the count for that letter. The X can be replaced by \ 2 6 2 to get a better looking graph with one of the IBM-PC's special characters. The particular printer used here ignores the \ 2 6 2 special character printing command, and so we used X instead).

The two buffers have been declared above m a i n ( ) as *global* buffers. Thus they will be available to any function which needs them. The function m a i n ( ) itself has been reduced to calls to three of the functions. The reader might find it interesting and informative to experiment with this program.

13.5   THE C PRINTF ( ) FUNCTION

We have been using p r i n t f ( ) since the very first C program in this book. Now we pause once again to review this useful and versatile function. Here is a simple program which illustrates some of the variety possible with the p r i n t f ( ) function:

```
main()
{
   int i = 1234;
   float r = 12.34;
   int b = (1234 > 12.34);
   char c = 'x';

   printf("\n i = %6d r = %8.3f b = %d c = %c",
          i, r, b, c);
}
```

The result of compiling and executing this simple program is a display on the monitor of:

```
i =    1234  r =    12.340  b = 1    c = x
```

We notice that b is evaluated as 1. We remember that the logical 0 is false and that anything else is true. However, C usually sets true equal to 1. In this program the variables are initialized as they are declared, which is impossible with a number of other programming languages such as Pascal.

There are two parts to the argument of the p r i n t f function:

```
printf(" text plus formatted variables here ",
             list of variables here )
```

The formatted variables are marked by the % sign. The rest of the text is printed as it is written. There are many possible formatted variables. A complete list is contained in the *Turbo C Reference Guide*. The ones we will generally use are listed next:

```
        %c      a character
        %d      an integer
        %f      a floating point variable
        %s      a string
        %u      an unsigned integer
        %x      a hex integer
```

As an example of the use of these formatted variables, we present a C program which uses p r i n t f to format and print a table. The data for the table is introduced by initializing arrays, something that we would not normally do. The data would probably be read from a file in most applications, but this is a quick way to illustrate data formatting and arrangement. Our program is:

```
main()
{
   int i;
   static char *growth[] = {"Ch. Margaux",
                            "Ch. Mouton-
                                Rothschild",
                            "Ch. Larose",
                            "Bourgeois growth",
                            "Peasant growth"};
   static float alcohol[] = {12.14, 11.82,
                            12.06, 12.71,
                            11.47};
   static float sugar[]   = { 1.93,  2.56,
                             3.97,  2.49,
                             1.20};

   printf("\n\
             VINTAGE OF 1900");
   printf("\n\
      Growth                Alcohol Sugar");
   printf("\n\
                            %%      g/ltr\n");
   for (i = 0; i < 5; i++)
     printf("\n%-22s %6.2f   %5.2f",
               growth[i], alcohol[i],
               sugar[i]);

   printf("\n\nSource: Encyclopedia
      Britannica,");
   printf(" 11th ed., vol.28, pg 722\n");
}
```

Execution of the program causes the screen to display:

```
          VINTAGE OF 1900
Growth                     Alcohol   Sugar
                           %         g/ltr
Ch. Margaux                12.14     1.93
Ch. Mouton-Rothschild      11.82     2.56
Ch. Larose                 12.06     3.97
Bourgeois growth           12.71     2.49
Peasant growth             11.47     1.20

Source: Encyclopedia Britannica, 11th ed.,
   vol.28, pg 722
```

The data are provided by the declarations of static arrays, which can be initialized. The variable growth is an array of strings. The p r i n t f statement uses the minus sign to left-justify the strings in 22-character fields. Notice that the percent sign was doubled for the table heading. This prevents its interpretation as format.

13.6 SYSTEMS PROGRAMMING

To further illustrate p r i n t f and to show how C allows penetration to the internal workings of the machine, we present a program which uses the same string data as our last program:

```
include <dos.h>
main()
{
   int i;
   char c;
   int segment;
   unsigned offset;

   static char *growth[] = {"Ch. Margaux",
                            "Ch. Mouton-
                              Rothschild",
                            "Ch. Larose",
                            "Bourgeois growth",
                            "Peasant growth"};

   printf("\nThe data segment address of the");
   printf(" program is %x hex",(segment = DS));

   printf("\nThe offset of the second
     vineyard");
   printf(" is %x hex", (offset =
     (unsigned)growth[1]));

   printf("\nThis can be verified by
     printing: ");

   for (i = 0;(c = peekb(segment, offset + i))
     !='\0';i++)
     printf("%c", c);

   printf("\n");
}
```

The result of compiling and executing this program is the display on the screen of the following messages.

```
The data segment address of the program is
  3599 hex
The offset of the second vineyard is b0 hex
This can be verified by printing: Ch.
  Mouton-Rothschild
```

We notice that the *value* of a pointer is simply its offset address within the data segment. The addressing organization used is just that of the Intel 8088. The pointer o f f s e t is defined within the parentheses in the second p r i n t f statement. It is given the name of its array element, in this case g r o w t h [1]. The function o f f s e t is declared to be an u n s i g n e d integer, and the conversion from the pointer address name is made by the type cast (u n s i g n e d).

The variable s e g m e n t is defined in the first p r i n t f statement using the pseudovariable D S, which returns the contents of the *ds* register.[2]

Finally, a f o r loop prints each character in the string at that address, using the function p e e k b (s e g m e n t , o f f s e t) to return the ASCII code that is stored there. C stores strings like this, with nulls separating them, end to end in the data segment.

This example illustrates the use of C as a systems programming language. C was first used to write the UNIX operating system and is well suited to manipulation of the internal registers and memory of the computer. As might be expected, such manipulation is not without danger, and it is well to save a program frequently during development of software which does this kind of thing. Programming errors at this level can write into the memory that is needed by the operating system. The usual result is a nonresponsive keyboard. Consequently, the machine must be rebooted (Alt Ctrl Del) or, in extreme cases, switched off and turned on to start over completely.

13.7   APPENDIX: PASCAL APPLICATIONS

A *menu* is an invitation for easy selection among multiple choices. Here is a Pascal program that offers four choices and then acts on the one chosen.

```
{$g1,p1,d-}
program menu;
const
   legal: set of char = ['a','b','c','e'];
```

---

[2]The segment register contents will probably be different on your machine.

```
var
  key: char;
procedure show menu;
  begin
    clrscr;  (* a turbo pascal procedure *)
    writeln('menu');writeln;
    writeln('a      select a');
    writeln('b      select b');
    writeln('c      select c');
    writeln('e      exit');writeln;readln;
  end;
function ch:char;
  var
    kbd:char;
  begin
    read(kbd);
    ch := kbd;
  end;
procedure pick(ch:char);
  begin
    writeln;
    if ch in legal then
      case ch of
        'a': write('you have entered a');
        'b': write('you have entered b');
        'c': write('you have entered c');
        'e': begin
               writeln('returning to DOS');
               exit;
             end
      end
    else
      write('illegal character');
    readln;
    writeln;
  end;
begin (* main *)
  show menu;
  repeat
    write('enter your choice: ');
    key := ch;
    pick(key);
  until key = 'e';
end.
```

Here is what the screen shows when a through e are entered:

```
MENU
a        select a
b        select b
c        select c
e        exit

enter your choice: a
you have entered a

enter your choice: b
you have entered b

enter your choice: c
you have entered c

enter your choice: d
illegal character

enter your choice: e
returning to DOS
```

With Pascal programs it is best to start reading in the (*main*) block, since the procedures which support a particular block must always precede it. In this program we use the Pascal expression procedure show menu to print the choices first, and then go into a repeat block to obtain choices until exit is chosen.

Within the repeat block, we obtain a keyboard response with the function ch. Then the procedure pick is used to provide the action. A case statement is used for the multiple-choice branch. In Pascal care must be taken to eliminate input choices to case, for which there are no provisions. C has a default for this purpose, but Pascal has none. We have solved the problem here by introducing a set of legal characters in const, and by testing the keystroke before allowing the case to consider it. If the key pressed is an illegal one, the else statement takes over.

Pascal has a set of type variable which can be used with the standard *set* manipulations. We can test a variable for membership in a particular set, as we have done in this example, or we may apply the operations of intersection, union, and others. C does not have set variables, however, and this is a potential shortcoming.

Our final observation on input/output is occasionally a consequential one. The very first line of the program is a *Turbo Pascal* compiler directive that is needed to set up input/output buffers for MS-DOS. We have met this before, and in this case the buffers are sized to one character in order to receive the letters that are entered in response to the menu. In turn, this required the insertion of a couple of read l n statements to clean out the buffers before they are used. These then required some adjustment to handle the newlines that come with the read l n's. For the casual user of Pascal these things are best done by trial and error. But they are a decided nuisance and reflect the immaturity of the Pascal language that we have noted before. C, with its UNIX background, does a better job of interfacing with the outside world than Pascal, at least in our experience.

Both C and Turbo Pascal provide functions which allow a program in either language to start another program. Here is a short Pascal program (hello.pas) which greets the world with a beep:

```
PROGRAM HELLO;
begin
   writeln('hello, world!', chr(7))
end.
```

This program is compiled using the chn option to produce hello.chn. If we check the directory, we will find that the executable program has only 81 bytes. The compiled code is small because the chn option depends on another program to supply the lengthy Pascal library functions. We can invoke hello from another program in this way:

```
PROGRAM RUN;
var
prog: file;
begin
   assign (prog, 'hello.chn');
   chain(prog);
end.
```

We should remember that the chain function is not standard Pascal, which has no counterpart to this function; chain is a special function that comes with *Turbo Pascal*. When the chain function is invoked, control is passed to the new program; and when the new program is finished, we are passed back to DOS.

We have been using writeln in Pascal and printf in C since the beginning of our programming efforts. Now it is time to look at these useful library functions more closely.

In a Pascal program the writeln function adapts itself to the declared type of the variable that is to be printed. We now present a short program that demonstrates the flexibility of writeln.

```
program wr;
var
  i: integer;
  r: real;
  b: boolean;
  c: char;
begin
  i := 1234;
  r := 12.34;
  b := (1234 > 12.34);
  c := 'x';
  writeln('   i = ',i:6,
          '   r = ',r:8:3,
          '   b = ',b,
          '   c = ',c);
end.
```

Here, the Boolean statement equates **b** to an expression which is **TRUE**. The four types have been mixed in one **writeln** statement. The result exhibits each in proper format:

```
i = 1234          r = 12.340   b = TRUE   c = x
```

Text has been mixed in with the computations (e.g, **i =**) in order to make the result readable.

PROBLEMS

13.1 Modify the histogram program so that it rounds a 1 occurrence to 2, but still shows 0 occurrences as 0.

13.2 Write a program which saves part of the screen (a window) in a buffer and restores it when a key is pressed. The new contents should be swapped with the old in the process.

13.3 Write a program which capitalizes all the words in *poem*. (How will you handle the word **'em?**)

13.4 Write a program that stores the words individually in a file. Print a list of words from the file.

PART III

OPERATING SYSTEMS

14

OPERATING SYSTEMS

14.0 INTRODUCTION

We have now reached the point in our efforts where very rudimentary applications programs have been produced in the C language. We have concentrated on programming and not on the internal activities needed for the computer to produce a running program. If you are using *Turbo C*, or any other program development system, many complicated operations occur when you type A l t r to run a program from the editor. This is a good place to pause to examine the role of the operating system in making all of these things happen.

We have also previously discussed some fundamentals of computers and computing, including the physical makeup of computers, their peripheral equipment, and the *primitive* operations carried out by the instructions that are built into the hardware. In a modern computer system applications program, *repetitive* operations of great complexity are continually required. Performance of these repetitive operations is enabled through *operating system software*. This collection of programs also performs mappings of program descriptions, from languages easy for the human to use to the *native language* of the computer. These tasks are essential if a single computer system is to handle many diverse applications effectively and efficiently. We will now introduce operating system concepts and indicate how they aid in enabling the computer to handle complex problems.

14.1 PREPARING FOR PROGRAM EXECUTION

The earliest computers used no programs except the one that represented steps needed to cope with the application itself. The programs were, of necessity, written in machine language. This did not even provide the programmer with the opportunity to use mnemonic's applications representation for data variables or subroutines. In those early days experienced computer programmers had no sensation that anything was missing or erroneous in their program except the ultimate realization that things did not work either as anticipated or perhaps at all. The end user was often the programmer and this did make program debugging an easier task than it otherwise would have been. Nevertheless, it was a very tedious and error-prone operation.

The input device, customarily a card or paper tape reader, was exercised in order to read a single word of data at a time into the computer. Once all needed data had been input, it was then manipulated by the arithmetic routines imbedded into the logic of the machine language program. These included homemade floating-point procedures which shifted mantissas and incremented or decremented the exponents of the data variables that were stored in a separate word location from the fixed-point component of the data. Subroutines were created for frequently used operations, such as *adjusting* floating point numbers.

Complex scientific problems could be solved on these early computers, whose memory was often only 1024 words of 32 bits each, and whose instructions dealt only with full words. Whenever an output word was produced, it was sent off to a card punch where all 32 bits were punched. Since interpreting results was rather difficult, users and programmers generally preferred output forms which also tested whether certain desired conditions were met. This provided at least a crude form of error checking.

Two major steps have been taken since those early days. The first was *mnemonic programming*, in which the programmer could use easily remembered word representations for instructions, data, and program branch destinations. This required a separate program, an assembler or compiler, to *translate* the program into a version which was suitable for the computer. The second step, which came years later, was to preprogram a wide variety of computer operations, most particularly those associated with housekeeping rather than the actual solution of the user's problem, into a series of programs. This collection of programs was referred to as an *operating system*.

It did not take long to realize that programmers repeatedly constructed very similar program sections for input, output, and floating point operations. Then as now, however, these individuals were proud of their work and were often reluctant to rely on that of others. It became clear, however, that libraries of subroutines would contribute to efficiency and effectiveness in programming. Some of these subroutines naturally found major use in *operating systems*.

It was not until the late 1950s that a fully integrated operating system became a normal expectation for a large computer system. By that time, the simple card reader and punch, which served as the only peripheral devices on early computers, had been augmented by early disk storage and output printers. Not only was the environment in which the programmer had to operate far more complex, but instruction sets were larger and the memory much larger—many thousands of words. In short, the need for relief from housekeeping chores was much greater, and there was increased need for automation of the task of switching from one computer application to another. As with most other technologies, operating system capabilities slowly emerged over a number of years. Our description will deal with the capabilities which have come to be expected in a full-fledged operating system.

14.2 JOB-CONTROL LANGUAGES

With busy computer centers receiving many programs to be run each day, the concept of a *job stream* becomes important. With this concept, programs which do not require the programmer or user to monitor or control execution are given to the operating system for execution. The operating system provides a management function that allows jobs which are individual and independent programs, with their data, to be entered into the system continuously. When a job uses programs and data which already exist as data files in the system, all that is required to accomplish job execution is a set of instructions that define which program and data are to be used, and how output data is to be handled, with respect to sending it to a printer or storing it in a file for later use.

This job information is not a computer program in the full sense of program, but it does require an unambiguous structure and format which can be read by the operating system programs. Hence the term *job-control-language* is applied to these operating instructions. Or in some computer systems, the term *command language* only is used. Traditionally, little care has been applied toward making these formats simple to use, since it was most often assumed that they would be prepared by computer programming professionals. This tradition remains in operating system command formats for large computers especially up to the present time.

Job-control, or operating-system command languages provide for defining:

1. the name and file location of the program to be executed,
2. the name(s) and location(s) of a file or files to be used for input when the program calls for input data, and
3. the name(s) and location of output file(s).

If the input or output is to be derived from, or directed to, some other device, such as a terminal or printer, this must be specified. In addition, there may be *parameters* (sometimes abbreviated as *parms*), which are used to give additional control directions to be used by the operating system. In the absence of specified parameters, a set of *default* parameters is used. In PCs the entire control statement or command is limited to a single line of terminal input. In running programs on large computers, there may be a series of lines for each of several *tasks* which collectively constitute the *job*. A *batch* job is defined as one which does not have a human and terminal operating together in an *interactive* manner with the program. The more capable operating systems also allow the user to program a job to be started at some time in the future, or even a job to be run on a scheduled, periodic basis.

Often, a program to be executed is defined by job-control statements or an operating-system command. A program called the *job scheduler* determines that a job is ready to be started. It assigns the next phase to a program, referred to as the *loader*, which undertakes the responsibility of locating the program. Such attributes as file name, normally ending with special characters which signify that it is a program and not data, are used to uniquely describe the program. When a job-control request is made, the input and output data file(s) are also located and their identity made known to the program by *binding* the program's mnemonic file references to specific files defined in the job-control commands.

The *binding* concept is an important one. Binding refers to the association of an entity, defined in one program or at one time, with one defined at a later time. It permits programs to be constructed in a less specific form initially and only tied or bound to specific files or input/output devices, at some later time. In the earliest machines data and program were always bound to specific memory locations at the time of writing, and all input or output devices were necessarily referred to in an absolute sense. Modern operating systems allow enormous flexibility in terms of *late binding*, so that the programmer can be very general in specifying many of the system resources which will be used.

After binding, the program is transferred into main computer memory by the loader. In many computers, the program is, at this point, incomplete. When initially prepared, the area of main memory that would be available to it was not known. Hence the loader might necessarily fill in some missing addresses.[1] It obtains needed information from another operating system program, often called the *memory-manager*, which assigns a region of memory for the program when this is requested and when memory is available. If sufficient memory is not available, a program of the same priority, but which requires less memory, may be loaded. Alternately, a program of lower priority may be swapped out of memory to make way for a more important program which needs to be executed.

A number of other important operating-system programs take part in this operation. In addition to the *memory manager*, a *file manager* may be called. The file manager determines whether the requested files are available, and whether the program has authorization to read or both read from and write to these files or to certain parts of them. If output must be directed to a high-speed printer, a program known as an *output spooler* will be invoked, though normally only after completion of the program execution. The job stream itself is often managed and retained in the form of a file in disk storage by a corresponding *input spooler*. Some of these *resource management* routines are relatively sim-

---

[1]For example, in the IBM-PC and related computers the *segment addresses* for the program and its data areas cannot be known until *execution time*, and must be completed then.

ple, but others are quite complex. In most operating systems they will often be assigned unique names by the software designer, but are usually present, in one form or another, in all modern operating systems. The user or the application program need have little concern with most of these details. The only observed evidence of their presence may come from an *error message* that is outputted when one of these resource managers discovers a problem with a program and aborts further execution.

The program and data may not be loaded into memory by an operating system unless all resources needed for its execution are available. This availability is reported by a variety of resource management software modules, based on the various job control statements or commands. Once an executable application is loaded into memory and ready to begin operation it comes under the powerful rule of the system executive and many *assistants* which govern program execution.

14.3   THE SYSTEM EXECUTIVE

The most critical, though as a rule not the largest, program in a full-fledged operating system is referred to as the *executive*. Simply stated, its function is to assign the processor, or several processors in a multiprocessor, in order to achieve timely execution of the multitude of tasks which must be carried out for all application and systems programs that need to be executed. The nature of the executive varies greatly, depending on the application focus of a particular operating system.

In terminal-driven operating systems, such as those for most PCs, which support only one program, or one task or separately executable part of a program at a time, there is no software executive. That function is fulfilled by the *computer user*. In most process-control applications, the executive may be a simple loop routine which calls each of a number of control and test routines after the previous one is completed. In large computers supporting concurrent execution of tens or even hundreds of programs, however, the executive plays a critical role.

Let us consider a typical multiprogramming or multitasking operating system. Any time that an application program initiates a step, such as calling for output to be written to a file, the executive program regains control while it is waiting for the step to be completed. Once in control it establishes whether any other program task is able to proceed *immediately*, that is, if all needed resources are available and an event for whose completion the executive was waiting has been completed. If there are several such tasks in ready status, and they are of different priorities, the executive will transfer control to the one of highest priority. In some systems the executive will assign the processor to that task which has least recently had processor time for tasks of uniform priority.

Let us suppose that the executive commits itself to a task. The task is off and running until, in turn, it needs to wait. Such a simple algorithm for an executive is, without some additional control feature, vulnerable to programmer errors: if a program enters an endless loop, the entire system could be tied up indefinitely. In some systems each executable task is assigned only a limited computer time, generally a few milliseconds or tens of milliseconds, before it is forcibly stopped. This is one, more or less brute force, way of avoiding this endless loop problem. In operating systems that contain this feature a count-down timer interrupts the processor, thereby giving the executive control once more. When the executive assigns a limited time interval to each executing program, the operating system is said to be *time-sharing*. This protects the system from endless-loop errors, as the program execution will finally be terminated by completion of an allotted time for program execution. This also allows other programs to continue execution, despite the presence of some program which would never complete executing.

In large computer systems that perform a variety of program execution tasks, the executive will generally be very flexible. For example, some programs which always operate without interactive user involvement, referred to as batch programs, may be prioritized as *background programs*. Programs operating from user terminals, and which generally need user input, are defined as *foreground programs*. Background programs operate only when no foreground programs are capable of execution. Generally, background programs are assigned a priority[2] less than foreground programs, all of which may have the same priority.

Capable operating systems must be prepared to handle situations in which a program, which is structurally a *single* application program, actually supports a large number of terminals. For example, data-file access and query-handling programs are prototypical examples of programs in which this is highly desirable. One way to handle such applications might be to let each terminal *separately* execute the program. This would require, however, that the operating system itself be able to understand and cope with the differences in priorities between currently active users, as well as with many other details best handled directly by those most familiar with the application. The *entire* application, including any or all terminal users, may be set up to run as a single *job* in such cases. A new *task* is defined whenever a terminal must be answered. In this case, the task management resources may all be used. These resources include executive, file manager, memory manager, and software of the operating system. Task *priorities* will be assigned by the application management routines. Alternatively, the entire application might be set up to run as a *single*, in which case it must do its own file management as a foreground high-priority task. It can however call upon the services of the various operating system routines to handle file input and output, and to make memory available, and to perform other housekeeping chores.

---

[2]Priority will typically be represented by a *number*, (e.g., from zero to 16 or 256), which is assigned to each program on entry to the system or because the task is associated with a particular input terminal.

14.4   CONTROL BLOCKS

The housekeeping functions of the operating system are seen as *tasks* by the executive, as are application program execution. Generally speaking, such a *system task* as memory allocation must be given higher priority than application tasks, since they are essential to efficient operation of the system. The system programs which perform necessary housekeeping, and the peripheral driver routines which actually perform input and output operations, make use of a large variety of data tables which are often referred to as *control blocks*.

A control block is used for essentially every operating system resource allocation or activity assignment. If a file is to be used by a program, a *file control block* will be created. This block identifies the file in terms of name, location, the program using the file, and the status of the file.[3] When the application program prepares to use a particular file, it will first request the system to *open* the file. The file driver will then make a record in the file control block. Each time a portion of the file is read or written, or an imaginary *pointer* to a current location in the file is changed, the control block will be changed accordingly to indicate this. When the program no longer requires further use of the file, the file is ordered to be *closed* and the memory allocated to the file control block may then be used for another control block.

In turn, the file driver routine may use an *event control block* to make a record of a task such as moving the read/write head(s) of a disk drive to a particular track. In a large system the I/O channel or disk drive controller may be given the address of the event-control block. It will, either through an interrupt process or direct memory access, store a *completion code* in that memory location to indicate success or the reasons for failure of the assignment. The details of particular operating systems vary greatly in structure and handling of control blocks as well as in other aspects of their overall complexity and resource management strategies. In all sophisticated operating systems a highly systematic scheme of resource allocation, task assignments, and event reporting is used, thereby making it possible to retrace steps in case of difficulty.

There is clearly an opportunity for tradeoffs between completeness and performance in operating-systems design. In minicomputer operating systems, which must respond quickly to a variety of external devices that are capable of interrupting the processor, control-block structures are generally simpler than in large mainframe computer operating systems. In the latter 1980s, with the bulk of PCs running under the MS-DOS operating systems, there is little multitasking. Those PCs running UNIX, however, are equipped to handle multitasking, and hence have the control structures found in large computer operating systems. For the future, the upper end candidate for the third generation of PC operating systems, OS/2, supports multitasking.

---

[3]DOS' predecessor CP/M used File Control Blocks, and early versions of DOS repeated their structure. After DOS 2.0 a handier scheme was added, but DOS still can use FCBs.

Operating system capabilities are not obtained without a cost; those portions of the more capable operating systems that must remain *resident* (i.e., remain stored in main memory) may occupy hundreds of kilobytes. It is normally possible to limit the quantity of routines which remain resident. However, if operating system routines are used frequently, a strong penalty is incurred if they must be repeatedly loaded into memory from file storage.

Ten percent, or more, of a processor's time may be occupied with operating-system tasks. Whether this time, as well as the memory reserved for resident operating-system routines, should be viewed as *wasted* depends on one's point of view. A majority of application programs are prepared with the assumption that operating system capabilities are readily available. Hence application programs need not contain those same software mechanisms and are, as a result, smaller than they would be otherwise.

In large operating systems, handling large numbers of concurrent tasks, large numbers of control blocks are needed. When one task goes to an inactive state while, for example, awaiting input from a file, the executive must make a comprehensive search of control blocks to determine which task(s) can be made active. *All* control blocks of a given type may need to be examined. Thus control blocks of a given type, such as memory allocation control blocks, are *chained* together. Each block in the chain will contain the address of the next block of the same type. The operating system will retain the address of the start of the chain. When a block is no longer needed, it is removed from the active chain and then attached as the start of a chain of *spare* control blocks that can be made available immediately when the next request for one of them occurs.

Operating systems for mainframe computers and minicomputers are essentially unique to one, or to just a few, machines. These programs are the result of long-term evolutions, some of which have been in use 20 years or more. Many OS features represented their original designers' views of optimal resource management strategies. Some may no longer be optimal, but cannot easily be altered because of the consequences for the overall system. Generally speaking, those operating systems for which the most care was taken in their original definition and design have been the most durable. They are however not the most economical in terms of memory and processing time requirements.

14.5 PROGRAM-PREPARATION SUPPORT

Operating-system programs have traditionally been written in assembly language (machine language, one instruction per line in mnemonic form) for the family of processors with which the operating system is to operate. Early *application* programs were also mostly written in machine language or assembly language, as we have often noted. It was soon recognized that the use of *high-level languages* could considerably reduce programming difficulties. But it was not until powerful operating systems became available that high-level languages achieved dominance. The simple reason for this is that the operating system could handle much of the detailed input/output and data conversion tasks which theretofore had to be part of the application program.

UNIX and related operating systems are an important exception to assembly-language coding, as they are written in the high-level language C. Although the system programs for computers using the DoD's *Ada* programming language are not referred to as operating-systems but as operating *environments*, these are written in Ada. The objective of being able to transport large portions of the operating system routines, as well as applications, from one computer design to another is the major motivating factor behind this—it is doubtlessly the wave of the future. Since most useful software is developed in an iterative fashion, it is not necessarily a major increase in complexity to interatively generate an operating system as well.

Operating systems may offer several distinct types of support for high-level language programming and execution. Let us esamine several of these.

14.5.1   Program Editors

Program editors are used to write and later modify programs conveniently. Most modern program editors, like word processors, permit the user to scan the complete program quickly and search for the occurrence of variable names and branch points. A program editor is similar to a *word processor* except that formatting for printout is of little interest and the ability to quickly compare two or more programs is more important. The editor in the *Turbo C* development package is a descendent of the early word processor, *WordStar*, which is among the most sophisticated and used word processors today.

14.5.2   Interpreters

Interpreters are programs which read each line of the source program, skipping comments, and which dynamically execute each instruction as it is read. The *compiler*, which is discussed below, converts the program into an executable machine-language program. Running a program on an interpreter typically takes from 10 to 100 times longer than executing an optimized machine-language program to perform the same functions. Interpreters are often used for writing short programs which will be used only a few times. Many BASIC programs are interpreted rather than compiled. There are compatible interpreters and compilers available and this leads to the use of the interpreter to develop programs, which are then compiled for more rapid execution.

An interpreter is *its own* debugging program, since most interpreters permit the program to be executed one *step* at a time and allow quick alteration of the program itself. Although an interpreter never changes the program sequence defined in the source program, some interpreters may store and execute the program in an abbreviated form in which mnemonic names and command names are replaced by numbers referring to an *index* stored as part of the program.

This substantially speeds execution without losing ability to debug and revise the program.

A *BASIC* interpreter is provided with PC-DOS and included in many MS-DOS operating systems as well. As mentioned, programs produced this way are slow to run. If an application is to be run often, it is better to *compile* it. However, some languages are normally furnished in interpreter form because it better fits the use of the language. Examples of generally interpreted languages are *LISP* and *APL*. Compilers do, however, exist for each of these three programming languages.

14.5.3 Assemblers and Compilers

Assemblers and compilers translate the program from the *source* form, as written with the editor by the programmer, to *object* program form, in which it is nearly ready for execution. The programs used to translate assembly-language source programs to executable code are referred to as *assemblers*. They are similar to compilers, but are less complex because the translation process is one-for-one: one source program instruction per machine-language instruction. Both assemblers and compilers *read* the source-language program; thereby recording each *name* of data or program location found in the source. Assemblers typically make two *passes* over the source code, the first to collect all the names (mnemonics) and the second to *resolve* them and assign address locations to them.

Compilers make one or more *passes* reading the source code. Since there is not a one-to-one relationship between the source program and compiled instructions, a compiler may make an additional pass or passes to alter the initial results. Often it optimizes them in terms of eliminating duplicative program sequences.

In addition to producing an object version of the program in machine language, both assemblers and compilers can normally produce a *cross-reference* tabulation. This identifies each of the mnemonic names used, what it is used for (e.g., program-location label, data variable, or data constant), and where it is referred to in the program. Probably the most important aspect of quality compilers and assemblers is their error-reporting function. Few programs longer than several lines[4] of source code are totally without error. Mnemonic names may be misspelled in some occurrences. Wrong *syntax*, such as order of writing

---

[4] The term *line*, though commonly used as a measure of program length, does not have uniform interpretation. Most assemblers and compilers allow or require programmers to state *directives* which inform the translator of the name given the program, how a printed listing is to be titled, where major subdivisions of the program begin and end, and other information which removes ambiguity. Most programs contain *comments*—notes written by the programmer as reminders of the program's intentions and limitations. Though these do not produce instructions in the assembled or compiled object program they are nonetheless *lines* in the source program. High-level language programs may produce from *four to ten machine-level instructions* for each high-level *command* which occupies a single source-program line, hence source-line count does not provide any absolute measure.

commands and their operands or punctuation, may be used. Some variables may be used, though not defined. While any *correct* compiler can compile a completely correct source code, it requires a more sophisticated compiler to identify correctly the *kind of error* a programmer has made. Even the best compilers may have difficulty understanding the convoluted errors made often by novices to a programming language however.

14.5.4 Linkers

Linkers are system programs which can combine *object* programs or *modules*, each written separately, into a single *executable* program. Where a DOS program is written in a single segment, although in fact the linker has no work to do, the linking step is required *pro forma*. In the more common situation in which a program has been separated into several parts (one containing subroutines, another containing data, etc.) to reduce the length of the source files or for other reasons, the responsibility of the linker is to identify the program or data locations, or values of constants which are *defined* in one module and also *used* in other modules. The linker strings the object program together from its several parts. It also inserts the proper cross-reference values into address references. The output of the linker is referred to as the *executable* program.

When the source program is written in a high-level language such as C, FORTRAN, or Ada, the compiler may identify certain *external* subroutines which are needed. Software floating-point arithmetic functions for a processor without built-in floating-point instructions is one example of such a need. These subroutines are *grouped* into object-program modules and collected in a library file. The linker is told the file name for that library, and if that mnemonic subroutine name is not found among the object modules of the user-written program, the support library for that programming language is examined and the module containing the needed subroutine (among others) is *included* in the executable program. Hence we have *link-time* support for the language, which is invoked by the presence of subroutine calls in the compiled program.

A linker program must also be capable of error detection. Generally these will be of a different type than those detected by an assembler or compiler. The principal type of error detected by a linker is the *absence of a mnemonic value* that has been referred to in one program module in any of the other source modules or the support library. If the programmer calls a subroutine called **PRINTIT** in a main program, declaring it to be *external* there, the compiler is happy. But if the linker does not find a program entry name P R I N T I T, which has been declared to be *public*, in any other module, it will complain that an external reference is *unresolved* and may refuse to produce an executable program.[5]

---

[5]Should it not refuse to produce a program, the program which it does produce will customarily have the missing address replaced by all zeros. If this obviously incorrect program is executed, very strange things will happen, since the memory address corresponding to all zeros may contain data or status information rather than a program instruction.

The *Turbo C* linker is called t l i n k. It is run every time the A l t r command is typed in the t c program.

14.6 RUN-TIME SUPPORT

Run-time support is a term applied to special subroutine programs which are loaded into memory from file storage *during execution* of the high-level language program. While these programs could alternatively be linked into the executable program itself, the executable user program can be kept smaller in size by not doing so. Routines which are handled as run-time support may, for example, interpret printing of data as lines of output on a printer; the executable user program needs to contain only a template which identifies the format to be used and the location of the data to be printed. The run-time support routine does the detailed work using the operating system's printer driver to actually output the characters. Because this is a separate file, the same memory space can be used for different run-time support routines (e.g., input and output formatting) that are not required at the same time.

14.7 DEBUGGING TOOLS

Debuggers are special programs that are designed to simplify the detection and location of logical errors in a program. Although some types of programming errors will be removed in the processes of assembly or compilation, many others cannot be detected at this time, since the compiler cannot know the programmer's full *intent*. Merely having correct syntax for program commands, having defined all data and program branch points, and having avoided spelling errors does not ensure correctness in the sense of the program always doing what the programmer intended. The program as written may jump to an unintended address, the algorithm used in some computation may be erroneous or fail to consider some particular case, and other similar errors will be undetected by an assembler or compiler. Some amount of debugging is needed for almost every program written. It can truly be said that most programmers are surprised if a program operates correctly without some repairs or *debugging*.

The process used in debugging ordinarily involves operating the program with specially prepared test data inputs and *incremental execution*. The program is entered and allowed to execute until it reaches a point in the instruction stream which is suspected by the programmer to contain an error. The program is then *stepped* through one or more instructions or high-level language commands at a time. After each step, the programmer is given an opportunity to *review the results*, that is, the new values of data variables or processor register contents. The program may also be *entered* at a selected point, often the beginning of a subroutine or some easily identifiable entry point. In this case, the values of data and register contents to be manipulated must be inserted by the programmer, prior to stepping the program through its operation. In either case, the programmer must have a clear view of what values the program will be working with and what the *expected* results should be.

If a debugging program is designed to work in connection with a specific version of a specific programming language and compiler, it may permit the program to be debugged *symbolically*, that is, with the programmer identifying data and program locations by the *mnemonic names* assigned them in the source program. The debug program must at least have access to the source program, which contains these names (the object program does not), or possibly a cross-reference listing of the names generated by the compiler. If the compiler has, in an optimization process, rearranged or altered source-code statements, it is not logically *possible* to work from the source. Accordingly, some symbolic debuggers will display to the programmer a *pseudosource* program listing which is derived from a symbolic cross-reference table and the actual executable program. Since this will not include all of the comments the programmer may have inserted into the source, it will generally be necessary to examine a printed version of the source as debugging proceeds.

Some symbolic debuggers do not attempt to debug using the final executable version of the program. Instead they use the source program and *interpret* it dynamically, command by command.

If no symbolic debugger is available, the programmer must revert to a much simpler (but more difficult to use) *absolute debugger*, which executes the actual executable machine-language program, one or more instructions at a time. We have already used DEBUG, which is provided with DOS, to assemble simple programs. Use of this limited debugging tool requires that the programmer comprehend the machine-language instructions and relate them to the original source. The debugger will show mnemonic names for the *instruction codes*, but not for data or for program or subroutine labels. Hence the program listed by the debugger closely resembles an assembly-language version of the program. Unless the programmer understands assembly language, DEBUG may be of little help. Programs written in assembly language are fairly easy to debug with an absolute debugger. Symbolic debuggers *are* available for use with programs written in assembly language, as well as higher-level language programs.

Invariably the *source* code will need to be changed in the process of debugging. Unless the debugger interprets the program in a stepwise execution fashion and includes a built-in source editor, on finding a program error (1) the debugging process must be terminated, (2) the source program edited then (3) compiled, and (4) linked following discovery of some error. This is inevitably a time-consuming process and quickly emphasizes to the programmer the importance of taking all reasonable steps to minimize careless errors in the original design of the program. The Turbo C development package includes this linking feature between editor, compiler, and linker. Syntax errors are identified with the text of the program, and their correction is relatively easy. If the program contains no syntax errors, the compiler will accept it. Logical errors can be found only by executing the program and examining the results. This often requires test data, which should include examples of all cases in which data is treated differently in the program.

For example, a letter-frequency counting program might first be tested by using it to read a file including both upper- and lowercase alphabets. If the result is other than a count of two per each letter, there is an error. Then one must examine the program to learn why the error occurred. This can be a time-consuming step, since the compiler has not shown where to start. In such a case one might add **printf** commands for each letter and use a shorter file to read. Only continued experience in writing and debugging programs in a particular class of applications will allow the programmer to develop speed in debugging.

14.8 SUMMARY

In this chapter we have examined some of the characteristics of operating systems. The complete listing, to follow, of MS-DOS (Version 3.2) operating system commands should provide a clear picture of the many features possible through use of a comprehensive operating system. In the DOS operating system, transient commands are located in an executable file that is recorded on disk. Resident commands are located within the operating system itself. Consequently, they will generally execute faster. The primary commands are:

APPEND	(*Transient*) Sets a search path for the data files.
APPLY	(*Transient*) Executes a command with substitution of the term that follows apply.
ASGNPART	(*Transient*) Assigns a Winchester drive partition to a logical drive name.
ASSIGN	(*Transient*) Temporarily reassigns logical drive names.
ATTRIB	(*Transient*) Modifies the read-only and archive attributes.
BACKUP	(*Transient*) Archiver which creates backup file(s). Terms can be added after the command to designate attributes of files to be backed up.
BOOTF	(*Transient*) Corrects problems with running some floppy disk programs on a microcomputer equipped with a Winchester disk drive.
BREAK	(*Resident*) Sets check for CTRL-BREAK or CTRL-C through use of the command BREAK ON or BREAK OFF.
CHDIR or CD	(*Resident*) Changes the current directory to the one specified.
CHKDSK	(*Transient*) Provides status of disk contents in terms of bytes used and remaining for the disk drive specified and the random access memory.
CLS	(*Resident*) Clears the screen.
COMMAND	(*Transient*) Makes EXEC calls on resident commands.
COMP	(*Transient*) Compares files on a byte by byte basis.

COPY	(*Resident*) Copies file(s) specified from one location to another. File attributes, including wildcards, may be used.
CTTY	(*Resident*) Changes the device from which commands are issued.
DATE	(*Resident*) Displays and enables one to set the date to a new value.
DEL or ERASE	(*Resident*) Deletes the file(s) specified.
DIR	(*Resident*) Lists the requested directory entries, as well as their size and the latest date modified.
DISKCOMP	(*Transient*) Compares disks on a byte by byte basis.
DISKCOPY	(*Transient*) Copies the contents of one disk to another.
ECHO	(*Resident, Batch-Processing*) Controls the echo feature to change whether items entered will be "echoed" to the screen.
ERASE	See DEL command.
EXE2BIN	(*Transient*) Converts executable files to binary files.
EXIT	(*Resident*) Exits COMMAND.COM and returns to previous level.
FC	(*Transient*) Performs a "File Compare" operation and lists the differences between the specified files.
FIND	(*Transient*) Searches for a constant specified string of text and indicates if and where it is found.
FOR	(*Resident*) Batch and interactive command extension command.
FORMAT	(*Transient*) Formats a disk such that it is then able to receive MS-DOS files.
GOTO	(*Resident, Batch-Processing*) Causes the CPU to branch out of execution of a program to some specified location.
GRAPHICS	(*Transient*) Outputs all graphic and special characters to the printer.
GRAFTABL	(*Transient*) Loads table of additional characters.
IF	(*Resident*) Allows conditional execution.
JOIN	(*Transient*) Joins a disk drive to a path name.
LABEL	(*Transient*) Creates, changes, or deletes disk volume label.
MKDIR or MD	(*Resident*) Makes a new directory, the directory specified.
MODE	(*Transient*) Configures MS-DOS for a peripheral monitor or printer. MODE MONO or MODE CO80 are typical commands to cause either a monochrome or color monitor to become active.
MORE	(*Transient*) Displays the output one screen at a time.
PATH	(*Resident*) Specifies the directories to be searched for transient commands. Usually this is entered as part of

	an AUTOEXEC.BAT file to indicate where often used software is stored.
PAUSE	(*Resident*) Suspends the execution of a program.
PRINT	(*Transient*) Prints hard copy of ASCII files.
PROMPT	(*Resident*) Designates the MS-DOS system prompt by the symbol specified after the PROMPT command.
RECOVER	(*Transient*) Recovers file or files specified.
REM	(*Resident*) Displays a batch file comment.
REN or RENAME	(*Resident*) Renames the first file noted after the command as the second file noted after the command.
REPLACE	(*Transient*) Updates previous versions of files.
RESTORE	(*Transient*) Restores archived files, or files that have been saved through use of the BACKUP command.
RMDIR or RD	(*Resident*) Removes a directory.
SEARCH	(*Transient*) Locates files within the directory structure.
SET	(*Resident*) Sets one string value equivalent to another value.
SORT	(*Transient*) Sorts data alphabetically or numerically.
SUBST	(*Transient*) Substitutes a virtual drive name for a path name.
SYS	(*Transient*) Transfers the system files IO.SYS and MSDOS.SYS to specified drive.
SYSCLR	(*Transient*) Clear all memory and reset machine.
TIME	(*Resident*) Displays and sets the time as indicated by the prompts that follow after execution of the command.
TREE	(*Transient*) Displays the subdirectory paths on a disk.
TYPE	(*Resident*) Displays the contents on the monitor of the ASCII file specified after the command.
VER	(*Resident*) Displays MSDOS.SYS and IO.SYS version numbers.
VERIFY	(*Resident*) Verifies that data is correctly written to disk. VERIFY ON turns on the verification and VERIFY OFF turns it off.
VOL	(*Resident*) Displays the disk volume label on the monitor.
XCOPY	(*Transient*) Copies files and directories, including subdirectories, using the full available RAM. The command operates much the same way as the resident copy command, which will not copy subdirectories.

PROBLEMS

14.1 A simple 16-bit-per-word computer has only 256 words of memory and a single register (traditionally referred to as *the accumulator*). It is to be used to add the ages of four individuals, which have previously been stored in four particular memory words. Each machine instruction is two bytes long, one byte designating the instruction and one the memory address. There are only four instructions in the repertoire.

```
01hh   READ contents of memory address hh
       into accumulator
02hh   WRITE contents of accumulator into
       address hh
03hh   ADD contents of address hh into
       accumulator
04hh   JUMP to address hh for next
       instruction
```

(a) Define the absolute memory locations which you will use for the four ages and the sum, and construct the absolute machine-language program (a series of 16-bit words) which will perform the function.

(b) Prepare a *mnemonic version* of the same program sequence, using READ, WRITE, and so on, as instruction mnemonics and assigning mnemonic names for the ages (AGE1, AGE2, etc.) and sum.

14.2 For the simple processor in Problem 14.1, define a small number of *additional* instructions to be added to the instruction set, to permit the four ages to be arranged, in decreasing order of age, in four additional memory locations. Write a mnemonic program routine to carry out this process.

14.3 Given a simple mnemonic program such as that prepared for the problems above, outline the steps which an assembler program, reading the mnemonic program as an input, would need to carry out in order to produce the set of absolute machine-language instructions for the routine.

14.4 A classical resource allocation problem in large computers which concurrently execute multiple jobs is *competition for system resources*. Two programs or on-line terminal users, of equal priority, may at the same time request use of a particular file for updating. Such a file (or at least the same data record in that file) cannot be *shared* for updating since each program would be unaware of changes being made by the other. Show (by simple analogy if you wish) that a resource allocation strategy in which *available* resources are allocated to one requestor while that requestor awaits availability of other resources can result in paralysis of the system.

14.5 Imagine yourself to be a memory-management routine in a large operating system, assigning memory in blocks of 4096 bytes, as requested by a job manager, loader, or application program. You will assign memory until it is *returned* by the requestor. Requestors may ask for "at least xx *contiguous* blocks, or up to yy blocks if available."

(a) What information will you need in order to make an assignment? What information will you return to the requestor, under different conditions? What records will you keep, and how will you update them?

(b) After several minutes (or perhaps hours) of operation, your available memory consists of a large number of blocks in groups of one or two blocks. *Assuming that it is the memory manager's responsibility to resolve this problem*, what strategies would you use? What system performance consequences could result from this strategy? How could these problems (if any) be resolved (e.g., by passing the buck, assigning requests for single blocks in a particular area of memory)?

14.6 In ordinary multitasking a program may be allowed to use the processor until it requires an I/O wait or until the user's estimate of execution time has been reached. In time-sharing the program may be interrupted after a few milliseconds of processor time. Any program may have a bug which causes it to execute repeatedly some unintended loop, which may however involve just a few instructions or a great many. In what clever ways might the system or human system operators detect when a program is operating in such an unintended loop? (NOTE: The problem is in general unsolved except for execution timeout based on expected run-time.)

14.7 Assume that as some operating-system resource management routine you keep records by means of control blocks (of fixed length, in bytes), each control block containing within it the starting address of the next control block in the chain of (independent) control blocks. You maintain two starting addresses, one of which is the first of a chain of control blocks in use, the second the address of the first of a chain of control blocks which are currently inactive (i.e., unused). The last block in each chain can be easily identified, since it contains all zeros in its next block address location.

(a) Indicate the specific control block chain altering steps you must perform when you need to activate a control block.

(b) Indicate the steps you must perform when a control block is deactivated.

(c) Considering the possibility of program or system errors overwriting some of your control blocks. What steps in the layout and content of the blocks could be taken to minimize the chances for catastrophe?

14.8 In any mnemonic programming language, a *forward reference* is the mention, at some point in the program, of a symbolic name which has not been defined up to that point. Show that, if it is clear from the way the name is used in the program, just what kind of data (e.g., a byte or a word) the name refers to, the forward reference can be *resolved* (made definite) by a second pass through the program, but that in cases where the name is involved in defining, for example, the length of a memory space set aside for a string of characters, additional "passes" would be required. (A two-pass assembler or compiler lays out the program in sequence on the first pass and defines all addresses on the second.)

14.9 Give several examples from everyday life in which a certain sequence must be followed in proper order or obtain the desired results, and in which you might have to *debug* the sequence on a step-by-step basis to find out what went wrong. What *aids* would you be likely to use in the debugging processes?

14.10 Programs which are executed *interpretively*, by scanning the original program, require considerably longer to execute than those that have been converted into binary computer codes and addresses. Describe additional steps which would be necessary in interpreting a program whose data variables and subroutine addresses are expressed only as names, for example, as below:

```
READ LENGTHMU = WIDTH
MULT BREADTH
WRITE VOLUME
CALL PRINT
RETURN TO OS
SUBROUTINE PRINT
READ VOLUME
OUTPUT
RETURN-FROM-SUB
```

14.11 One very simple sort is known as a *ripple sort*. The first two in a list of N items to be sorted are compared and reversed in position if their order is wrong, then the second and third items are compared and reversed if in wrong order. When the end is reached, the process may be repeated until a *pass* is made during which NO reversals of order are required.

   (a) For a list of N numerical items such as social security numbers, how many passes may be required, as a maximum, to put all of the items in increasing order? How many compares does this require?

   (b) If you had 10 additional areas available into which you could move and sort items beginning with a 0,1,2,..9, by what specific steps could you significantly reduce the amount of comparing and moving the items, and by approximately what factor?

14.12 For some particular small operating system such as MS-DOS or PC-DOS, examine a user's manual and make separate lists of those operating-system programs (they may be called *commands*) that are involved with: (a) checking for proper operation or condition of the system and its parts; (b) manipulating individual *files*; (c) examining the contents of storage devices; (d) setting operating *modes* of the *hardware*; and (e) setting operating *modes* of the system *software* used to execute programs. Include a few-word description of the functions of the command. If a command could be in one of several categories, place it in a primary category.

PART IV

DATA STRUCTURES AND ADVANCED TOPICS IN C

15

THE C-LANGUAGE VOCABULARY

15.0 INTRODUCTION

At this point in the development of the high level language C, we will summarize its vocabulary. Like other computer languages, C has a *reserved word* list containing words that have special meaning in the language and which should be used for nothing else. The word **double** is an example; it should never be used for a variable or function name. C has a very short reserved word list, as we shall see.

The other kind of vocabulary consists of words that specify a function which copes with the need to deliver items to the outside world (like **printf**), or that provides some kind of internal housekeeping (like conversion from an ASCII string to an integer). Strictly speaking, these functions are not part of the formal languages. But they have been standardized and are commonly treated as if they were. We will categorize and summarize these functions here. In this chapter we will also discuss *storage classes,* the ways variables are stored and communicated between blocks of a C program, as this concept forms an important part of a broad interpretation of vocabulary.

15.1 RESERVED WORDS

One characteristic of a computer language is its reserved vocabulary. These are words that have special meanings in a program, like f o r, and which cannot be used for anything else.

C has a short list of reserved words, only 27 in the standard C of Kernighan and Ritchie, which suggests that much has been left to the programmer to define. By contrast, Pascal has 36 reserved words and Turbo Pascal has 44. We have met all but one of the reserve words that deal with variable types and control flow in C. They are presented in Table 15.1.

The reserved word g o t o was discussed in Section 10.9. It has the same function as the instruction of the same name in BASIC and FORTRAN. Use of this direction to an absolute address transfers control of the program to a place marked by the label or absolute address. In the philosophy of block languages, it is held that g o t o is seldom necessary. There are times when it is particularly useful, such as exit from a program under error conditions that require a return to the operating system. Statements such as b r e a k or c o n t i n u e are special g o t o ' s which direct the computer to specific places near the block. It is generally always possible to avoid using the g o t o expression, and we will not generally discuss it or use it further here,[1] despite the occasional need or desirability for this command.

Other categories and reserved words in C are presented in Table 15.2.

Structures are the subject of our next chapter, and we will soon discuss storage classes. The other category is named *other*. Here is a program that uses both t y p e d e f and s i z e o f :

```
typedef int number;
main()
{
   NUMBER x;
   int y, z;

   x = 5;
   y = sizeof(long);
   z = sizeof(NUMBER);

   printf("\n x = %d", x);
   printf("\n a long type has %d bytes", y);
   printf("\n a NUMBER type has %d bytes", z);
}
```

The t y p e d e f (*type definition*) statement makes **NUMBER** an *alias* of i n t. Some people use t y p e d e f to simplify C programs. But the result can often be confusing. This expression results in more declared types that need to be remembered. It should, therefore, be used sparingly.

---

[1]A short discussion of proper uses for g o t o will be found in Kernighan and Ritchie, *The C Program Language*, Prentice-Hall, Englewood Cliffs, NJ, 1978, pp. 62–63.

TABLE 15.1 Reserved Words in C

Variable Types	Control Flow	
int	goto	do
char	return	while
float	break	switch
double	continue	case
long	if	default
short	else	
unsigned	for	

TABLE 15.2 Other Reserved Words in C

Structures	Storage Class	Other
Struct	Auto	Typedef
Union	Extern	Sizeof
	Register	
	Static	

The function `sizeof()` returns the storage size in bytes of a variable or a type. The foregoing program writes the following to the screen:

```
X = 5
a long type has 4 bytes
a NUMBER type has 2 bytes
```

The last two statements are true for an IBM-PC and *Turbo C* or Microsoft C compilers with which the program was run. The size is returned in units of bytes.

When applied to an array, `sizeof` returns the number of members. For example, the program:

```
main()
{
printf("\n%d",sizeof("hello, world"));
}
```

writes **13** to the screen. The text uses 12 bytes and the terminating null character is the thirteenth.

15.2 LEAVING THE LOOP

Here is a program which uses all three methods to leave the inside of a loop:

```
main()
{
char code;

   loop('a');
   loop('b');
   loop('c');
   loop('g');
}
loop(c)
   char c;
{
   int i;

   printf("\n%c: ", c);
   for (i = 0; i < 4; i++)
   {
     if (i == 2)
     {
       if (c == 'a')
          ;
       else if (c == 'b')
          break;
       else if (c == 'c')
          continue;
       else if (c == 'g')
          goto end;
     }
     printf(" %d", i);
   }
   printf(" end of loop ");
   end: return;
}
```

MAIN() calls the function loop() four times, each with different instructions. The loop() function counts toward 3, checking when i is 2 to see whether action is required. In the a case nothing is done. In the others, control is transferred outside the loop. Here is the result:

```
a:    0 1 2 3 = d of loop
b:    0 1 end of loop
```

```
c:    0 1 3 end of loop
g:    0 1
```

In the case of **b r e a k** (**b**), the count is terminated and the loop exited via the **p r i n t f** statement at the end. With **c o n t i n u e** (**c**) the loop continues at the next value of **i** . Then **g o t o** transfers control directly to the label **e n d :** , skipping the **p r i n t f ( )** entirely.

There is enough variety here to fill any loop-leaving requirements. Once again, the use of **g o t o** can generally be avoided, and should be reserved for cases of transfer to error messages and the like.[2] Indiscriminate use of anything is usually bad practice. Indiscriminate use of the **g o t o** may undo much of the useful support that block structure provides in making programs correct and easy to follow.

15.3 LIBRARY FUNCTIONS

Library functions have a standard for the C language in UNIX, and many compilers such as *Turbo C* and Microsoft C have libraries which are compatible. Our experiments with UNIX C programs in *Turbo C* have been successful in that the programs compiled without any changes. The same is true of Microsoft C, with the single exception of features which interface directly to DOS functions.

We have used the **p r i n t f** library function extensively. There are several others. Tables 15.3a and 15.3b present a list of some of the C library functions provided in the *Turbo C* library.

The table is not a complete list of functions available, but rather a sampling. Version 1.5 of *Turbo C* includes screen-handling functions, and so does *Microsoft Quick C*. UNIX has a set of terminal-handling functions called CURSES, and a version of that should be available soon. The *Turbo C Reference Guide* has 230 pages of functions similar to these. The best way to get familiar with these is to use them in programs.

15.4 STORAGE CLASSES

The C language makes distinctions, depending on the physical location of the block of the program and use for which it is intended, among variables and functions. Storage classes are the names used in making the distinction. Here are four of them:

1. **A U T O** This is the default storage class for C variables. On entry into a block (function) automatic variables contain garbage and must be initial-

---

[2]When unrecoverable errors occur it is usually most convenient to move immediately to the end of the program, **p r i n t f** an error message, and terminate.

TABLE 15.3a Turbo C Library

File Functions	Function Name
Open a File	fopen, open
	creat
Read	fread, read
Write	fwrite, write
Set File Position	lseek
Close a File	fclose, close
Input/Output	
Read Character	fgetc, getc
	getchar, getcnb
Write Character	fputc, putc
	putchar, putcnb
Read a string	fgets, gets
Write a String	fputs, puts
Formatted Output	printf, fprintf
Formatted Input	scanf, fscanf
Keyboard	kbhit
Character Functions	
Type Check	isalpha, isupper, isdigit
Conversion	toascii, toupper

TABLE 15.3b Turbo C Library

Math Functions	Function Name
Absolute Value	abs
Logs	log, log10
Exponentials	exp, pow
Trig	sin, cos, tan, asin, acos, atan
String Functions	
String To Number	atoi
Number To String	fcvt
Copy	strcpy
Concatenate	strcat
Compare	strcmp
Memory Functions	
Allocate memory	malloc, free
Insert/extract	poke, peek
Miscellaneous	
Sort	qsort
Random numbers	rand
Size	sizeof
DOS	
Register contents	_AX etc.
Execute program	spawn.., exec..
Terminate	exit
Get the time	time
Systemcall	geninterrupt

ized. Simple variables can be initialized in declaration (e.g., `int x=5;`); arrays cannot. `auto` variables disappear when the function is exited and are unknown elsewhere; they are local variables.

2. `STATIC` We have used the `static` storage class in examples to allow initialization of an array in a function. This class retains its values from one invocation of a function to the next.

3. **REGISTER** When speed is important it is sometimes possible to keep a variable resident in a register by declaring it this way. There are a limited number of registers in the PC, so the declaration may be ignored if there are no registers available.

4. **EXTERN** This class allows reference to a variable declared outside the function (a *global* variable). If the declaration is made outside the function, but in the same file, and if the declaration occurs before use of the function, it need not be explicitly declared.

For example, the use of x in the prog0 below is acceptable, even though it is not declared inside the program itself.

```
/* file prog0.c */
int x;
main()
{
   x = 5;
   printf("\nprog0 says x = %d", x);
}
```

However, if declaration is in another file, the keyword extern must be used, as in the second example, which has two separate files. Notice that there can be only one main, so the second program is named prog2.

```
/* file prog1.c */
int x;

main()
{
   x = 5;
   printf("\nprog1 says x = %d", x);
   prog2();
}
/* file prog2.c */
prog2()
{
   extern int x;

   printf("\nprog2 says x = %d too.", x);
}
```

The two programs are compiled by creating a *Turbo C* project file called prog.prj containing:

```
prog1
prog2
```

The project facility is activated by naming prog.prj when asked, and typing Alt r as usual. Both prog1 and prog2 are automatically compiled and linked; the output is:

```
prog1 says x = 5
prog2 says x = 5 too.
```

External static variables can be used to keep a variable *local* to a file, but global within it; the reader is referred to the K & R text for the details of this usage.

15.5   COMPLEX DECLARATIONS

The C-language variable declarations are made in a form that mimics the use of the variable in the program itself. Sometimes, this leads to program lines that are hard to understand. One such declaration is char *argv[]. This is an example of one of C's common, but complicated declarations. This one is used to declare an array of strings which contain command line arguments. We will discuss this subject further in our next Chapter. One way to interpret it in words is: *argv[] is a char. The [] and () operators are bound more closely to the variable argv than the *. Therefore we can write argv[] is a pointer to char. Finally, the [] is removed, leaving argv is an array of pointer to char.

This procedure works on more complicated examples as well. The declaration is *peeled* a layer at a time, thereby keeping track of the result each time an operator is removed, and also observing the precedence of () and [] over *.

In a program using this declaration, the first character of the first of the strings would be assigned to first with the line:

```
first = *argv[1];
```

which illustrates the way the declaration reflects use.

15.6   APPENDIX: PASCAL VOCABULARY

Pascal has reserved words also. A partial list of these follows in Table 15.4.

We have not used goto or label in our examples up to this point for the same reasons we have discussed relative to the use of the C language. Use of nil, record, and with will come in our next chapter, where structure is

TABLE 15.4 Reserved Words in Pascal

and	file	not	type
array	forward	of	to
begin	for	or	until
case	function	packed	var
const	goto	procedure	while
div	if	program	with
do	in	record	
downto	label	repeat	
else	mod	set	
end	nil	then	

discussed. The word p a c k e d is an artifact from Pascal's origin, when memory was more expensive than it is now. A p a c k e d   a r r a y had two characters per 16-bit word for efficiency of storage. Turbo Pascal allows the word to appear in programs, but does nothing with it, and we will generally not use this expression. C stores characters one byte at a time, so the issue doesn't come up there.

Turbo Pascal provides a library of functions. Some of them are listed in Tables 15.5a and b.

15.7 SUMMARY

An important characteristic of a language is its vocabulary. We have discussed the vocabulary of both C and Pascal in this chapter.

TABLE 15.5a Turbo Pascal Library

File Functions	Turbo Pascal Function Name
Open a File	assign, reset, rewrite
Read	read
Write	write
Set file position	seek
Close a File	close
Input/Output	
Read Character	
Write Character	
Read a string	
Write a string	
Formatted Output	write , writeln
Formatted Input	
Keyboard	keypressed
Character Functions	
Type check	
Conversion	upcase
Internal code	ord, char

TABLE 15.5b Turbo Pascal Library

Math Functions	Turbo Pascal Function Name
Absolute Value	abs
Logs	ln
Exponentials	exp
Trig	sin, cos, arctan
Truncate	frac, int, round, trunc
Ordinals	pred, succ
String Functions	
String To Number	val
Number To String	str
Copy	copy
Concatenate	concat
Compare	
Memory Functions	
Allocate memory	new, mark, release
Insert/ extract	memw, mem
Miscellaneous	
Sort	
Random numbers	randomize, random
Size	sizeof
Clear the screen	clrscr
Cursor position	gotoxy
DOS	
Register contents	cseg
Execute program	chain
Terminate	exit
Get the time	
System call	msdos
Command line	paramcount, paramstr

PROBLEMS

15.1 Write a C program that echoes a string that you enter from the keyboard.

15.2 Write a C program to print the sizes of various objects: `long`, `float`, `double`.

15.3 What is the description of the variable `x`:

   (a) `int *(x[])`

   (b) `double (*x)[]`

   (c) `char *(*x[])`

16

ASSEMBLY LANGUAGE AND
MACHINE INTERFACES IN C

16.0 INTRODUCTION

In this chapter, we will discuss the important subject of communicating with a C
program at *run time* using the DOS command line. We will also cover *unions*,
which allow sharing of a memory location by two or more variables. Then we will
begin our study of data structures by investigating the stack in detail. We have
discussed the stack before in Chapter 2, but here we will develop it in more depth
and also look at the hardware stack facility on the 8088. We will investigate data
structures in much more detail in our next chapter and the discussion here provides some background. The reader may well question the need for this material
in the midst of discussions about a high-level programming language. The answer of course is that C needs to incorporate many assembly-language type calls
because of its incompleteness relative to communications with the external
world.

16.1 COMMAND-LINE INPUT

Command-line input is the normal way that data is passed to a program at invocation. For example, in MS-DOS the command D I R causes execution of the
internal operating system D I R and results in a listing of the files in the default
directory. However, D I R b : \ results in a listing of files on the root directory of
drive b. The drive name (b :) was provided to the program D I R via the command line.

   In C programs the command line inputs are identified by including the variables `argc` and `argv` in the parentheses after `main`. The number of parameters entered at invocation will be stored in `argc`. The path name of the program itself is the first parameter,[1] so that `argc` is `1` if there is nothing at all entered on the command line. Pointers to the strings are written after the program's name and are stored in the array `argv`. These two variables must be declared in the same way that any function parameters are declared outside of the program block.[2]

The program to follow reads an integer from the command line. The name of the program source file is `cline.c`. The C computer compiles it into an executable file called `cline.exe`. To run the program with an integer `1234` as input, we write after the DOS prompt:

```
C:> cline 1234
```

The program is:

```
/* program cline.c    demonstrate command line
    input */

#include  <ctype.h>

main(argc, argv)
   int argc;
   char *argv[];
{
   int error;

   if (argc == 1)
     printf("\nno parameters on command line");
   else if (argc > 2)
     printf("\ntoo many parameters - only one
       allowed");
   else
   {
     printf("\nthe first parameter is %s",
       argv[1]);
     if ((error = checkup(argv[1])) == 0)
       printf("\nthe value is %d",
         atoi(argv[1]));
```

---

[1] Prior to DOS version 3.0 this parameter was empty, since the operating system did not preserve the source of the program.

[2] Under a proposed ANSI standard, function declarations can appear inside the parentheses as prototypes. Both *Turbo C* and *Microsoft Quick C* implement this feature, but we will stay with the K&R form. The second edition of the K&R text presents this ANSI standard.

```
      else
        printf("\nthere is a problem in position
          %d", error);
  }
}


checkup(str)
  char *str;
{
  int i = 0;

  while (1)
  {
    if (str[i] == '\0')
      return(0);
    else if (isdigit(str[i++]))
      ;
    else
      return(i);
  }
}
```

In this program, the file ctype.h. is included to support the function
isdigit, which will return a 1 if the argument of argc is an ASCII character 0 through 9. The program tests argc and responds to no arguments, too
many arguments, and so on. When argc is set at the correct value, 2, the
string argv[1] must be tested to be sure that argv[] is an integer. The
function checkup() is created for this purpose.

The function checkup tests each character of the string str. If it is an
integer, nothing is done because of the presence of the lone ';'. If it is not an
integer, the function returns with the position of the offending character. If the
null marking the end of the string is reached, a zero is returned, thereby signaling success. The function includes an infinite loop, while(1), but has provisions for escape under all circumstances.

Here is a sample dialog with the program:

```
C:>cline 12345
the first parameter is 12345
the value is 12345

C:>cline 12 34
too many parameters - only one allowed

C:>cline
no parameters on command line
```

```
C:>cline 12.34
the first parameter is 12.34
the parameter has a problem in position 3
```

16.2   THE COMMAND-LINE DECLARATION

We discussed the declaration of the array of pointers to command-line strings in
our last chapter. The declaration is:

```
char * argv[];
```

It should be emphasized that the values are filled in by the MS-DOS operating
system. All the programmer need do to have access to the name and command-
line input is to declare argc and argv.

To understand what an array of pointers to strings looks like, we next write a
short program that prints out information about such an array.

```
main(argc, argv)
   int argc;
   char *argv[];
{
   printf("\nargc = %d", argc);
   printf("\nargv[0] points at %s; argv[1] at
     %s", argv[0], argv[1]);
   printf("\n**argv = 1st letter of program
     name: %c", **argv);
   printf("\npointers: argv=%x, argv[0]=%x,
     argv[1]=%x", argv, argv[0], argv[1]);
   printf("\naddr: argv[0]=%x argv[1]=%x
     argv[0][0]=%x", &argv[0], &argv[1],
     &argv[0][0]);
   printf("\n                    argv[0][1]=%x",
             &argv[0][1]);
   printf("\n &argv = %x", &argv);
}
```

Here is the output of the program when 1234 is entered on the command line:

```
argc = 2
 argv[0] points at C:\WD\FINAL\ARG.EXE;
   argv[1] at 1234
 **argv = 1st letter of program name: C
 pointers: argv=ffe0, argv[0]=ffe6,
   argv[1]=fffa
```

```
addresses:  argv[0]=ffe0  argv[1]=ffe2
   argv[0][0]=ffe6  argv[0][1]=fffa
&argv = ffdc
```

The program name includes the *full path name* of the directory where the C compiler was invoked.[3] The full path name consists of the names of all the directories including the one in which the source code is located, separated by backward slashes. If we run the program on our system, it will surely also have another directory. The a r g c is 2 for the program name and the input of 1 2 3 4. The two strings are printed on the second line, and the third verifies that a r g v is really a pointer to a pointer.

The next three lines develop information about offset addresses where the various variables are stored and about the contents of the addresses themselves,[4] and are depicted in Figure 16.1.

The strings themselves have been displayed end to end, with each terminated by an ASCII null ('\0'). It is easy to verify that the 1 2 3 4 is stored in the proper number of bytes beyond the name of the program.

16.3 UNIONS

Sometimes it is useful to store more than one piece of data in the same place in memory. The C language makes provisions for this in an arrangement called a u n i o n. Specific application usage of u n i o ns tends to be complicated, but the idea itself is simple enough.

One such example is the invocation of DOS functions via C. The registers used for inputting and outputting variables are the same, but each needs to be named as a variable. Using a u n i o n declaration is one way of invoking DOS function calls.

This cooccupation, or u n i o n, is declared as shown in the following simple program in which a l o n g, 2 i n t s, and 4 c h a rs all occupy the same memory location:

```
union
  {
    char ch[4];
    int in[2];
    long lo;
  } combo;
```

---

[3]With DOS 2.0 the file name is not available; it is replaced by NULL.

[4]Some compilers ignore the & request for the address of an array or function since the name *is* the address. They make an exception in the case of the a r g v.

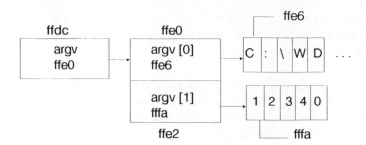

FIGURE 16.1   Typical array of pointers.

The memory location is identified with the name c omb o. The occupants of this memory location are recovered by using the name of the un i on, which is connected to the component wanted with a *period*. A typical expression is c omb o . l o, which refers to the l o ng form of the occupant. Enough storage is automatically set aside by the C compiler to accommodate the largest member present.

Here is a short C program that sets the contents equal to the long constant 0 x 1 2 3 4 5 6 7 8 L (note the letter L for l o ng) and then exhibits the occupant as i n t and c h a r.

```
include <dos.h>

main()
{
   int  j = 0;
   int  ds;
   unsigned offset;

   union
   {
     char ch[4];
     int  in[2];
     long lo;
   } combo;

   ds = (int)DS;
   offset = (unsigned)combo.ch;
   combo.lo = 0x12345678L;

   printf("\n%lx\n\n",combo.lo);
```

```
while (j < 2)
   printf("%x  ", combo.in[j++]);
printf("\n\n");
for (j = 0; j < 4; j++)
   printf("%x  ", combo.ch[j]);
printf("\n\n");

printf("offset = %x   dseg = %x\n",
   combo.ch, ds);
for (j = 0; j < 4; j++)
   printf("%x  ", peekb(ds, offset + j));

printf("\n\n");
}
```

The variable d s is used to hold the data segment address obtained from the C pseudo variable D S. This variable is *coerced* to an integer by a type cast for use by p e e k b, a library function which returns the byte value for a given address. The values printed out for the data segment and offset (the latter obtained from c o m b o . c h) are the ones for the machine that are used to run the program. Different values are provided by MS-DOS for different machines. The term o f f s e t is also coerced by a type cast, in this case to u n s i g n e d, as required by p e e k b ( ).

The result of executing this program is:

```
12345678

5678    1234

78   56   34   12

offset = ffd6    dseg = 359c
78   56   34   12
```

The last line in the foregoing display simply confirms that the byte values stored are the same as the ones provided by the c h a r version of the u n i o n. We notice that the numbers are stored with the most significant byte given last, at the highest memory address, in accordance with the rules of the Intel 8088. The words are stored in reverse order as well, that is, offset first.

The memory where the number 0 x 1 2 3 4 5 6 7 8 L is stored would look like that illustrated in Figure 16.2.

In our next chapter we will use a u n i o n to work with the printer hardware status via *bit fields*.

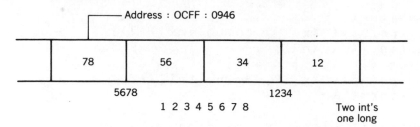

FIGURE 16.2   Actual physical storage of a value.

16.4   THE STACK: A DATA STRUCTURE

We now turn to the *stack*, one of the simplest and most widely used storage mechanisms. Suppose that we create an array of integers for storage within a program. We are free to invent our own rules for moving data in and out of our stack. Our simple example will use a structure like that shown in Figure 16.3.

If the integer 123 is stored on the stack (*pushed* on the stack), the picture looks like that shown in Figure 16.4. The number is stored in the place pointed to by stkptr, and stkptr is advanced to the next empty position. The number can be retrieved, or *popped* from the stack, by assigning the number that is pointed to by stkptr to some other variable, and by moving stkptr back one position. It is not necessary to erase the popped number because the next push will overwrite it.

In an earlier chapter we used the cafeteria-line plate holder as an example of a stack. The plates have the same first-in-first-out behavior, except that our com-

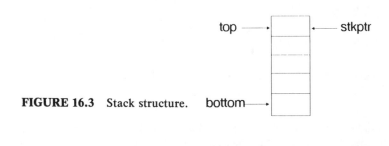

FIGURE 16.3   Stack structure.

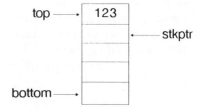

FIGURE 16.4   Stack structure with storage of 123.

puter stack uses a copy of the number, which is not really removed by popping. The top and bottom of the stack are marked by pointers which are used to detect errors caused by pushing onto a full stack or popping from an empty one.

A program that pushes **123** onto the stack and then recovers it is next given. The pushing and popping is handled by functions.

```
int stack[5]; /*define global stack outside
  main() */
int *top = stack;
int *bottom = stack + 4;
int *stkptr = stack;
main()
{
  int i = 0;

  printf("\nstack=%x top=%x bottom=%x
    stkptr=%x", stack,top,bottom,stkptr);
    /* diagnostic */

  while (i++ < 4)  /* fill stack with zeros */
    push(0);
  clear();

  display(top);
  printf("\npushing %d", 123);
  push(123);
  display(top);

  printf("\nresult of popping is %d", pop());

  printf("\nbut doing it again results in an
    error:");
  pop();
}

clear()
{
  stkptr = stack;
}

push(i)
  int i;
{
  if (stkptr < bottom)
    *stkptr++ = i;
```

```
    else
    printf("\nstack full; no push");
}

pop()
{
  if (stkptr > top)
    return (*(--stkptr));
  else
    printf("\nstack empty; no pop");
}

display(p)
  int *p;
{
  int *ptr = p;

 while (ptr < bottom)
  {
    printf("\n%x  %d",ptr, *(ptr));
    ptr++;
  }
  printf("\n");
}
```

The results of executing the compiled program are printed with some of the diagnostics that are used in writing the program. This is a good example of the use of pointers. It also demonstrates how pointers can be compared and displaced by adding and subtracting integers. Arithmetic operations are legal with pointers; but they must also make sense.

Here is the result of executing the compiled program:

```
stack = 28A top=28A bottom=292 stkptr=28A
28A   0
28C   0
28E   0
290   0

pushing 123
28A   123
28C   0
28E   0
290   0

result of popping is 123
but doing it again results in an error:
stack empty; no pop
```

The compiler complains that p o p ( ) uses both return and return of a value. This is somewhat sloppy programming practice, but causes no harm here. It could be corrected by adding a return statement at the end of p o p ( ), but we will not do this here.

16.5   THE 8088 INTERNAL STACK

The Intel 8088 microprocessor produces a stack in memory which is used during subroutine calls and also with the assembly language p u s h and p o p instructions. To illustrate the operation of the 8088 stack, we will use an assembly language program running under DOS DEBUG. The program uses the DOS utility i n t 2 1 to send an ASCII b e l character to the terminal, thereby causing it to beep. Five beeps are sent, each with a delay between them. Figure 16.5 lists the program as assembled by DEBUG, with the two loops of the program marked.

The segment address 1 2 B 7 was provided by DOS for the compiler system we used here. Your result will probably be different.

The registers are set up for the first beep with i n t 2 1 at offset address 1 0 7; then the delay routine is called.[5] The c a l l instruction transfers control to the address specified. It then returns to the instruction following c a l l when r e t (for return) is reached.

The delay comes from the l o o p instruction and the large number (f 0 0 0 hex) in the c x register. In this case, the loop is *to itself*. The purpose is to instru-

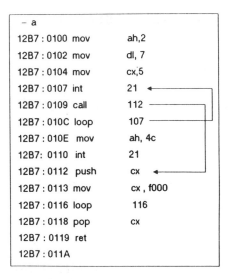

FIGURE 16.5   Program assembled by DE-BUG. Segment address 12B7 is provided by DOS and may vary.

---

[5]The amount of time wasted depends on the speed of the processor, that is, a PC will add more delay than an AT. To make delays independent of processor, one must add a user-written routine which uses the internal clock of the machine.

ment a delay. Here `loop` decrements the `cx` register and then tests it; if the contents of `cx` are not zero, control is transferred to the address specified in `loop`. Otherwise, the following instruction is executed. Before the delay is started, the original count value of `cx` is first `pushed` on the stack. After the delay, the beep-delay cycle is repeated five times.

To check progress the process is stopped by a break at address `107`. We obtain the display:

```
-g 107

AX=0200   BX=0000   CX=0005   DX=0007   SP=FFEE
   BP=0000
SI=0000   DI=0000   DS=12B7   ES=12B7   SS=12B7
   CS=12B7
IP=0107      NV UP EI PL NZ NA PO NC
12B7:0107 CD21                  INT    21
```

The stack pointer is set at `FFEE`, which is one word down from the top of was the segment, the location specified by MS-DOS rules for `.COM` files. Next we stop at `113` and obtain the display:

```
-g 113

AX=0207   BX=0000   CX=0005   DX=0007   SP=FFEA
   BP=0000
SI=0000   DI=0000   DS=12B7   ES=12B7   SS=12B7
   CS=12B7
IP=0113      NV UP EI PL NZ NA PO NC
12B7:0113 B900F0              MOV    CX,F000
```

When we dump memory addresses starting at the original stack pointer, we obtain:

```
-d ffea ffef

12B7:FFE0                       05 00 0C 01 00 00
```

From this dump we can draw a picture of the stack, as shown in Figure 16.6.

Now the stack pointer is two words further down. The stack contains the backward data in 8088 format for the count in the outside loop (`0005`) and the address for return after the call (`010C`). This stack behaves differently from the software stack we discussed in the last section in the way it grows as data are pushed. We are free to choose the rules for the software, but we cannot change the way in which the hardware will respond for a given command.

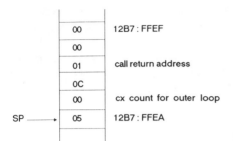

FIGURE 16.6   Stack structure display.

16.6   APPENDIX: PASCAL COMMAND LINE INPUT

Both C and Pascal allow parameters to be passed to a program at the time of invocation by including these parameters on the command line. A Pascal program which recognizes such an input is:

```
{g512,p512,d-}
program cl;
var
  count, value, code: integer;
begin
  count := paramcount;
  if count = 0 then
    writeln('no parameters on command line')
  else if count = 1 then
    begin
      writeln('the first parameter is ',
        paramstr(1));
      val(paramstr(1), value, code);
      if code = 0 then
        writeln('the value is ', value)
      else
        writeln(' parameter has problem
          position ', code)
    end
  else
    writeln('too many parameters - only one
      allowed')
end.
```

The usual *Turbo Pascal* compiler directive line has been included at the top to make the program compatible with MS-DOS. The function `paramcount` returns the number of command line entries; and the function `paramstr(n)` returns the nth entry itself. The string is converted to an integer with the built-in procedure v a l. This sets the value of c o d e to zero if no problems are encountered, or to the location of the problem character in the parameter string if there is a problem.

Provisions are made for handling the various command line inputs that might be encountered. The program is invoked by entering its name and a parameter separated by a space. The result is identical with that of the C program c l . c which we presented in Section 16.1.

16.7   SUMMARY

In this chapter we illustrated some simple C applications to machine input-output interfaces. Clearly, this is very error prone programming work. It raises the interesting speculation of software productivity in C. In particular, it suggests that C may be a very suitable language for the development of software to be produced in many copies and where assembly-language-like execution speed and transportability across operating systems and machines are important.

PROBLEMS

16.1   Write a DEBUG assembly language program that pushes a string on the stack and then prints out the string backward.

16.2   Write a C program that accepts an integer from 0 to 999 on the command line and prints out the value in English. Include error trapping (e.g., for negative numbers).

16.3   Write a C program that prints out all the command-line arguments, no matter how many.

16.4   Write a C program that opens a file and prints it. The name of the file should be specified on the command line.

16.5   Check the C stack program in Section 16.4 for pushing when the stack is full.

16.6   Modify the stack program in Section 16.4 to store pointers to strings and use it to select messages to be printed.

16.7   Write a C program using a u n i o n to pick out a particular fives-letter word from a group of five of them.

17

DATA STRUCTURES

17.0 INTRODUCTION

Many, if not most, serious applications of computer technology make use of data which has been organized into various structured groupings. The contents of a spreadsheet cell are one such grouping of numbers or text, format information, and formulas grouped according to the headings in the various rows and columns of the spreadsheet matrix. The File Control Block described earlier is another example. Word processors deal with text as groups of strings, formatting, fonts, and the like. In this chapter we will look at several of the ways the C language handles such groupings.

17.1 STRUCTURES

Until now, we have generally dealt with data that has been organized into one or more bytes or words. At this point, we begin a study of the organization of data into structures. For example, data about a person might contain name, address, phone number, height, and so on.

The C language uses structural declarations or definitions (keyword: struct) for this process of associating related data elements. The form or the definition of a structure is much like that of the union, which we described in the last chapter. A simple structural declaration is:

```
struct descrip
{
  char name[20];
  char eyes[5];
  int height[2];
} person;
```

In this case, we have allocated 20 characters for the name, 5 for the color in eyes, and a 2-integer array for height in feet and inches. The word descrip is a *tag* for the structure. It is not a variable, but just a name by which to refer to the structure. The word person is a variable name. In this case, the variable is a structural one which is invoked by the reserved word struct and denoted descrip.

Access to the *members* or parts of a structure is obtained in a similar way as that used in unions. The name of the structure variable, person in this case, and the name of the member, separated by a *period*, are used together for this purpose. For example, the expression

```
person.name
```

is appropriate.

The struct data elements are stored in contiguous memory locations. They are not stored on top of one another, as with the union expression. A program that fills in and prints one record of information is:

```
main()
{
  struct
  {
    char name[20];
    char eyes[5];
    int height[2];
  } person;
  persp = &person;

  strcpy(person.name,"My Gal");
  strcpy(person.eyes,"blue");
  person.height[0] = 5;
  person.height[1] = 2;
  printf("\nName: %s; Eyes: %s; Height: %d
    feet %d\
 inches", person.name, person.eyes,
    person.height[0], person.height[1]);
}
```

In this example the p r i n t f line was too long for the page. So we used the backslash to undo the carriage return in the middle of the line. The library function s t r c p y is used to move the strings for name and eye color into the proper places. When the program is run, the following information is printed to the screen:

```
Name: My Gal; Eyes: blue; Height: 5 feet
   2 inches
```

17.2   POINTERS TO STRUCTURES

C provides another way to refer to members of a structure. This method is one in which a pointer to the structure is declared. Here is the preceding program with the p e r s p pointer used instead of p e r s o n:

```
main()
{
   struct
   {
     char name[20];
     char eyes[5];
     int height[2];
   } *persp, person;

   persp = &person;

   strcpy(persp - name,"My Gal");
   strcpy(persp - eyes,"blue");
   persp - height[0] = 5;
   persp - height[1] = 2;

   printf("\nName: %s; Eyes: %s; Height: %d
      feet\
%d inches", persp - name, persp - eyes,
   persp - height[0], persp - height[1]);
}
```

In the foregoing, as well as C in general, the little arrow —> is treated as a single symbol. It connects the name of the pointer and the member that is being accessed. This version of the program is identical with the first one, and it produces the same result.

The pointer is declared with *p e r s p. That is, p e r s p is a pointer to a truct, as defined in the declaration. This is analogous to the declaration i n t *x, which means that x is a pointer to an integer.

The declaration of the pointer provides storage *only* for the pointer. It does not provide storage for the structure itself. A second variable person is declared to provide storage, and its address is assigned to the pointer persp. This activity is generally called *setting* the variable persp.

This is an important point, and one that is often missed, even by experienced C programmers. We restate it. Assigning a value to the place pointed to by a pointer which has not been set will lead to trouble. This results in an insidious bug because sometimes the program will work correctly and at other times it will not. C assumes that a pointer defined in this way will be set by another part of the program, a part which is separately compiled. If that is not the case, the pointer points nowhere in particular, and the filling of that space will only lead to trouble.

This example also illustrates the *only* two things that can be done to a structure in C. We can set or examine the values of the members of the data structure or we can examine its address with the & operator. Some compilers, including *Turbo C*, also let a structure be passed to, or returned from, a function. We will stick with the K & R definition, which does not allow this.

17.3 BIT FIELDS

Even though the price of memory has dropped dramatically over the years, there are still times when the use of individual bits to indicate some particular condition is convenient,[1] if not mandated, because the grouping of bits that comprises a word may also need to be considered as a *group*. The bits that comprise a word are often used as *flags* to keep track of the status of hardware status or software events. An example comes from the way the MS-DOS operating system stores the status of the printer. Let us examine this by means of an example.

This example combines the union and the bit-field specification in a structure. The program is:

```
#include <dos.h>
struct prstatus    /* printer status */
{
    unsigned timeout        : 1;
    unsigned                : 2;
    unsigned ioerror        : 1;
    unsigned selecte        : 1;
    unsigned paperout       : 1;
    unsigned ack            : 1;
    unsigned notbusy        : 1;
};
```

[1]The low price of memory may be less than fully meaningful as a design constraint if the operating system imposes a limit to RAM that is too low for a particular application.

```
main()
{
  unsigned prst();
  union
  {
    struct prstatus status;  /* printer bit
      template */
    unsigned stat;
  } result;

  result.stat = prst();
  printf("\nprinter status: ");
  putb(result.stat);
  result.status.paperout ?
        puts("\nout of paper") :
          puts("\npaper ok");
}
putb(x) /* print a byte in binary */
  unsigned x;
{
  unsigned pwr;
  int i;

  pwr = 1 << 7;
  for (i = 7; i >= 0; i--)
  {
    x & pwr ? cputs("1 ") : cputs("0 ");
    pwr >>= 1;
  }
}
unsigned prst() /* get the printer status
  byte */
{
  AH = 2;
  DX = 0;
  geninterrupt(0x17);
  return (unsigned)AH;
}
```

The program printed this when printer was on, but out of paper:

```
printer status: 1 0 1 0 1 0 0 0
out of paper
```

This program includes d o s . h so that the printer status can be obtaind from one of the BIOS services via the p r s t ( ) function. The BIOS interrupt command i n t 0x1 7 causes a return of 8 bits of status information in register a h. In turn the p r s t ( ) returns it as an u n s i g n e d integer. We use an unsigned integer in this case because the most significant bit of the integer represents a printer condition, and not the sign of a number.

The printer status information is defined in the BIOS code in the *Technical Reference* for the IBM PC,[2] and that definition is reflected in the status request p r s t a t u s. For example, the out-of-paper condition sets bit 5 to 1. The declaration of the structure does not include variables. They will be declared next.

The individual bits are named as members of the structure by means of the colon. Unneeded bits are skipped by passing them by, unnamed. Bits 1 and 2 are skipped in the present example.

Inside m a i n ( ), the function p r s t ( ) is declared and returns an u n s i g n e d integer. Next, a u n i o n variable called r e s u l t is constructed. This variable contains two members: the variable s t a t u s of type s t r u c t p r s t a t u s and s t a t, the return from BIOS. We can load the actual status into the member r e s u l t . s t a t by means of the union and then read out one bit at a time from the member r e s u l t . s t a t u s.

A picture of the union that emanates from our 8-bit word is shown in Figure 17.1. The member r e s u l t . s t a t u s is called a *template*. It overlays the data expression r e s u l t . s t a t by means of the u n i o n and also provides the means for interpretation.

The last line of the foregoing program uses the ? construction in order to test the p a p e r o u t bit to print a message about the condition of the paper.

The status word itself is printed in binary form by the function p u t b ( ). In the p u t b ( ) function a *mask* called p w r is created which has one bit set to 1

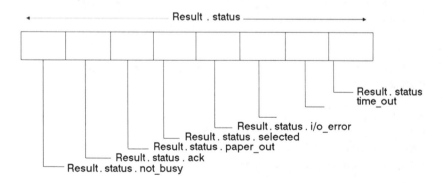

FIGURE 17.1 Interpretation of the eight bits of I/O information. Interpretation of each of the eight bits of example. The member "result.status" is called a template. It overlays the data expression "Result.stat" by means of the union, and also provides the means for interpretation.

[2]This information also appears in other references, such as *Advanced MS-DOS* by Ray Duncan, Microsoft Press, Redmond, WA, 1986.

and the rest set to zero. The loop starts with the leftmost bit set. The mask is ANDed with the input variable x and a 1 or 0 is printed, depending on the result of this logic computation. The reader should study this small function by trying it and experimenting with it in test programs.

17.4   ARRAYS OF STRUCTURES

We will now write a program that creates two structures and then links them together. We will accomplish this with two different programs. In the first version the storage for the structures will be allocated by declaring an array of two structures. The program is marked with roman numerals for our explanation to follow:

```
#include <stdio.h>

main()
{
  struct stag                           /* I */
  {
    char letter;
    struct stag *next;                  /* II */
  } element[2], *first, *dummy;         /* III */

  first = &element[0];                  /* IV */

  element[0].letter = 'A';              /* V */
  element[1].letter = 'B';
  element[0].next = &element[1];
  element[1].next = NULL;               /* VI */

  dummy = first;                        /* VII */
  do
  {
    printf("%c", dummy -> letter);      /* VIII */
    dummy = dummy -> next;
  }
  while (dummy != NULL);
  printf("\n\n");
}
```

The program prints the letter members of the two structures.

AB

There a number of important comments which should be made:

I. The declaration s t r u c t includes the *tag* s t a g identifies the struc-
    ture for future reference. For example a second declaration s t r u c t
    s t a g x; would create the structure x without the listing of the details
    of organization.

II. The structure consists of a c h a r and a pointer to another structure of
     the same type. Here is where s t a g is used to identify the object
     pointed to.

III. The declaration of element, an array of two structures, creates storage.
      The other two objects declared here, f i r s t and d u m m y, are
      pointers to structures of type s t a g.

IV. As mentioned in the foregoing, only two things can be done legally with
     a structure. We can take its address with &, as we are doing here, or we
     can refer to its members, as we will do in the next line. Since
     e l e m e n t is an array, we specify the first structure with the index 0:
     by means of the expression e l e m e n t [0].

V. Now we fill the structures with values for the c h a r and pointer parts.

VI. NULL is a pointer, which points at nothing, defined in s t d i e . h .

VII. The word d u m m y is used in the loop that follows in order to point at
      each member of the array. The program prints the letter held in the
      c h a r part and the loop terminates when the last structure is reached.

VIII. Here the little arrows — > are used to refer to members of the structure
       via the pointer d u m m y.

Actually this example is a little more than a linked list of two members. The
link is the pointer part of the structure, and it is the link that shows the way to
the next member. In this version of the program the storage allocation was provided by declaring an array of structures.

Another way to allocate storage is to use the C library function called
m a l l o c (s i z e), which returns a pointer to the character in memory which
begins an allocated block of the requested s i z e. In this second version of the
program, we declare pointers to the structure and use m a l l o c ( ) to provide
the storage. The program is:

```
#include <stdio.h>

main()
{
   struct stag
   {
      char letter;
      struct stag *next;
   } *first, *dummy;
```

```
first = (struct stag *) malloc(sizeof(struct
   stag));
first -> next =
   (struct stag *) malloc(sizeof(struct
      stag));
first -> letter = 'A';
(first -> next) -> letter = 'B';
(first -> next) -> next = NULL;
dummy = first;

do
{
   printf("%c", dummy -> letter);
   dummy = dummy -> next;
}
while (dummy != NULL);
printf("\n\n");
}
```

The lines using the malloc() expression require some further comment. Generally, we have been remiss in this book by not providing sufficient comments in our programs to make them more self-explanatory. Of course we have to have a considerable amount of text that describes the somewhat cryptic C code and makes it less than fully necessary to provide remarks with our code. We recognize this as less than the best programming practice. Most of our longer programs are indeed more fully documented. Our next program and those in subsequent chapters do reflect this aspect of good programming practice. The size requested in malloc() is enough space to hold a stag structure. This expression is associated with the sizeof operator. Since malloc() returns a pointer to the first byte of the space requested, we use the type cast (struct stag *) to coerce the pointer to a char to also become a pointer to a structure. Failure to make the conversion results in a complaint from the compiler, and this would not be good programming form.

17.5   A LINKED LIST

We will continue with our next C-language example to illustrate how elements can be added and deleted to linked lists. The program has been modified to print the whole alphabet instead of just two letters. A function called add() is included. It adds a letter, s2, to the list in the position that follows the letter s1. To delete an element, we use the drop() expression. This removes the element following s1. The method of addition is illustrated in Figure 17.2.

An element can be removed by removing its pointer and reattaching it to the following member. This is what the function drop() does.

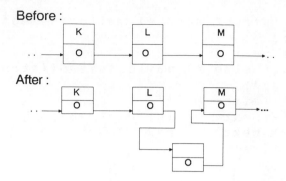

FIGURE 17.2   Addition with two linked lists.

The main part of the program to come first adds a **$** following element **L** and then removes it. The function **show()** displays the linked list as this list exists before, during, and after the program is run. The library function **free()** is used to return the storage used by the removed element to the pool of available memory. If this were a lengthy program, it is quite possible that we could exhaust our RAM before program completion.

Here is the program:

```
#include <stdio.h>
struct stag    /* definition of structure stag
                  outside */
{              /* main where it is available to
                  all    */
   char letter;
   struct stag *next;
};
main()
{
   char find = 'L';
   int i;
   struct stag *first, *dummy;
/* link up the alphabet */
   first = (struct stag *) malloc(sizeof(struct
     stag));
   dummy = first;

   for (i = 0; i < 26; i++)
   {
     dummy -> letter = 'A' + i;
```

```
    if (i < 25)
      dummy -> next = (struct stag *)
                             malloc(sizeof(struct
                               stag));
    else
      dummy -> next = NULL;

    dummy = dummy -> next;
  }

  show(first);

  if (add(first, find, '$') == 0)
    show(first);
  else
    printf("\ncan't find %c", find);

  drop(first,'L');
  show(first);
}

show(sptr)   /* display members of linked
  list */
  struct stag *sptr;
{
  struct stag *dummy;

  dummy = sptr;
  do
  {
    printf("%c", dummy -> letter);
    dummy = dummy -> next;
  }
  while (dummy != NULL);
  printf("\n\n");
}

add(sptr, s1, s2)   /* add s2, a new member,
  after s1 */
  struct stag *sptr;
  char s1, s2;
{
  struct stag *dummy, *temp;
```

```
    dummy = sptr;
    while ((dummy -> letter) != s1 && dummy !=
      NULL)
      dummy = dummy -> next;

    if (dummy == NULL)
      return(1);
    else
    {
      temp = dummy - next;
      dummy -> next = (struct stag *)
                         malloc(sizeof(struct
                           stag));
      (dummy -> next) -> letter = s2;
      (dummy -> next) -> next = temp;
      return(0);
    }
}


drop(sptr, s1)   /* drop the member following
  s1 */
  struct stag *sptr;
  char s1;
{
 struct stag *temp;

/* look for s1 */
  while ((sptr -> letter) != s1 && sptr !=
    NULL)
    sptr = sptr -> next;

  if (sptr == NULL)
    return(1);   /* can't find it */
  else
  {
    temp = sptr -> next;   /* disconnect */
    (sptr -> next) = (sptr -> next) -> next;
    free(temp);
    return(0);
  }
}
```

This program is a long one. By using block structure and documenting the code in an appropriate manner, it can be digested a function at a time. When compiled and executed, we obtain the screen display:

```
ABCDEFGHIJKLMNOPQRSTUVWXYZ
ABCDEFGHIJKL$MNOPQRSTUVWXYZ
ABCDEFGHIJKLMNOPQRSTUVWXYZ
```

The rationale behind the output obtained is as follows. First we print the alphabet, each letter being a member of the linked list. Next $ is inserted after the L. Finally, $ is removed and the alphabet is displayed for the third time.

17.6   SEARCHING A LINKED LIST

Here we present a modification of the C program just discussed. We use a search function search(), instead of the one used in the foregoing program in order to add and remove an element. Searching is accomplished by starting at the beginning (first) and looking until we reach the end (NULL). This is not a very efficient search, as we shall see next. Here is the program:

```
#include <stdio.h>
struct stag
{
   char letter;
   struct stag *next;
};

main(argc, argv)
   int argc;
   char *argv[];
{
   char find = ' ';
   int i;
   struct stag *first, *dummy;

   first = (struct stag *) malloc(sizeof(struct
      stag));
   dummy = first;

   for (i = 0; i < 26; i++)
   {
     dummy -> letter = 'A' + i;

     if (i < 25)
       dummy -> next = (struct stag *)
                        malloc(sizeof(struct
                        stag));
```

```
    else
      dummy -> next = NULL;
      dummy = dummy -> next;
  }

  if (argc == 2)
    find = argv[1][0]; /* 1st letter of
      command line */

  show(first);

  if ((i = search(first, find)) != 0)
    printf("\n%c is letter number %d",
      find, i);
  else
    printf("\ncan't find %c", find);
}
show(sptr)
  struct stag *sptr;
{
  struct stag *dummy;

  dummy = sptr;
  do
  {
    printf("%c", dummy -> letter);
    dummy = dummy -> next;
  }
  while (dummy != NULL);
}

search(sptr, s1) /* search for s1, return
  position */
  struct stag *sptr;
  char s1;
{
  int i;

  i = 1;
  while (sptr -> letter != s1 && sptr != NULL)
  {
    sptr = sptr -> next;
    i++;
  }
```

```
    if (sptr == NULL)
      return (0);
    else
      return (i);
}
```

The output that results from compiling and then executing the program is next shown. The program is executed twice, first with L entered on the command line and then with x: entered on the command line. A lowercase x is not in the alphabet of uppercase letters. We obtain:

```
ABCDEFGHIJKLMNOPQRSTUVWXYZ
L is letter number 12
ABCDEFGHIJKLMNOPQRSTUVWXYZ
can't find x
```

17.7 BINARY SEARCH

Actually, there is a faster, more efficient way to do this kind of search in a *sorted* list, generally called the *binary search*. If the list to be searched is alphabetical, and this one is, we can proceed as follows, using Knuth's algorithm from page 407 of his book on sorting and searching,

```
/* bs.C  binary search using Knuth's algorithm
   from p. 407 of Sorting and Searching.  */

char alphabet[] = "ABCDEFGHIJKLMNOPQRSTUVWXYZ";
int tries = 0;

main(argc, argv)
   int argc;
   char *argv[];
{
   int n;
   char k;
   if (argc == 2)
     k = argv[1][0];
   else
   {
     printf("\nusage: bs letter");
     exit(1);
   }
```

```
    if ((n = bsearch(k)) == -1)
      printf("\ncan't find %c", k);
    else
      printf("\n%c found in %d tries in
        position %d", k, tries, n + 1);
}

bsearch(k)
  char k;
{
  int l = 0;
  int u = 25;
  int i;

  do
  {
    tries++;
    i = ((l + u) / 2);   /* integer division */
    if (k < alphabet[i])
      u = i - 1;
    else if (k > alphabet[i])
      l = i + 1;
    else
      break;
  }
  while (l <= u);
  if (l > u)
    return(-1);
  else
    return(i);
}
```

The output for **M** and **N** is:

```
M found in 1 tries in position 13
N found in 4 tries in position 14
```

The algorithm is implemented in the function s e a r c h ( ). The range of 26 letters is divided in half, and the half containing the target is divided until the objective is reached (or not found). The maximum number of comparisons in this case is 5. Note that the end-to-end search performed above could take 26 comparisons if the target letter is **Z**. Evidently, the binary search algorithm is a good deal more efficient. The data need not be *sorted* before the search is begun. Generally, this is done as part of arranging a binary tree. This structuring allows us to provide an almost immediate response to location requests. In particular, sorting before search allows us to examine questions of relative location as well.

An interesting question concerns how much more efficient this search algorithm is than the one we used initially. After the first division of range the new range is half of the original; after the second, it is one-quarter; and so on. The search must end when the size of the search range drops to less than one:

$$N/2^n < 1$$

which can be written

$$2^n > N$$

Using the log_2 function, the relationship can be written in terms of n:

$$n > log_2 N$$

The function log_2 is implicitly defined by the identity:

$$n = 2 log_2 n$$

When N is large, the advantage of using a binary search is substantial. For example, a list of a million items can be searched in no more than 20 steps ($log21,000,000 = 19.9$).

17.8   MORE OF THE DATA STRUCTURE STORY: SORTING

There is much more to the story than we have told thus far. In our last section we had a beginning look at the important subject of searching. Searching for something is generally aided if the elements over which we must search are first sorted. Since sorting and searching are such fundamentally important tools for virtually all information systems applications, we will continue our discussion of these important topics. As we have noted, searching for something is usually easier if the various elements over which to search have been sorted. Now that we have discussed a bit about searching, we will discuss sorting.

As we have noted, sorting is the process of arranging similar entities into some sort of order based on numerical value or alphanumeric sequence, generally increasing or decreasing. In particular, we wish to arrange a set of elements in an ordered relation

$$a_1 \quad a_2 \quad a_3 \quad \ldots \quad a_n$$

where the elements to be sorted were presumably unsorted initially.

We can sort arrays that are stored in RAM, or we can sort sequential files on disk. We will restrict our coverage here to sorting across arrays. Also, we will concentrate our discussion on sorting across character strings. The extension to other more general forms of data structures is generally quite simple.

Three general methods may be used to sort an array. They are: **Exchange, Insertion** *and* **Selection.**

It is convenient to define each of these in terms of sorting a common 52-card deck of playing cards. To sort by exchange, we spread the cards across a table face up in a row. We examine two cards. If they are not in the proper increasing or decreasing order, we exchange their location. A simple exchange-sort algorithm is the bubble sort.

In sorting by insertion, we place the entire deck of unsorted cards face down on the table. We proceed to draw the cards one at a time and then place them into a new deck on the table. We do this in such a way that each card is placed in the new deck that we are forming in the correct order. When we uncover the last card from the original deck and put it into the proper place, the entire deck is then sorted. The insertion sort is the prototypical example of this type of sort.

Finally, the selection sorting process is accomplished by speading the 52 cards on the table face up and then searching and selecting the lowest, or highest, card and placing it in our hand. We then research the deck and pick the then-lowest or highest card and place it just behind the first one that is in our hand. When we have taken the last card from the table, the process is completed and all of the cards are sorted.

As we might expect, a large number of sorting algorithms is available. A primary concern with selecting one of them is efficiency. The answers to four questions are important:

1. *On the average, how fast can information be sorted?*
2. *What is the maximum speed of sorting?*
3. *What is the minimum sorting speed?*
4. *Does the algorithm always exhibit natural behavior?*

Clearly, the speed with which an algorithm searches will be directly related to the number of comparisons and exchanges that are required. Sorting times depend, in many cases, on the initial condition of the information to be sorted. If there is a large difference between the maximum and minimum sort time, the variation in performance of the algorithm may be unacceptable, especially if the best and worse cases occur often. In evaluating any sorting algorithm, it is desirable to determine the number of comparisons and exchanges that need to be made under the best, worst, and average conditions for the (perhaps many) different generic classes of elements that will need to be sorted.

One would normally expect that the sort time for information that is already sorted would be much less than for information initially very unsorted. It is important that an algorithm possess this characteristic, especially if information to be sorted arrives sequentially. This is what we mean by *natural behavior* and there is no guarantee that an algortihm will behave this way. We would judge the performance of an algorithm to be very poor if the addition of a single new element to be sorted into a sorted set of elements causes the entire data base to be resorted, unless we knew that the data base is very small.

This notion of natural behavior extends to sorts where there exists more than one index field or key. In this case, it is particularly important that the addition of a new element to the data base does not cause a rearrangement of any of the elements previously sorted on more than one index key.

The **bubble sort** is probably both the best known and one of the least efficient sorting algorithms. It is based on the exchange sort principal. Repeated comparisons and exchanges of adjacent elements are made starting from one end of the list and going to the other. The name of the algorithm probably comes from the analog to bubbles in a tank of water, where each bubble would seek its own level, depending upon the volume of air contained in the bubble. The algorithm works as follows: We start at the one end of the array and compare each adjacent pair of values. If the lower member of the pair being compared is greater than the upper member, we change the position of these elements or values. Once we work our way to the other end by continuing this process, the element at the far end will have to be the largest or smallest element, or number if we are dealing with numbers, in the array. Next we repeat this process with the newly formed array. This time we stop one element short of the top, since we already know that the element now at the top is the largest. We continue this process until, on the last pass, the array that we are examining contains only two elements. There is a modified bubble sort algorithm in which we alternately *bubble* in different directions.

A simple bubble-sort algorithm is shown next.

```
bubble(item,count) /* simple Bubble Sort
                        program */
char *item;
int count
{
    register int a,b;
    register char c;
      for (a=1;a<count;++a)
      for(b=count-1;ba=a;--b)
        {
            if(item[b-1]item[b]
              {
                c=item[b-1]; /* exchange
                  elements */
                item[b-1]=item[b];
                item[b]=t;
              }
        }
    }
}
```

The bubble-sort algorithm is basically driven by the two loops in the program statement. The outer loop will cause the array to be scanned $n - 1$ times, where there are n elements in the array that will be sorted. The inner loop will perform all of the actual exchanges and comparisons, with the outer loop acting as a bookkeeper to insure that every element is in the proper sorted position when program execution stops.

A possibly unfortunate feature of the bubble sort is that the number of *comparisons* will always be the same, regardless of the initial sortedness of the array. The number of exchanges will, however, vary with the degree of sortedness. The inner loop will need to execute n - 1 times for each execution of the outer loop. The outer loop must execute a total of (n-1) times. Thus the bubble sort will always need

$$C = (n-1)^2$$

comparisons, where n is the number of elements in the sort. This is the case regardless of the initial sortedness of the array to be sorted.

The number of element exchanges will be zero if the array is already sorted. It turns out that the number of exchanges is given by

$$E = K(n-1)^2$$

where K is a number that depends upon the orderliness of the initial array to be sorted. It turns out that $K = 1.0$ in the worst case, and 0 for the best case.

The fact that the sort time is of the order of n^2 renders the bubble sort very inefficient for other than quite small data base sorts. There have been some modifications, such as the shaker sort, which improves performance somewhat. The shaker sort moves in alternating directions. Still, this will continue to remain a very inefficient sort because the n^2 performance characteristic cannot be avoided.

The operation of insertion sort is relatively simple. We pick two elements and place them in the proper order. Then we pick a third element and put it into the proper location. This continues until the entire array is sorted. Quite unlike the operation of the bubble sort, the insertion sort is able to recognize an initially sorted set of elements. Thus the number of comparisons and exchanges that will need to be made depends upon the initial orderliness of the elements to be sorted. We see that the insertion sort resembles the way we might sort a poker or bridge hand that has been dealt to us face down. We pick up one card at a time and each card that we pick up is placed in its correct position relative to the cards that have already been sorted.

The actual number of exchanges, or interchanges, and comparisons is:

Exchanges	Comparisons	
$2(n - 1)$	$(n - 1)$	Best case
$0.25(n^2 + 9n - 10)$	$0.25(n^2 + n - 2)$	Average case
$0.50(n^2 + 3n - 4)$	$0.50(n^2 + n) - 1$	Worst case

We see that these efficiency numbers are little different from those for the bubble sort, except for the best-case performance. Thus we need only to insure best case performance and we will have an algorithm that is much better than the bubble sort. This is not as self-evident as it might sound. For the insertion sort also has another property. It behaves naturally, and the bubble sort does not necessarily do this. The bubble-sort algorithm may perform very poorly when a sort has already been obtained and then another element added that is smaller than any other element in the list, but the new element is added at the very high end of the list of elements. The new element may immediately bubble up to the right position at the first inner-loop pass. Alternately, depending upon the direction the bubbles are moving, there may only be one exchange of position for two elements at each time the outer loop is exercized. Thus the basic bubble sort is not naturally well behaved. This is true both for the basic version as well as the shaker sort.

Insertion sorts have good performance when the array size is small, generally less than 50 elements, or when it is already nearly sorted. A nearly sorted array is where either very few elements are out of place or, alternately, when those elements that are out of place are above and very close to where they should be. For an already sorted array, an insertion sort performs in an amount of execution time linearly proportional to the number of elements to be sorted. Generally, this is written as $O(n)$. In the worse case, which occurs when we have an array that is sorted in inverse order, the performance is $O(n^2)$.

This discussion suggests that the insertion sort may be quite good if it is used, after initial sorting by some other approach, to sequentially update a data base. Indeed, this is the case where the insertion sort is most used. A simple ascending insertion sort is shown next:

```
insert(item,count) /* insertion sort */
char *item;     /* address of array to be
                   sorted */
int count;      /* number of elements in
                   array */
{
    register int a,b:
    char c;
    for (c = item + 1; c   item + count; c++)
    {
        i = c;              /* init to current
                               element   */
        swap = *c;          /* save the value        */

        for ( ;             /* iterate over array */
           (i>item)&&        /* still in array        */
           (*(i-1)swap);    /* out of place          */
           i--)[            /* next element          */
```

```
            *i=*(i-1);      /* bubble value up   */
            }
        }
    if (i != c)         /* there was a swap?  */
  *i = swap;
   }
}
```

The selection sort idea consists of taking an array that is unsorted, selecting the lowest element, and placing it at one end of a new array to be formed. Then the process is repeated. The program next shown will accomplish a simple version of a selection sort.

```
select(item,count) /* simple selection sort
   program */
char *item;
int count;
{
   register int a,b,c
   char d;
   for(a=0;a<count-1;++a)
   {
     c=a;
     d=item[a]
     for(b=a+1;b<count;++b)
     {
       if(item[b]<>)
       {
          c=b;
          d=item[b];
       }
     }
     item[c]=item[a]
     item[a]=d;
   }
}
```

Sorting using a selection sort requires that the outer loop compare elements n - 1 times. The inner loop must compare elements 0.5n times. The total number of comparisons, $C = 0.5(n^2 - n)$, renders it too inefficient for a large number of elements. It turns out that the number of element exchanges for the selection sort may be quite a bit less than for the bubble sort however.

Each of these sorting algorithms has the distinct disadvantage of requiring n^2 comparisons. Only one of them, the insertion sort, could be considered suitable for any realistic large application. This has led to the development of many new algorithms for data sorting. The shell sort and the quick sort are among these.

The shell sort was invented by Donald L. Shell. The approach also resembles the sorting of shells of various sizes that have been placed on top of one another in an unsorted order. This popular sorting method compares and swaps those elements, characters or numbers, that are some greatest distance from each other in physical location first. Then the distance measure is decreased according to some prescribed relation and the sort is repeated. This relation causes a shrinking of the distance between numbers until we obtain the ones in closest proximity to each other. Suppose that we initially have an array of n integers. There are various ways in which we could decrease the distance between the integers that we are comparing. To start with a reasonably large number in the sequence

$$I = 2^i - 1, \quad i = 1, 2, 3, 4, \ldots$$

or the sequence

$$I = 2^i + 1, \quad i = 1, 2, 3, 4, \ldots$$

and then decrement I by one each time is an appropriate way to accomplish the shell sort. This results in starting with numbers or elements that are 1, 3, 7, 15, ... units apart. An alternate approach is to compute the sequence

$$I_{j+1} = 3I_j + 1, \quad I_1 = 1, \quad j = 1, 2, 3, \ldots$$

until we get a number greater than I_{j+1} n, the number of elements in the array. We start the shell sort with elements V_j apart and then divide the separation I by three at the start of each iteration. Figure 17.3 and 17.4 presents two simple illustrations of the shell sort on 6 letters using the sequence 3,2,1 and the sequence 5,4,3,2,1. Also presented in the figure is some indication of the number of computations involved.

A moderately complete version of a shell-sort algorithm is presented next. This uses the foregoing relation to determine the initial width between elements. We obtain the series 1, 4, 13, 40, 121, ... The program is:

```
ssort( item, noel, width, comp )
                            /*simple shell sort */
char      *item;
int       noel, width;
int       *comp;
{
          register int i, j;
          int          gap, k, temp ;
          char         *a, *b;
```

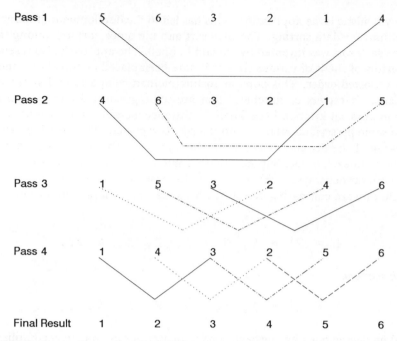

FIGURE 17.3 An illustration of a shell sort with initial width 5. Four passes, nine comparisons, and five exchanges are needed.

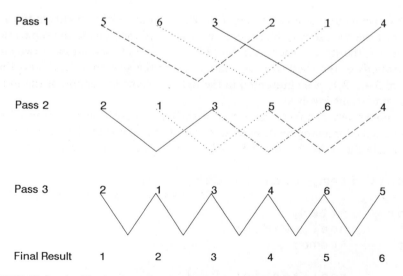

FIGURE 17.4 An illustration of a shell sort with initial width 5. Three passes, twelve comparisons, and five exchanges are needed.

```
for( gap=1;  gap <= noel;  gap =
   3*gap + 1 )

for( gap <= 3;   gap > 0  ; gap >=
   3 )
      for( i = gap; i < noel; i++ )
         for( j = i-gap;  j = 0 ;
            j -= gap )
         {
            a = item + ( j* width);
            b = item + ((j+gap) *
            width);

            if( (*comp)( a, b ) <=
               0 )
            break;

            for( k = width;  --k >=
               0 )
            {
               temp    = *a;
               *a++ = *b;
               *b++ = temp;
            }
         }
      }
}
```

While shell sort will execute quite quickly for a small number of elements, the execution time of $n^{1.2}$ will still be perhaps unacceptably large for large n. It turns out that the quick-sort algorithm will generally execute faster.

For most purposes, the quick-sort algorithm is a best choice. The operation of the standard quick-sort algorithm, first discovered by C. A. R. Hoare, is as follows:

1. A pivot point, or comparand value, is located in the center of the array to be sorted.

2. The array is partitioned by exchanging equal or larger elements, working from the left, with equal or smaller elements, working from the right. This procedure is repeated until the array has been organized such that every value to the left of the pivot point is smaller than every value located to the right of the pivot point.

3. If there is more than one element to left of the pivot point, we call the quick sort algorithm to function, recursively or nonrecursively, on the left-hand side of the array.

4. If there is more than one element to the right of the pivot point, we call the quick sort algorithm to function, recursively or nonrecursively, on the right side of the array.

5. The two arrays are effectively partitioned such that each element in one array is now guaranteed to be larger (or smaller) than an element in the other array.

6. We now proceed to consider the two arrays as independent and partition each, just as we have done in the foregoing, and repeat the procedure until every array is of size three. One last sort on an array of size three completely sorts that array. If we obtain an array of size two, an artificial element at one extreme end of the elements in the array may be introduced.

The number of comparisons and exchanges that need to be made in a quick sort are essentially $E = (n \log n)/6$ and $C = n \log n$.

Unfortunately, functioning of the quick-sort algorithm is very dependent upon the value chosen for the comparand. If the value chosen is at the end of the range of elements in the array, it turns out that the number of comparisons and exchanges is proportional to n^2. Usually, it is a relatively simple task to choose a value that is close to the middle of the range of elements to be sorted. In practice, a quick-sort algorithm is used initially to partition a large array into a number of smaller arrays. When these smaller arrays contain a sufficiently small number of elements to make insertion or shell sort efficient, a switch is often made to one of these algorithms.

A recursive quick-sort algorithm is:

```
qsort(item,count) /*Quick sort algorithm
                      initialization*/
char *item;
int count;
{
    qsort(item,0,count-1);
}

qsort(item,i,j) /* Quick sort algorithm */
char *item
int uppr,lwer;
{
    register int a,b;
    char x,y;
    x=item[(uppr+lwer)/2];
    do{
        while(x<item[j] && j>lwer) j--;
        while(item[i] && i<upper) i++;
```

```
     if(i<=j)
        {
        y=item[i];
        item[i]=item[j];
        item[j]=y;
        j--;
        i++;
        }
   }

   while(i<=j);

   if(i<uppr ) qsort(item,i,uppr);
   if(lwer<j)  qsort(item,lwer,j)
}
```

There are a variety of other sorting algorithms. Some of the specialized texts that deal with data structures, especially Knuth (1983) and Sedgewick (1984), may be consulted for a discussion of some of these.

17.9 APPENDIX: RECORDS IN PASCAL

In Pascal the element `record` provides the same combination of data that structures do in C. Here is the Pascal counterpart of the C program in Section 17.4.

```
program 11;
type
  elptr = ^element;                (*      I *)
  element = record                 (*     II *)
              letter:char;
              next:elptr;
            end;
var
  i: integer;
  first, second, dummy : elptr;    (*    III *)

begin
  new(first);                      (*     IV *)
  new(first^.next);                (*      V *)

  first^.letter := 'A';            (*     VI *)
  dummy := first^.next;            (*    VII *)
```

```
dummy^.letter := 'B';
dummy^.next := nil;                          (* VIII *)

(*   structure as in Figure 17.5: *)

dummy := first;                              (*   IX *)
repeat
  write(dummy^.letter);
  dummy := dummy^.next;
until dummy = nil;
end.
```

Here is a tour of the Pascal program that is keyed to the Roman numerals found in it:

I. The caret (^) is used to designate a "pointer-to". In this case we have a pointer to type element, which we will define next.

II. The word element is defined as a record consisting of the combination of a character and a pointer to another record of the same type (an element). A record is a combination of related pieces of data. It is the counterpart of the C struct. We notice that the record can contain a pointer to an object of the same type as itself. This kind of definition is called *recursive*. Recursive functions are very important, as we have seen in our previous efforts.

III. Several variables are declared to be elptr; which represent pointers to records of type element. Pascal requires that new types like this be previously defined in the type statement.

IV. The Pascal function new(pointer) creates storage for the object pointed to by pointer. C allows pointers to refer to existing objects by use of the & operator.

V. The use of the caret (^) on the right side of a variable means *contents of*; this is the counterpart of the C *indirection* operator *. This statement creates, through the use of the new() function, an object to be pointed to by the second member of the first structure.

VI. Now that the structures themselves have been created, we assign values to their members. Here the letter A is placed in the first record.

VII. Pascal puts limits on the complexity of expressions, so the dummy variable dummy is used here to hold the value of the contents of the

FIGURE 17.5   Structure of the Pascal program.

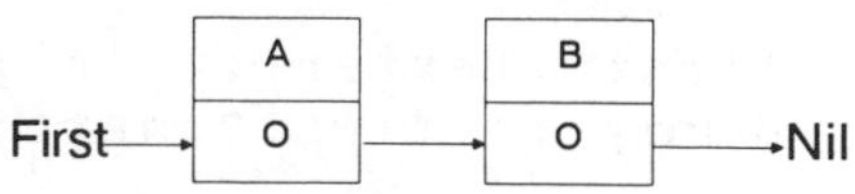

pointer member of the first record. Its value is the address of the next record obtained in Step V from the `new()` function.

VIII. The pointer in the second record is set to point at *nothing*. This is provided by Pascal through use of the `nil` expression. This is similar to the use of `NULL` in C.

IX. In the final step, we print out the contents of the letters stored in the records. We start at the first record, using the pointer `first`, and repeat until we come to the last record, which is the one with the pointer pointing to `nil`. The variable `dummy` is used a second time in this process.

The program prints:

A B

Almost all of our discussion concerning data structures, searching, and sorting in C can be repeated in the context of Pascal. There is little to be gained here by doing this. Nevertheless, some indications of simple sorting programs may be of value.

A simple bubble-sort program, which is written from the same perspective as our program in C is:

```
program bubblesort;

type
  ary = array[1..Max] of real;

var
  no-change: boolean;
  j,n: integer;
  a,p,q,hold: real;

procedure swap (var p, q: real);
begin
  hold:=p;
  p:=q;
  q:=hold
end;(*   exchange elements *)

begin   (* Bubble sort procedure *)
      repeat
        no-change:=true;
        for j:=1 to n-1 do
```

```
             begin
               if ary[j]>ary[j+1] then
                 begin
                   swap(ary[j],ary[j+1]);
                   no-change:=false
                 end
             end
         until no change
end;
```

A basic version of the shell sort algorithm is also rather brief. It is:

```
program shell sort;

type
  ary = array[1..Max] of real;

var
  j,n: integer;
  a,p,q,hold: real;

procedure swap (var p, q: real);
begin (* exchange elements *)

  hold:=p;
  p:=q;
  q:=hold
end;

begin (* Shell sort *)
  jump:=n;
  while jump1 do
    begin
      jump:=jump div 2;
      repeat
        done:=true;
        for j:=1 to n do
          begin
            i:=j+jump;
            if ary[j]>ary[i] then
              begin
                swap(ary[j],ary[i]);
                done:=false
              end
```

```
         end
     until done
   end
end;
```

For illustrative purposes, we will also present a recursive version of the quick sort algorithm. The recursive version is:

```
Recursive Quick sort algorithm;
type
  ary = array[1..Max] of real;

var
  done : boolean;
  jump,i,j,m,n: integer;
  left, right: integer;
  a,p,q,hold,pivot: real;

procedure swap (var p, q: real);
begin (* exchange elements *)
  hold:=p;
  p:=q;
  q:=hold
end;

begin {locate pivot point}
  pivot:=ary[(left+right)div 2];
  i:=left;
  j:=right;
  while i <= Max do
    begin {partition}
      while ary[i]<pivot do
        i:=i+1;
      while pivot<ary[j] do
        j:=j-1;
      if i<=j then
        begin
        swap(ary[i],ary[j]);
        i:=i+1;
        j:=j-1
      end
    end
  end (* end partitioning *)
```

```
begin        (* Quick sort *)
  if m<n then
    begin
      partit(x,i,j,m,n); (* divide array in two *)
      qsort(x,m,j);      (* sort left side of
                            array *)

      qsort(x,i,n)       (* sort right side of
                            array *)
    end
end;
```

An interesting nonrecursive quick-sort algorithm is described by Grogono (1976). It would be of interest to rewrite this program in C and then to contrast and compare the performance of the recursive and nonrecursive versions of the quick-sort algorithm both in Pascal and in C.

PROBLEMS

17.1 Write a C program that creates an array of structures containing names of states, state capitals, and postal abbreviations (California = CA). Put in a few states and print out a table.

17.2 Write a C program that creates an index to words in poem that allows retrieval of the nth word. Use a linked list.

17.3 Write a C program that stores the hex, octal, and binary numbers for decimal 0 through 64. Use an array of structures. Print a table from the array.

17.4 Do Problem 17.3 using pointers.

17.5 Use bit fields to find the status of the shift keys on the IBM PC keyboard.

17.6 Use a union as a template to extract the upper and lower halves of the ax register and print the contents of al and ah.

17.7 Write a function which displays the octal form of a decimal number and test it.

17.8 Write a program with a linked list of project activities and a way to add to and delete from it from a menu.

17.9 Write a C program that obtains the number of bytes from malloc() specified on the command line and prints the starting and ending addresses.

17.10 Write a program that lists the words in *poem* in alphabetic order: use bubble sort.

17.11 Contrast and compare performance of the several algorithms for sorting a character string of your choosing.

17.12 Prepare a brief discussion concerning how we might go about sorting groups of data. In particular, suppose that we have a structure for a typical mailing:

```
structur mail
{
      Char  Name [65];
      Char  Company [65];
      Char  Street [65]
      Char  City [40]
      Char  State [3]
      Char  Zip [6]
};
```

and discuss how we might sort an address data base on zip codes, states, names.

17.13 Prepare a brief discussion concerning how the sorting algorithms that we have discussed need to be modified in order to deal with random access disk files. Discuss how this may be done when the disk file is sufficiently small such that it can be read into memory, as well as when it is sufficiently large that this cannot be done.

17.14 Repeat Problem 17.13 for the case of sequential access disk files.

PART V

NUMERICAL ANALYSIS AND COMPUTATIONAL COMPLEXITY

18

NUMERICAL COMPUTATIONS

18.0 INTRODUCTION

In this lengthy chapter we will provide an introduction to one of the core subjects in computer science and engineering analysis—the solution of mathematical problems using approximation procedures from numerical analysis. While our detailed discussions of programming in the high level languages C and Pascal may be about to convince the reader that this is a programming text, this is not really the case. In this chapter we will shift our emphasis to software applications, and will examine a number of aspects relative to solving problems that require numerical approximations.

We can generally characterize most computing efforts as being symbolic or numeric. In the early days of computing, almost all interest was in the numeric. The early computers were coded in machine language, and after the mid 1950s, in such early high level languages as Fortran. It was fairly natural that these early efforts at numerical computing would be on a "new program for every new problem" philosophy. Libraries of numerical subroutines were certainly written, but these were often personal libraries more appropriate for use by the person who wrote them than for wide-scale reuse.

As we have noted in earlier chapters, there were certain drawbacks to machine code and early programming that made the application of modern programmer productivity practices difficult. For example, Fortran has a single looping construct, the DO loop, which is relatively inflexible. To be sure, looping can still be accomplished with nonnumeric looping logic. Usually this is done by the artifice of transforming something not initially in numeric form into something that is numeric, or through use of a program construct such as **IF** − **THEN** − **ELSE** − **GOTO** − **ENDIF** like statements. Generally, these make interpretation of a program very difficult. Fortran contains two types of data structures, scalars and arrays, only; this can make the organization of even numerical data quite difficult.

There are a number of desirable attributes for a language to be useful for numerical software purposes. The language should have

1   very fast and very accurate mathematical functions, such as exponentiation and logarithms;
2   a rich selection of numeric data types, such as double size reals that provide more significant digits for precise data;
3   recursion capabilities for iterative goal seeking, and searching routines;
4   a full range of structured control-flow constructs, including dynamic data structure and user-definable structure capabilities; and
5   portability across popular operating systems and hardware.

C is very well equipped to meet the criteria that we have just described. Just as with any complex and sophisticated tool, the use of C should be approached with caution. Users of C that are more experienced with *forgiving* programming languages should be especially cautious since, just as with closely related assembly languages, C is not very forgiving and will attempt to follow instructions blindly, even instructions that would be flagged as silly by other languages. This is the price that apparently must be paid for achieving execution speed and functionality in different operating environments. It is an advantage that is generally not possessed by more forgiving languages.

Numerical analysis is that branch of applied mathematics, computer science, and engineering that is concerned with procedures and techniques that enable us to obtain approximate solutions to problems that have been modeled in mathematical form. Numerical analysis is a very important part of modern computer science and engineering, including information systems engineering. It has been somewhat neglected in computer science of late with the increasing emphasis that has been placed on symbolic computation. This is unfortunate, as there are many problems in business, finance, industry, and defense for which numerical software is indispensable.

In this chapter we will present a brief introduction to numerical computing and numerical analysis. First, we will discuss some of the many types of numerical analysis methods that are available and then introduce the Taylor series approximation as a fundamental tool that provides a basis for most numerical analysis algorithms. We will then examine just a few numerical algorithms, paying particular attention to those most useful for financial computations. The subject of algorithms for financial and economic systems analysis concludes the chapter.

18.1   FUNDAMENTALS OF NUMERICAL ANALYSIS

Among the many functions we can perform using numerical algorithms, the following are among the most valuable:

- interpolation of data,
- approximation of functions,
- differentiation of functions,
- integration of functions,
- solution of systems of linear and nonlinear algebraic equations, and
- solution of differential equations.

A major reason why numerical methods are needed is that it is often either not possible or not feasible to obtain exact solutions to a mathematical problem. The important subject of approximation errors in the use of numerical methods then arises. We will not be able to examine this important subject in any depth here. Nevertheless, some summary comments are important.

Discretization error, or truncation error, is said to occur when a given function is approximated by another one. These errors would occur regardless of whether or not numerical methods were used. For example, we might approximate the exponential e^{-x} by the simpler relation $1 - x + 0.5x^2$. The truncation error is just the difference between these two and is

$$\mathtt{error} = e^{-x} - 1 + x - 0.5x^2.$$

Figure 18.1 illustrates the error in this approximation. As we see, the error is really quite small for small x. Much of the rationale for use of numerical methods can be seen in this very simple example. It is *difficult* to compute e^{-x}. It is *easy* to compute $1 - x + 0.5x^2$. Thus it is appealing to use the second computation as an approximation to the first *whenever the error involved is small*. In using numerical methods, it is generally very important to know when various approximations are valid.

Another important error that results in using a digital computer with finite word length is that of round-off error. As we have noted in earlier chapters, computers perform the arithmetic operations of addition, subtraction, multiplication, and division using representations of numbers with a limited number of digits. In general, all arithmetic operations in a computer will contain errors, unless it is known that the input numbers are very restricted—such as being between 0 and 256.

For example, if we wish to add 1.0200 to 1.0249 using a computer that can only retain two decimal digits, then we can only add 1.02 and 1.02 to get 2.04. The percentage error due to the *round off* is very small. We know that computers generally use the binary system, with the exception of some older machines

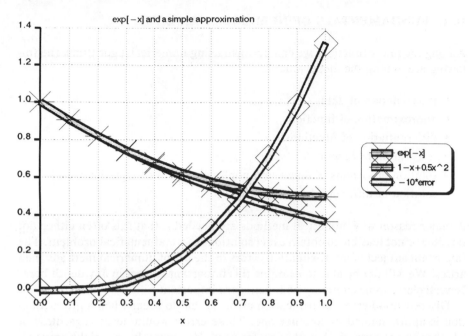

FIGURE 18.1 Truncation error versus X for Taylor approximation to exp[$-x$].

which may use a binary coded decimal system. Here it is just as well to think of adding two decimal numbers. In many instances, this round off error causes no problem.

However, round off errors may cause problems. For example, we might wish to subtract the smaller number from the larger number in the foregoing example. It might get us in a lot of trouble to use the number 0.00 when we really wish to obtain the *correct result* of 0.0049. Sometimes, it is possible to arrange the order of computations such that we retain significant information, like this residual. Since there may be millions of arithmetic operations in many calculations, it is important that this be done.

Accumulation of round-off errors depends greatly on the numerical method used. Methods which allow round off errors to accumulate in an unacceptable way are called numerically unstable. It is very important, from the standpoint of realistic applications, to understand how computational methods behave with respect to the possible errors that may exist. Generally, we will not wish to use numerically unstable methods. Unfortunately, some methods may be quite stable with one class of inputs and quite unstable with another. For example, one of the simplest and oldest methods to solve a set of linear algebraic equations is the method known as Gaussian elimination. This method may be numerically unstable and may yield unacceptable answers to computations. This can occur, as we shall illustrate later, even with only two equations. It is important to note that once the cause of the instability had been found, numerical analysts modified the basic method. With these modifications it turns out to be an efficient and a numerically stable method.

Even if a numerically stable method is used for a computation, erroneous results will be obtained if the problem is *ill conditioned.* In ill-conditioned problems, very small changes in the input data will often cause much larger changes in the solution than should occur. A system of linear algebraic equations is said to be ill-conditioned if small changes in the constant parametric coefficients of the system of linear equations will cause large and erroneous changes in the results. Ill-conditioned numerical analysis problems are often very difficult to solve. A further complication often occurs in that the model used to represent the problem is only an approximation.

On other occasions, the input data used for a given problem are only approximations. In these cases, the possibility of ill-conditioning should lead the analyst to either a better model, or better data, or both.

The Taylor series provides a very useful tool with which to introduce numerical analysis methods. It is instructive to examine some aspects regarding the derivation of the Taylor series. The fundamental definition of the derivative of variable y with respect to variable x is

$$dy(x)/dx = \lim_{h \to 0} [y(x+h) - y(x)]/h \qquad (1)$$

We can obtain an approximation to the derivative by using a small but finite (generally positive) h. For convenience, we let $x = nh$. The foregoing equation, with the finite h approximation, becomes

$$y'_n = [y_{n+1} - y_n]/h \qquad (2)$$

where we use the subscript n to denote the variable $x = nh$, and the subscript $n+1$ to denote the variable $x = (n+1)h$. If we solve for y_{n+1} we obtain

$$y_{n+1} = y_n + hy'_n \qquad (3)$$

It turns out that this expression represents the first two terms in a Taylor series expansion. This relation is also known as the rectangular rule. It is very useful for numerical integration, as we shall also see. We can integrate a constant over any interval with zero error, and that is why this is called the rectangular rule. It *integrates* a constant over a fixed interval, and this takes the shape of a rectangle.

The complete form of Taylor's series may be obtained by a continuation of these ideas. This derivation may be found in any introductory calculus book. The series is

$$y_{n+1} = y_n + hy'_n + h^2 y''_n/2 + h^3 y'''_n/6 + \cdots \qquad (4)$$

In actual practice, the higher terms in the series are virtually never used directly. They are used, however, in order to derive numerical algorithms that have error properties such that the error is zero for some number of derivative coefficients.

One of the most common needs for numerical methods is to find the roots, or solutions, of polynomial equations. This amounts to solving the equation

$$y = f(x) = 0 \qquad (5)$$

for the various values of x that satisfy the equation. We can use the simple version of Taylor's series given by Eq. (3). We assume that we are given some x_n which does not satisfy the equation $f(x_n) = 0$. We will iterate the solution such that we obtain a value x_{n+1} which (we hope) does better satisfy the equation. We will force y_{n+1} to go to zero in Eq. (3). The interval here is just the difference between the old value x_n and the new value x_{n+1} which does force y_{n+1} to go to zero. From Eq. (3) we obtain

$$0 = f(x_n) + h f'(x_n)$$

or

$$x_{n+1} = x_n - f(x_n) / f'(x_n) \qquad (6)$$

There are, as might be expected, more sophisticated versions of this equation, which is called Newton's equation or method (and occasionally the Newton Raphson method). Most of the extensions to this simple equation result from the observation that the derivative expression $y'(x)$ could really be replaced by some generic function $m(x_n)$ and that this could be more complex than just $y(x_n)$. For example, it could involve the average of the derivative at the end points x_n and x_{n+1}. It turns out that the convergence of this algorithm will be quite rapid when we are near a root, but potentially not very good at all when we are far from a root. Thus it would be useful to find a method that would perform better when we are far from a correct root. We would then switch to a method with rapid convergence properties, such as this method, when we are near the root. Rather than involving ourselves in these potentially complicated discussions, which would truly require an entire book, we will concentrate on elementary numerical algorithms here.

If we wish to obtain the solution to the polynomial equation

$$y = f(x) = x^3 - 6x^2 + 11x - 6 = (x-1)(x-2)(x-3)$$

we can do this through numerical iteration using Eq. (6), which becomes here

$$x_{n+1} = x_n - [x_n^3 - 6x_n^2 + 11x_n - 6] / [3x_n^2 - 12x_n + 11]$$

The computations should proceed quite rapidly. They should be terminated whenever we obtain x equal to 1, 2, or 3, as these are the correct roots to the equation. In general, we will never obtain precisely these values; and so we need to have some test that enables us to know whenever we are close to a root of the equation. This might be obtained by stopping the iterations whenever there is change below some threshold level from one iteration to the next. This approach is often used. As we know, there are three roots to this equation. The root that we will converge to, if any, is determined by the initial value of x_0 that we use to start the iterations. If we pick this value very far from the true root, the algorithm becomes ill-conditioned and the solution diverges. Figure 18.2 illustrates some behavior patterns for the simple third order polynomial considered here. Once we have obtained a single root, we still need to evaluate two more of them. Although this can be done by repeating the computations using the same algorithm, it is generally much more efficient to divide out the root that we have just obtained and obtain a polynomial of lower order. Another small caution is in order here. It is entirely possible for some, occasionally all, of the roots of a polynomial equation to appear in complex conjugate form. In this case, we should extract quadratic terms from the polynomial equation if we wish to evaluate these complex conjugate roots. We will not examine this extension here.

The first C language program that we will write in this chapter is one which will evaluate the roots of the polynomial f (x) of degree N whose coefficients

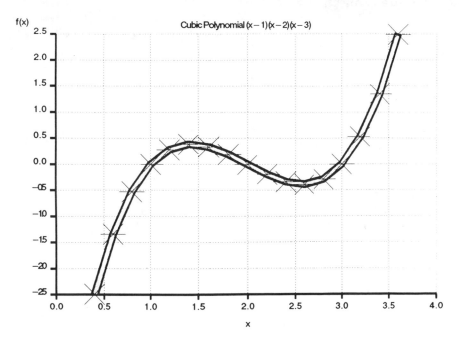

FIGURE 18.2   Cubic for use of Newton's formula.

are represented by the stored array a[j] for j = 0,1,2,...,N. In symbol form, where we use vf to denote value of the function, this is

$$vf = y = f(x) = a[0] + a[1]x + a[2]x^2 + a[3]x^3$$
$$+ \cdots + a[N]x^N$$

If we wish to use our algorithm, Eq. (6), to evaluate the roots of the polynomial, we will need to know the first derivative. This is just another polynomial, where df denotes derivative of the function

$$df = y' = f'(x) = a[1] + 2a[2]x + 3a[3]x^2 + \cdots$$
$$+ Na[N]x^{N-1}$$

Our program will call a function, fun(x,vf,df), which must be supplied by the user and which contains the value of the function and the derivative at the point x. Our program is

```
/* newton.c    demonstration of Newton's
   method */
/* usage: newton [range] */

#include <stdio.h>
#include <math.h>

/* IMAX is maximum number of iterations */
#define IMAX 25

/* 3rd degree polynomial */
#define DEG 3

/* accuracy of calculation */
#define ACC .001L

double vf = 0, df = 0; /*vf is function val;
   df, derivative */
double x1 = .5, x2 = 1.5; /*default range for
   expected root*/

main(argc, argv)
   int argc;
   char *argv[];
{
   double guess, atof(), fabs();
   int i;
```

```c
  if (argc == 3)
  {
    x1 = atof(argv[1]);
    x2 = atof(argv[2]);
  }

  guess = (x2 + x1) / 2;
  printf("initial guess = %6.2lf", guess);

  for (i = 0; i < IMAX; i++)
  {
    fun(guess, &vf, &df);

    if (fabs(vf) < ACC)
      break;
    else
      guess -= vf / df;
  }

  if (i < IMAX)
    printf("\nroot at %5.2lf after iteration
      %d\n", guess,i);
  else
    printf("\nsearch terminated after %d
      iterations\n", IMAX);
}

fun(x, afp, dfp)
  double x, *afp, *dfp;
{
  int i;
  double pow();
  static int poly[DEG+1]={1,-6,11,-6};
    /*f(x)=x^3-6x^2+1x-6*/
  *afp = *dfp = 0;

  for (i = DEG; i >= 0; i--)
    *afp += pow(x, (double)i) * poly[DEG - i];

  for (i = DEG - 1; i >= 0; i--)
    *dfp += pow(x, (double)(i)) * (i + 1) *
      poly[DEG - i - 1];
}
```

The reader may have noticed the appearance of a potentially new include statement in this program which calls ma t h . h. This is a library of math subroutines, invariably a part of a C compiler, that provides either source code in C or the equivalent assembly code to calculate various mathematical relations. The compiler will extract those portions of ma t h . h that are necessary for the particular problem in question and include them in the executable code. The C language code for the various routines in the ma t h . h include routine is not unlike the various numerical analysis programs in C that we write here.

It is possible to improve on this algorithm and the resulting code by detecting when the calculation of a root is ill-conditioned and then branching to some other numerical method until we are near convergence.

We can write many algebraic equations in the form of polynomial equations and solve them using Newton's method. For example, we can replace the problem of finding the square root of a number

$$x = M^{0.5}$$

by the problem of solving the polynomial equation

$$x^2 = M$$

or

$$y = x^2 - M = 0$$

and then use the root-finding algorithm that we have just obtained.

18.2 SOLUTION OF LINEAR ALGEBRAIC EQUATIONS

One of the most useful numerical algorithms is that for solving a set of linear algebraic equations. In general, a set of linear algebraic equations can be written as

$$a_{11}x_1 + a_{12}x_2 + a_{13}x_3 + \cdots + a_{1N}x_N = b_1$$
$$a_{21}x_1 + a_{22}x_2 + a_{23}x_3 + \cdots + a_{2N}x_N = b_2$$
$$a_{31}x_1 + a_{32}x_2 + a_{33}x_3 + \cdots + a_{3N}x_N = b_3 \qquad (7)$$
$$\cdots$$
$$a_{N1}x_1 + a_{N2}x_2 + a_{N3}x_3 + \cdots + a_{NN}x_N = b_N$$

There are N unknowns $x_1, x_2, \ldots, x_N$ and they are related by the N equations. Of course, there may be more or fewer equations than they are unknowns. If there are fewer equations, then the set of equations is underspecified and there will be no unique solutions. If there are more equations, then there may not be any consistent set of solutions, although we can use various approximation techniques, such as least-squares curve fitting, to find a *best fit* set of solutions.

When the number of equations and the number of unknowns are equal, we will, more often than not, be able to find a unique solution to them. There are some few pathologies, however, and these are invariably treated in books on linear algebra.

The potentially most straightforward approach to solving a set of linear simultaneous algebraic equations is by the method of systematic elimination of variables. The task that confronts us is to rearrange Eq. (7) by weighted addition of the equations such that the last equation is of the form $k_{NN}x_N = p_N$. Then we can immediately solve for x_N and backtrack to determine the other unknown variables.

The steps in the process are relatively simple. In the first phase of the process we:

1. Divide the first equation in Eq. (7) by a_{11} and rewrite the result as the new first equation
2. Multiply the resulting equation first by a_{21} and subtract the result from the second equation of the set, replacing the initial equation with the one that results from this operation
3. Repeat Step 2 until all of the equations in the initial set have been processed.

The resulting array looks like

$$x_1 + c_{12}x_2 + c_{13}x_3 + \cdots + c_{1N}x_N = d_1$$
$$c_{22}x_2 + c_{23}x_3 + \cdots + c_{2N}x_N = d_2$$
$$c_{32}x_2 + c_{33}x_3 + \cdots + c_{3N}x_N = d_3 \qquad (7a)$$
$$\cdots$$
$$c_{N2}x_2 + c_{N3}x_3 + \cdots + c_{NN}x_N = d_N$$

To continue the process to phase two, we ignore the first row of Eq. (7a) and repeat the procedure that we have just described on the reduced set of equations

$$c_{22}x_2 + c_{23}x_3 + \cdots + c_{2N}x_N = d_2$$
$$c_{32}x_2 + c_{33}x_3 + \cdots + c_{3N}x_N = d_3 \qquad (7b)$$
$$\cdots$$
$$c_{N2}x_2 + c_{N3}x_3 + \cdots + c_{NN}x_N = d_N$$

such that we now obtain

$$x_2 + e_{23}x_3 + \cdots + e_{2N}x_N = f_2$$
$$e_{32}x_2 + e_{33}x_3 + \cdots + e_{3N}x_N = f_3 \qquad (7c)$$
$$\cdots$$
$$e_{N2}x_2 + e_{N3}x_3 + \cdots + e_{NN}x_N = f_N$$

and this is continued until, after the last (Nth) phase, we have but a single equation in one unknown that we can easily solve.

The procedure is easily illustrated through use of an example. Suppose that we have the equations

$$-2x_1 + 1x_2 + 1x_3 + 4x_4 = 1$$
$$1x_1 + 1x_2 + 1x_3 + 1x_4 = 10$$
$$1x_1 + 2x_2 + 3x_3 + 4x_4 = 20$$
$$1x_1 + 2x_2 - 3x_3 - 4x_4 = 0$$

and wish to solve for the four components of the vector x

$$x = [x_1 \; x_2 \; x_3 \; x_4]^T$$

$$= \begin{bmatrix} x_1 \\ x_2 \\ x_3 \\ x_4 \end{bmatrix}$$

To use systematic elimination, also known as Gaussian elimination, we rewrite the four linear equations as the matrix

$$\begin{bmatrix} -2 & 1 & 1 & 4 & 1 \\ 1 & 1 & 1 & 1 & 10 \\ 1 & 2 & 3 & 4 & 20 \\ 1 & 2 & -3 & -4 & 0 \end{bmatrix}$$

We then proceed to reduce the equations in phases, as we have discussed. We obtain as a result of the first stage effort

$$\begin{bmatrix} 1 & -.5 & -.5 & -2 & -.5 \\ 0 & 1.5 & 1.5 & 3 & 10.5 \\ 0 & 2.5 & 3.5 & 6 & 20.5 \\ 0 & 2.5 & -2.5 & -2 & .5 \end{bmatrix}$$

We apply the same procedure again to the bottom three rows and obtain

$$\begin{bmatrix} 1 & 1 & 2 & 7 \\ 0 & 2/5 & 2/5 & 6/5 \\ 0 & -2 & -14/5 & -34/5 \end{bmatrix}$$

The procedure is repeated again on the bottom two rows such that we have

$$\begin{bmatrix} 1 & 1 & 3 \\ 0 & 2/5 & 2/5 \end{bmatrix}$$

We are now in a position to determine x_4 from the last equation. It is simply

$$x_4 = 1$$

We substitute this value of x_4 in the row above the last row and have

$$x_3 = 3 - x_4 = 2$$

Then we use the top row of the equation set above that and have

$$x_2 = 7 - 2x_4 - x_3 = 3$$

Finally, we use the top row in the equation set next above and have

$$x_1 = -.5 + 2x_4 + .5x_3 + .5x_2 = 4$$

and we have solved the problem. To illustrate the procedure, we have used the fractions that we would obtain in a precise solution rather than the decimal values that the computer would print out.

This is a good point in our discussions to return to the concept of ill-conditioned problems. It is a simple matter to see that solution of the equations

$$x_1 + x_2 = 2$$
$$x_1 \qquad = 1$$

poses absolutely no problems at all. Suppose that we form a new second equation by multiplying both sides of the original second equation by 0.01 and adding the result to the first equation. We now obtain the revised equivalent set of equations

$$x_1 + x_2 = 2$$
$$1.01x_1 + x_2 = 2.01$$

and now we are in real trouble in attempting to apply systematic elimination or most numerical approaches. In vector matrix form, we write the foregoing equation as

$$Ax = b$$

where

$$A = \begin{bmatrix} 1 & 1 \\ 1.01 & 1 \end{bmatrix}$$

$$b = \begin{bmatrix} 2 \\ 2.01 \end{bmatrix}$$

The solution to the problem is

$$x = A^{-1}b$$

and we are in trouble because the determinant of the A matrix is $(1 - 1.101)^{-1}$. Although the matrix inverse is just

$$A^{-1} = 100 \begin{bmatrix} 1 & -1.01 \\ -1 & 1 \end{bmatrix}$$

we might well not obtain the 100 in front of the matrix, owing to round-off errors, unless we take care with respect to all aspects of the solution procedure. The difficulty here is that the A matrix is *almost* singular.

In general, a matrix A is said to be singular if there does not exist any matrix Q such that

$$I = QA = AQ$$

Q is referred to as the inverse of A. The systematic elimination, or Gaussian elimination, method does not attempt to find the inverse of A. Indeed, this is unnecessary and computationally intensive if all we really need is a solution to the equation $Ax = b$ for x. Instead, we operate on rows by either of two permissible, or legal, operations: dividing a row by a scalar quantity; and adding or subtracting a multiple of one row from another.

The usual implementation of Gaussian elimination involves *partial pivoting* or *full pivoting*. In the implementation that we suggest here for students, the algorithm scans over one column at a time, beginning with the left-most column and iterating one column at a time to the right. It examines the augmented $[A|b]$ matrix for each row in the matrix and selects the largest element in the particular column that is being scanned. This is the first *pivot*, and it is used in the first phase of the process. After this is through, we have a reduced matrix and we use this to proceed. Again, we locate the row with the largest value, this time in the second column, and bring it to the top row. This becomes the new pivot. We continue the process until we obtain the desired result. Not only is this systematic elimination method quite simple for computer use, it is actually quite easy to use for pencil and paper computations up to perhaps a sixth-order set of linear algebraic equations.

18.3 INTERPOLATION

One very useful numerical procedure is that called interpolation. In general, this refers to the approximation of intermediate values between known values. The interpolation of data, and the associated approximation of functions, are usually brought about through the use of approximating polynomials. Occasionally *trigonometric interpolation* is used to approximate data within a region.

It might seem that a better fit to data could be obtained through the use of higher-order polynomials. It usually turns out that low order polynomial curve fitting, with the joining together of adjacent polynomial segments, is better. The term *spline* is often used to describe the two or more polynomials that have been fit together.

When we extend data beyond a range in which it is initially given, we call the process *extrapolation*. Both interpolation and extrapolation are quite important. In particular, the process of forecasting is much enhanced through the use of various extrapolation techniques.

It is possible to show that there is a unique straight line through any two points. In a similar way, there is a unique quadratic that can be passed through three points that are not in a straight line. A little thought convinces us that the equations which represent these curves are

$$P_1(x) = y_1(x-x_2)/(x_1-x_2) + y_2(x-x_1)/(x_2-x_1)$$

and

$$P_2(x) = y_1(x-x_2)(x-x_3)/[(x_1-x_2)(x_1-x_3)]$$
$$+ y_2(x-x_1)(x-x_3)/[(x_2-x_1)(x_2-x_3)]$$
$$+ y_3(x-x_1)(x-x_2)/[(x_3-x_1)(x_3-x_2)]$$

For the straight line, we see that $P_1(x_1)=y_1$ and $P_1(x_2)=y_2$. For the quadratic term, we have $P_2(x_1)=y_1$, $P_2(x_2)=y_2$, and $P_2(x_3)=y_3$. We see that knowledge of the $x_i y_i$ pairs is sufficient to enable us to calculate the polynomial. Computation through use of the stated algorithm is fairly straightforward. Identification of an appropriate C-language program is left as an exercise.

As an example of the computations, suppose that we take the three points (0,0), (1,1) and (2,4) for $(x_i, P(x_i))$, $i=1,2,3$ and fit a second-degree polynomial. From the foregoing equation, we have

$$P(0) = y_1 = 0$$
$$P(1) = y_2 = 1$$
$$P(2) = y_3 = 4$$

such that the polynomial becomes

$$P(x) = (x-0)(x-2)/[(1-0)(1-2)] + 4(x-0)(x-1)/$$
$$[(2-0)(2-1)] = x^2$$

which is the equation for a second-degree polynomial fitting the three data points.

By extending this reasoning we can write down the general polynomial in degree n that passes through $n+1$ points. This is a bit cumbersome in appearance and so we will not give it here. The basic equation that we have obtained here is often called LaGrange's interpolation and extrapolation equation. An implementation due to Nevill is often programmed as it is simpler to implement and provides an estimate of errors involved in the procedure.

There are many functions that are not well approximated by polynomials, but which may be quite well approximated by a ratio of polynomials or, as it is sometimes called, a rational function. The general definition of a rational function is

$$R_{m+n+1}(x) = P(x)/Q(x)$$
$$P(x) = p_0 + p_1 x + p_2 x^2 + \cdots p_m x^m$$
$$Q(x) = q_0 + q_1 x + q_2 x^2 + \cdots q_n x^n$$

where the $m+n+1$ subscript is used on R to indicate that the resulting rational function can pass through precisely $m+n+1$ points.

The numerical integration or differentiation of a function is easily accomplished if we approximate the function to be integrated or differentiated by a simpler one that can be easily, typically exactly, integrated or differentiated. Polynomials are especially useful functions as the operations of differentiation and integration are easily accomplished. Alternately, we can approach the problem through the direct use of numerical integration formulas. Generally, numerical differentiation of functions is accomplished through approximation of the function by a polynomial, or perhaps a transcendental or rational function. This approximate function is then analytically differentiated.

18.4   NUMERICAL INTEGRATION

Numerical integration is one of the very oldest numerical analysis topics. It was studied so early because it is such a fundamental problem for such a large number of applications. The accumulation of money in an interest bearing account is fundamentally a problem in integration.

The problem of evaluating the integral

$$J \; = \; \int_a^b \; f(x) \, dx$$

is exactly that of solving the differential equation

$$\frac{dy(x)}{dx} \; = \; f(x)$$

with the initial condition $y(a) = 0$. To obtain the integral, we evaluate the solution of the differential equation at $y(b) = J$. We see that there is a close relationship between numerical integration and numerical solution of differential equations. This fact has also provided motivation for the study of numerical integration.

Earlier in this chapter we derived a simple rule for numerical integration known as the rectangular rule. This rule, given by Eq. (3) is just

$$y_{n+1} = y_n + h y'_n \tag{3}$$

where we note that the derivative y' is just the function f. Thus we have

$$J \; = \; \int_a^b \; f(x) \, dx \; = \; [b-a] f(b)$$

or

$$J \; = \; \int_a^b \; f(x) \, dx \; = \; [b-a] f(a)$$

and we see again that we must assume that the derivative y', or the function f, is constant throughout the interval a to b.

Higher order integration formulas are very desirable. We can obtain one such higher-order rule from Taylor's series, written to include the third derivative term

$$y_{n+1} = y_n + hy'_n + h2y''_n/2 + h3y'''_n/6 + \cdots \quad (4)$$

If we differentiate this expression with respect to x and then multiply the result by $-h/2$, we obtain

$$-y_{n+1}'/2 = -hy_n'/2 - h2y''_n/2 - h3y'''_n/4$$

The *trick* in this is that we can now add these two expressions and get the second derivative terms to vanish. By doing this, we obtain

$$y_{n+1} = y_n + 1/2h[y'_{n+1} + y'_n] + TE$$

and where

$$TE = \Theta[h^3y'''_n/12]$$

is known as the truncation error. The symbol Θ, (theta), is just used to indicate a smooth function. This is the *order of the* error that results from the terms left out. It is proportional to h^3 and the third derivative of the function. This suggests that the error will be zero if the third and higher derivative terms are zero. Usually, the truncation error is not calculated, as it cannot be calculated exactly. Knowing the order of the truncation error does provide us with valuable information in terms of how this error may increase very rapidly with increases in the integration interval.

An alternate way to obtain this formula is to assume that we want a polynomial fit to three points, obtain the polynomial approximation from our results in the last section, and integrate this. Again, we will obtain the trapezoidal rule.

We can continue this procedure and establish a number of numerical integration formulas. Figure 18.3 presents the situation assumed in the determination of the various integration formulas. The resulting formulas are given in Table 18.1. The truncation errors associated with these approximate integration algorithms are $h^2f'(s)/2$, $h^3f''(s)/12$, $h^5f^4(s)/90$, and $3h^5f^4(s)/80$. The value of s is some value of x within the integration interval. It is interesting to note that there is some error cancellation in the 3 point Simpson's rule, such that it has a truncation error that is lower than the truncation error for the higher order 3/8 rule.

More often than not, the evaluation of an integral will be over a considerable number of data points, such as shown in Figure 18.4. The various integration rules that we have just discussed can easily be *extended* to cover this situation. In effect, we just integrate over subintervals and then add up the results. We easily obtain the following table, which assumed equally spaced sampling intervals and with each constant width sampling interval given by

$$h = x_i - x_{i-1}.$$

We obtain Table 18.2.

There are many ways in which these algorithms can be combined. We could have used the trapezoidal rule in one subinterval and Simpson's rule in the immediate next subinterval. We could then continue this alternating pattern throughout the range of integration. A major question in any numerical analysis effort concerns whether or not we have obtained the desired accuracy. This is a fairly simple matter to deal with in numerical integration problems. If we use the extended trapezoidal rule, we note that we can change the sampling interval, h, without losing the benefits of any of the calculations that we have already made. This suggests a simple method for numerical integration and maintaining error control at the same time. We perhaps start with the crudest form of integration in which we use only the two end points a and b of the integration interval. Then we split the interval in half. A little thought convinces us that this only adds to the average value of the function, which is the basic computation of the trapezoidal rule, the value of the function to be integrated at the midpoint of the integration interval. Next, we would divide the interval into half again. We note, however, that this merely results in the addition of the values of the function to be integrated at the 1/3 and 3/4 points. Figure 18.5 illustrates the nature of the computations. We stop the integration when there is no significant change in the values of the computed integral as a result of halving the integration interval.

A relatively straightforward program which uses the extended trapezoidal rule is now presented. Here m is the number of intervals used in the computation. If we set m = 1, we simply obtain the integration using the basic trapezoidal rule. Our C language program is:

```
/* integr.c    trapezoidal integration example:
   exponential integrated from 1 to 5 */

main()
{
   double integral(), expon(), exp();
   double a = 1, b = 5, current, last;
   int i, number;

   for (i = 1; i <= 200; i += 16)
   {
```

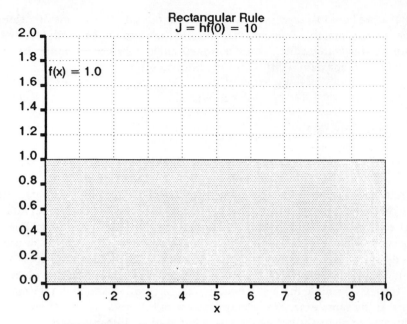

FIGURE 18.3a   Feasible curve for use of rectangular rule.

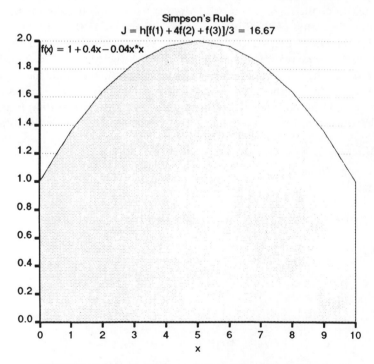

FIGURE 18.3c   Feasible curve for use of Simpson's rule.

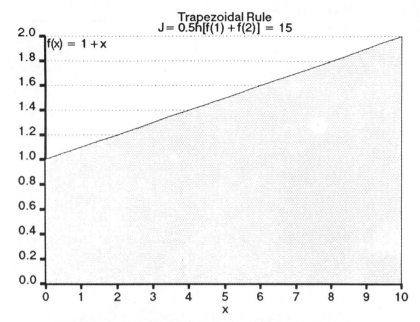

FIGURE 18.3b   Feasible curve for use of trapezoidal rule.

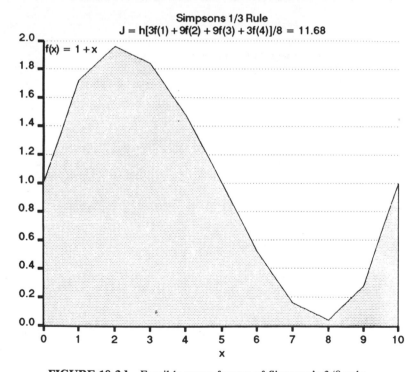

FIGURE 18.3d   Feasible curve for use of Simpson's 3/8 rule.

TABLE 18.1 Integration Formulae

Rectangular Rule

$$J = \int_{x1}^{x2} f(x)dx = hf_1$$

Trapezoidal Rule

$$J = \int_{x1}^{x2} f(x)dx = 1/2h[f_1 + f_2]$$

Simpson's Rule

$$J = \int_{x1}^{x3} f(x)dx = h[4f_1 + 4f_2 + f_3]/3$$

Simpson's 3/8 Rule

$$J = \int_{x1}^{x4} f(x)dx = h[3f_1 + 9f_2 + 9f_3 + 3f_4]/8$$

TABLE 18.2 Extended Integration Formulae

Extended Rectangular Rule

$$J = \int_{x1}^{xN} f(x)dx = h[f_1 + f_2 + f_3 + \cdots + f_{N-1}]$$

Extended Trapezoidal Rule

$$J = \int_{x1}^{xN} f(x)dx = h[1/2f_1 + f_2 + f_3 + \cdots + 1/2f_N]$$

Extended Simpson's Rule

$$J = \int_{x1}^{xN} f(x)dx = h[f_1 + 4f_2 + 2f_3 + 4f_4 + 2f_5 + \cdots + 4f_{N-1} + f_N]/3$$

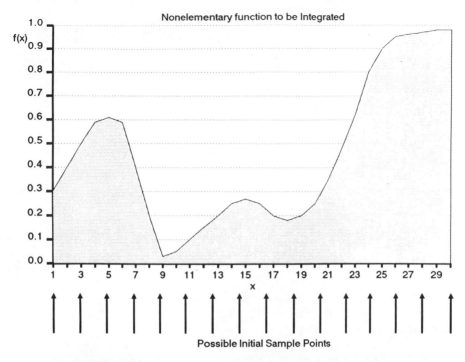

FIGURE 18.4   Prototypical function for extended integration.

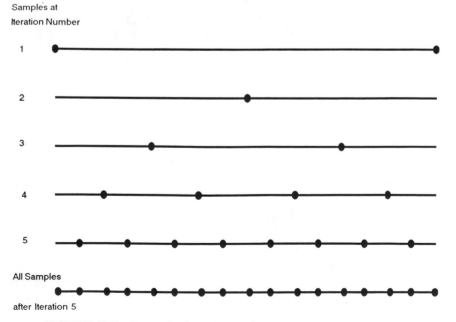

FIGURE 18.5   Successive iterations to improve integration accuracy.

```
      current = integral(expon, a, b, i);
      printf("\nintegral with %3d intervals is
        %8.5lf", i, current);
      if (i > 1)
        printf("    %8.5lf", last - current);
      last = current;
   }


   printf("\n\nCheck:exp(5.0)-exp(1.0)=%8.5lf",
     exp(5.0)-exp(1.0));
}


double integral (fcn, start, finish, number)
   double (*fcn)();
   double start, finish;
   int number;
{
   int i, j;
   double integral = 0, slice;
   double expon();

   slice = (finish - start) / number;

   for (i = 0; i < number; i++)
     integral += (((*fcn)(start + i * slice) +
       (*fcn)(start + (i + 1) * slice)) / 2)
         * slice;

   return (integral);
}


double expon(arg)
   double arg;
{
   double exp();

   return exp(arg);
}
```

We have included the functional form that we wish to integrate in the program.
This reduces its generality. It can easily be modified, however, to work with most
general forms. We are asking for calculation of the integral from 1.0 to 5.0 of the
function e^x. This is just $e^{5.0} - e^{1.0}$. We obtain the approximate results as a
function of the number of intervals

Number of Intervals	Calculated Value	Error
1	302.26288	
17	146.36644	155.89644
33	145.87322	000.49322
49	145.77578	000.09744
65	145.74085	000.03492
81	145.72448	000.01637
97	145.71552	000.00896
113	145.71009	000.00543
193	145.70009	000.00099
True value	145.69488	000.00000

We provide a number of exercises at the end of the chapter that should be performed in order to demonstrate the usefulness of this integration rule.

Numerical integration of a function of a single variable is a well researched and well understood area within numerical analysis. However, integration of functions of several variables is an area where not as much is known.

As we have noted, one of the major uses for numerical integration routines is in the solution of differential equations. Let us briefly examine this topic.

18.5   DIFFERENTIAL EQUATIONS

In the physical sciences and engineering especially, it is often necessary to solve differential equations. These often occur in business applications as well, especially when simulation models of the flow of money and products through an organization are being considered. In this section we will briefly examine the subject of numerical solution of differential equations.

The general format in which ordinary differential equations are written is typified by the equation

$$\frac{dy}{dx} = f(y, x)$$

with an initial condition

$$y(x_0) = y_0$$

This is a first-order differential equation. A prototypical first order differential equation is

$$\frac{dy}{dx} = f(y, x) = ay$$

with an initial condition

$$y(x_0) = y_0$$

This is spoken of as a linear first order differential equation with constant coefficients. This differential equation could be used to model the growth of money in an interest bearing account, where the rate of change of money over time is proportional to the money present at the time. Alternately, it could represent ideal population growth, where the rate of change of the number of people present in a given area at a given time is proportional, with the constant of proportionality being the birth rate minus the death rate. It is a simple matter to verify that the solution to this equation is

$$y(x) = y_0 e^{a(x-x0)}$$

The straightforward way to do this is to substitute the solution to the differential equation in the differential equation.

A more general representation of a set of N first order differential equations is

$$y_1' = f_1(y_1, y_2, \cdots, y_N, x)$$
$$y_2' = f_2(y_1, y_2, \cdots, y_N, x)$$
$$\vdots$$
$$y_N' = f_N(y_1, y_2, \cdots, y_N, x)$$

with the initial conditions

$$y_1(x_0) = y_{10}$$
$$y_2(x_0) = y_{20}$$
$$\vdots$$
$$y_N(x_0) = y_{N0}.$$

This can be represented as a single Nth order differential equation, however, the notation is quite cumbersome in the general case and will not be stated here. It is not needed, as a higher-order differential equation can always be rewritten as an equivalent number of first-order differential equations. For example, we may rewrite the second-order differential equation

$$y'' + g(x)y' = m(x)$$

as the first order equations

$$y'_1 = y_2(x)$$
$$y'_2 = m(x) - g(x)y_2(x)$$

through the substitution

$$y(x) = y_1(x)$$
$$y'_1 = y_2(x)$$

For convenience, a set of first order differential equations just given may be written as the vector differential equation

$$y' = f(y, x)$$

and the initial condition as

$$y(x_0) = y_0.$$

This neat and compact method is often very useful, particularly for conceptual purposes. It is generally quite convenient to think in terms of a first order differential equation and then to carry out actual implementations using the full vector set of equations.

There are three basic approaches to the numerical solution of differential equations:

1. Methods in which future ordinates are expressed as linear combinations of present or past ordinates and slopes
2. Methods in which a future ordinate involves only a memory of the present, and with no past memory
3. Methods which involve the calculation of one or more higher-order derivatives.

Although most modern software for numerical solution of differential equations uses methods in category 2, such as one of the several Runge-Kutta algorithms, we will only describe one method in the first category in any detail.

It turns out that methods in category 3 are computationally inefficient except for very special problems. The Runge-Kutta methods work very well, but are somewhat less computationally efficient, than methods in category 1. They are generally the best category two routines to use when we know very little about the characteristic of the differential equation that we are trying to solve. Methods in category one are often called predictor—corrector methods. They are computationally efficient but are often difficult to start because of the need to use higher-order integration formula that require a knowledge of the solution at several back points and not just at the initial condition.

The particular algorithm we will describe is a *predictor-corrector* algorithm that uses a modified form of the rectangular rule as a predictor and the trapezoidal rule as a corrector. The rectangular rule is an *open ended* rule and can predict the value of y at the end point of an interval without knowledge of the value of y ' at the end of the interval. This will be used as the predictor. The trapezoidal rule, which is a closed end rule, can then be used as a corrector. It will be used to improve on the prediction initially obtained. Actually, the trapezoidal rule could be used several times as a corrector.

We obtain our more accurate version of the rectangular rule by subtracting the two Taylor series expressions

$$y_{n+1} = y_n + hy'_n + h^2 y''_n/2 + h^3 y'''_n/6 + \cdots$$

$$y_{n-1} = y_n - hy'_n + h^2 y''_n/2 - h^3 y'''_n/6 + \cdots$$

to obtain the modified form of the rectangular rule

$$y_{n+1} = y_{n-1} + 2hy'_n + h^3 y'''_n/3$$

where the last term represents the truncation error. As we have noted, this term is usually not calculated. It is important to note that the truncation error for this modified rectangular rule is the same order as for the trapezoidal rule. Our predictor corrector algorithms for computational solution of a differential equation are

$$y_{n+1} = y_{n-1} + 2hy'_n$$

$$y_{n+1} = y_n + 1/2h[y'_{n+1} + y'_n]$$

The particular steps needed in the solution of a first order differential equation are:

1. Predict y_1 from the crude formula
   $y_1 = y_0 + hy'_0$
2. Compute y'_1 from the given differential equation
3. Correct y_1 using the trapezoidal rule
   $y_1 = y_0 + 1/2h[y'_1 + y'_0]$
4. Repeat steps 2 and 3 until the change from iteration to iteration is very small. We are now in a position to use the stated predictor corrector formulas.
5. Predict y_{n+1} from the modified rectangular rule
   $y_{n+1} = y_{n-1} + 2hy'_n$
6. Compute y'_{n+1} using the given differential equation

7. Correct y_{n+1} using the trapezoidal rule
   $$y_{n+1} = y_n + 1/2h[y'_{n+1} + y'_n]$$
8. Repeat steps 6 and 7 until the change from iteration to iteration is very small.
9. Continue the computation by means of steps 5 through 8.

The extension of these steps to equations of order higher than the first is quite straightforward. From the highest order derivative, the next lower in order is predicted. This is repeated with the order being reduced by one each time until we obtain y_{n+1}. This will be after N repetitions, where N is the order of the differential equation in question. The value of the highest derivative is then determined from the predicted data and the corrector formula is then used to obtain a better approximation to y_{n+1}. Of course, the corrector formula must be used N times for each iteration, once for each n.

The detailed program that performs these operations will not be stated here. It is an extension to the trapezoidal rule program already given and is left as an exercise for the interested reader.

There are many methods available for the numerical solution of ordinary differential equations. When these have boundary conditions, the solution is made somewhat more difficult, but not overly so. Partial differential equations are those differential equations which involve unknown functions of two or more independent variables. Often, these are very difficult to solve.

18.6 FINANCIAL ANALYSIS

In this section we will discuss four important financial analysis calculations. The first of these is the computation of the future value of a series of constant deposits. Using this we will also determine the net present value of the same series of investments. Then we will examine the internal rate of return calculation and an algorithm for amortization of a loan.

18.6.1 Simple Interest Calculations

If we invest a sum of money, (present value, PV) at time 0 and at interest rate i per unit time, then the amount of interest that we have earned one period later is i PV. If we assume simple interest, then the amount of interest that we would have in N periods is just N times this amount, or N i PV. The total amount of money that we would have at time N is just the principal invested, PV plus the interest that we have earned, or future value (FV):

```
FV = PV (1+Ni)       [simple interest]
```

It is rare that interest is calculated this way. The reason is that after the first period the amount of money that we have is PV(1+i). It would be foolish of us to let this amount stay invested and earn interest just like it was a smaller amount, the initial amount PV. For this reason compound interest calculations are almost always made and used to determine the present value of an investment. The calculation is still very simple. It is based on the fact that, under compound interest, an amount P_n at time (or period) n will become an amount

$$PV_{n+1} = PV_n(1+i)$$

If we start with amount $PV_0n = PV$, then the total accumulation of money is easily determined as

$$PV_0 = PV$$
$$PV_1 = PV_0(1+i) = PV(1+i)$$
$$PV_2 = PV_1(1+i) = PV(1+i)^2$$
$$PV_3 = PV_2(1+i) = PV(1+i)^3$$

.

.

.

$$PV_N = PV_{N-1}(1+i) = PV(1+i)^N \quad (compound\ interest)$$

or

$$FV = PV(1+i)^N \quad (compound\ interest)$$

and this is the most basic relationship in financial calculations for economic systems analysis. It turns out that almost all financial algorithms that are based on interest calculations can be obtained from this relation.

This same relation follows as an approximation to the solution to the elementary first-order differential equation for continuous compounding. If we assume that the growth rate of a quantity, $P(t)$, at time t is linearly proportional to the amount of the quantity present at time t, we have the differential equation

$$dP(t)/dt = r\ P(t)$$
$$P(t_0) = P_0$$

The solution to this differential equation is easily determined to be

$$P(t) = P_0 e^{r(t-t0)}$$

as we easily verify by substituting the solution into the differential equation. If we let $t = nT$, $t_0 = 0$, and use the first-order derivative approximation

$$dP(t)/dt = (P_{n+1}-P_n)/T$$

we see that the first-order differential becomes the first order difference equation

$$P_{n+1} = P_n(1+rT)$$

which is precisely the same as the difference equation we used to determine compound interest values. Thus we see that there is an equivalence between the discrete time accumulation of periodic interest and continuous time compounding. Further, we see that the accumulated principal does not become infinite at all when we use infinitesimally small compounding intervals. It is simply determined by the solution to the differential equation given above. Also, we see that we may use the approximate equality

$$e^{in} = (1+i)^n$$

for sufficiently small i.

A C language program for determining the amount of the interest amount one period later is easily written. As is the case throughout this chapter, we assume that the library header file, **math.h**, and the standard I O header file **stdio.h** are available for use in programs. Our program is

```
/* Future Value of a Present Quantity */
/* inter.c    determine interest */

#include <stdio.h>
#include <math.h>

main()
{
   double interest, pv, periods, fv;
   double pow();

    printf("\nenter present value, annual
       interest rate, years: ");
   scanf("%lf,%lf,%lf", &pv, &interest,
     &periods);

    printf("\n\nPresent value of %8.2lf at
     %5.2lf pc for %3.0lf years\
  yields %8.2lf\n",
       pv, interest, periods, pv * pow(1 +
         interest/100, periods));
}
```

The program in C just presented will prompt for the present value and the annual interest rate as a number, rather than as a fraction. It will then divide that number by 12 and then again by 100 to determine the true monthly interest rate. The number of periods is the number of years multiplied by 12. We make the assumption that monthly compounding of interest occurs. It is a simple matter to modify the program for other, perhaps more general, cases. Since the power function pow in Turbo C and in Microsoft C will only take doubles as arguments (along with exp, sin, log and almost all of the other math functions), all variables are doubles. Since the scanf input routine takes only floats as arguments, a temp variable of type float is introduced. Also it should be noted that we pass the address of the variable to the routine [i.e., scanf ("%f",&temp)] and not the variable itself when we read with the scanf routine. Some compilers such as Turbo C will alert you if you forget to pass the variable reference and not the address of the variable. In true C tradition, however, most of them will just let us suffer for our carelessness.

18.6.2 Present and Future Value of Regular Deposits

In many financial analysis situations, we make a number of deposits at a fixed interest rate at regular-time interval deposits over a certain number of periods. The amount of money that accumulates at the end of N periods, and just prior to any interest accumulating for that period, is the future value of the investment at that time. It is a relatively straightforward matter to show that the formula for the future value of this stream of deposits is

$$FV = PMT[(1+i)^N - 1]/i \quad (future \ value \ of \ deposits)$$

where PMT is the periodic deposit, i is the interest rate per period, and N is the number of periods. The C program is a slight modification of that just presented. We have

```
/* Future Value of Regular Deposits */
#include <stdio.h>
#include <math.h>
main()
{
    double int, md, pd, fv;
    float temp;
    printf("Monthly Deposit                : ");
    scanf("%f",&temp); md=temp;
    printf(" % Annual Interest");scanf
       ("%f",&temp);int=temp/100/12;
    printf("Number of Years of Deposits    : ");
    scanf("%f",&temp); pd=temp*12;
    fv=md*((pow(1+int,pd)-1)/int);
```

```
    printf("Future Value of Investment after
       Deposits:.2f\n",fv);
}
```

It is a simple matter to modify this program to cope with other than monthly compounding, or to determine the value of the investment at other than the time in the future when the last deposit is made. One way to do this would be to consider the future value obtained from the present program as the present value for a future value of money calculated using the first program of this section.

One such extension is to determine the present value of the deposits that will start at the present time and continue to be made N periods into the future. This is simply the last FV expression discounted back to the present. From the fundamental interest equation

$$FV = PV(1+i)^N \quad \text{(compound interest)}$$

and

$$FV = PMT[(1+i)^N-1]/i$$
$$\text{(future value of deposits)}$$

we obtain

$$PV = PMT[1-(1+i)^N]/i$$
$$\text{(present value of future deposits)}$$

It should be quite apparent that we could make this calculation through combination of the foregoing two programs. If speed is of any concern, it would be better to write one program to accomplish the task. A program in C to do this is:

```
/* Present Value of a Sequence of Future
   Deposits */
#include <stdio.h>
#include <math.h>
main()
{
    double int, md, pd, pv;
    float temp;
    printf("Monthly Deposit          : ");
    scanf("%f",&temp); md=temp;
    printf("Annual Interest : "); scanf
       ("%f",&temp); int=temp/12000;
    printf("Number of Years          : ");
    scanf("%f",&temp); pd=temp*12;
    pv=pmt*((1-pow(1+int,-pd))/int);
```

```
printf("Present Value of of Future
    Deposits : %1.2f\n",pv);
}
```

There are many cases in economic systems analysis where the future and the present value are known and either the interest rate or the number of needed monthly deposits should be calculated. If we take the natural logarithm of the present and future value equations, we obtain a simple way to do this. Developing a C language program to accomplish this is left as an exercise for the interested reader.

A major and needed extension to these results arises because the periodic (monthly) deposits to an account may not be at precisely the same level. Not only may they differ, some may actually be withdrawals. The net present value (NPV) concept generally addresses the present worth of a series of unequal cash flows. The NPV formula is easily obtained from the fundamental compound interest equation, where we use CF_n to represent the cash flow at the nth period. Figure 18.6 illustrates the nature of the calculation. We have

$$PV[n] = CF_n(1+i)^{-n}$$

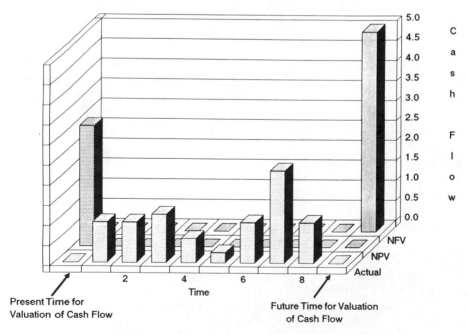

FIGURE 18.6 Present-value and future-value concepts.

as the present value of the cash flow (CF) occurring at the nth period. The total cash flow is just the sum of these over all considered periods. So we obtain

$$NPV = \sum_{n=1}^{n=N} PV[n] = \sum_{n=1}^{n=N} CF_n(1+i)^{-n}$$

A program in C to calculate net present value, NPV, follows:

```
/* Net Present Value of a Sequence of Cash
   Flows */
#include <stdio.h>
#include <math.h>
main()
{
double pv(a,int,numfl)
double a[],int; int,numfl;
    printf("Cash Flows                    : ");
    scanf("%f",&temp); CF=temp;
    printf("Annual Interest : "); scanf
      ("%f",&temp); int=temp/100/12;
    int j;
    double temp=0;
    for (j=1;j<=numfl;j++) {
     if (int==0) temp +=c[j-1];
     else temp +=(c[j-1]/pow(1+int/1200,i)); }
    return(temp);
    printf("Net Present Value of Sequence of
      Flows : %1.2f\n",fv);
}
```

It should be instructive for the reader to repeat this program for a number of interest rates and cash flows to determine the behavior of the net present value. Of particular importance is the fact that money at the present time is worth more than money at any future time for any positive interest rate. Also, as the interest rate becomes larger, the net present value becomes smaller.

18.6.3 Amortization

Amortization refers to the constant amount of money that must be paid periodically in order to reduce the future value of an amount borrowed to zero within a specified amount of time. During the initial period of payment on a mortgage, one typically pays a very small amount toward the principal and a large amount for interest due. After some time, the situation reverses and a large portion of the mortgage payment goes towards the principal.

Derivation of the equations for amortization of a mortgage is a relatively straightforward effort. The present value is just the mortgage amount. The interest rate is given, as is the number of years over which mortgage payments will be made. Thus we can easily use the equation previously obtained for present value of future equal deposits

$$PV = PMT[1-(1+i)^N]/i$$

(present value of future deposits)

and solve for the payments to obtain

$$PMT = iPV[1-(i+1)^N]^{-1}$$

The C-language program to follow will calculate the monthly payment for a given total amount financed at a fixed interest rate. It will also calculate other generally needed items including the principal balance after each payment, the amount of each payment that is applied to the principal and the amount applied to the interest. The program will prompt the user for the value of the three necessary variables, PV, i, and N. As with the other effort in this section, the i and N variables refer to the interest per period, expressed as a decimal, and the number of periods of the loan. The values requested in the program are the number of years and the interest rate per year. Monthly compounding is assumed. Our program is

```
/* Simple Mortgage Program /*
#include <stdio.h>
#include <math.h>
main ( )
{
    printf("Amount Borrowed            : ");
    scanf("%f",&temp); ab=temp;
    printf("Annual Interest : "); scanf
       ("%f",&temp); int=temp/12000;
    printf("Number of Years            : ");
    scanf("%f",&temp); pd=temp*12;
    double int,pd,pmt,intpaid,principal,
       initprin,prinpaid;
    int cpd;
    }
    pmt=ab*(int/(1-1/(pow(1+int,pd)))); cpd=0;
    principal=ab;
    intpaid=int*principal;
    prinpaid=pmt-intpaid;
    printf("Monthly Payment     :%1.2f\n",pmt);
```

```
printf("Monthly Balance Interest
  Principal\n\n");
while (cpd<=periods);
{
  printf("%3d %9.2f %7.2f %7.2f\n",
    cpd++,principal,
  intpaid,prinpaid);
  initprin=principal;
  principal=initprin-(pmt-(int*initprin));
  intpaid=int*principal;
  prinpaid=pmt-intpaid;
}
}
```

A very natural question to ask at this point is *Why should I do all of this when my favorite spreadsheet or database program will do all of this?* The answer is that the C-language program will execute much faster. That could be very important for some uses. If all we want to do is calculate a monthly mortgage payment, it would make little sense to develop these programs. On the other hand, if we are developing an information system for financial analysis, it may be very necessary to incorporate programs such as those presented in this section.

18.7 SUMMARY

This chapter is one of the longest in this book. Yet it has only scratched the surface with respect to discussing some of the many numerical analysis procedures that are currently available. We have attempted to provide a discussion of some of the more important topics and some insight into how one goes about resolving numerical mathematics problems. There is much more that could be done. We have provided a number of references to other texts that contain these discussions in the Bibliography.

PROBLEMS

1. A very common routine that is invariably found in a *math.h* library is one that calculates the exponential. The Taylor series for this is given by

$$\exp[x] = \exp[(x-x_0)+x_0] = \exp(x-x_0)\exp(x_0)$$
$$\exp[(x-x_0)] = 1 + (x-x_0) + (x-x_0)^2/2!$$
$$+ \cdots + (x-x_0)^n/n!$$

Here, x_0 is a quantity for which $\exp(x_0)$ is known. x_0 is sufficiently close to x that the series converges rapidly. Please write a brief paper outlining how you would incorporate a routine for exp[x] in a math.h library that you are preparing. Please investigate error and other properties of the configurations that you investigate.

2. Use Newton's method to write a C-language program that will extract the cube root of a real number.

3. Write a C-language program to obtain the solution to three linear algebraic equations. Evaluate the performance of your program for the example

$$x_1 + x_2 + x_3 = 6$$
$$x_1 + x_2 + 2x_3 = 9$$
$$2x_1 + x_2 + x_3 = 7$$

4. Write a C-language program to implement the systematic elimination approach to the solution of N linear algebraic equations in N unknowns.

5. Write a C-language program that will implement Lagrange's interpolation for a quadratic polynomial.

6. Derive Simpson's rule and Simpson's 3/8 rule. Be sure to indicate the truncation errors for each rule.

7. Write a C-language program to implement the algorithms in Problem 6.

8. Investigate the integration of $y(x) = sin(x)$ over the interval 0 to b for the four integration rules discussed in this chapter. Discuss the performance of the rules in terms of the sampling interval used and the integration interval, b.

9. Write a C language program to implement the predictor corrector scheme for integrating differential equations discussed in the text. Use this program to solve the differential equation

$$\frac{dy}{dx} = ax(1-x) \quad , \quad x(0) = 0.5$$

for several different values of a and sampling intervals.

10. You have the option of receiving one of the three cash flows illustrated in Figure 18.6. Use the net present value program to assist you in preparing a report, explaining which cashflow is best and why.

11. Prepare a table showing the monthly payments and total payments to service a loan of $100,000 for 10, 15, 20, 25, and 30 years at interest rates of 8%, 9%, 10%, 11%, and 12%. Does the total amount paid grow linearly with interest rate, ie. will the total amount paid to retire the mortgage grow by 25%? If you increase the interest rate by 25%. Why or why not?

19

PROBLEM SOLVING AND SYSTEMS ANALYSIS

19.0 INTRODUCTION

Our objective for this book is to study a broad and useful variety of computer systems analysis-based approaches for problem solving. Our earlier chapters were primarily concerned with describing the architecture of typical computer systems; and a presentation of C and Pascal, with primary emphasis on C, as programming tools that support the production of useful codes for problem solving. The latter chapters in the book have taken on more and more of a problem-solving orientation. We have examined some fundamentals of data structures for database management systems and numerical analysis applications. In this chapter, we will continue with this problem-solving theme. We will not be able to discuss many of these in any great depth, but we will attempt to provide the essential characteristics of several approaches, such that we will be in a much better position for continued study in more specialized areas and for appreciation and use of the many problem-solving approaches.

19.1 PROBLEM-SOLVING STRATEGIES—INTRODUCTION

To set the stage for a general discussion of problem-solving strategies, it is helpful to provide a brief overview and review of computers and programming. As we know very well by now, a computer program is a set of instructions to a computer that will enable it to solve some identified problem. The typical computer program directs the computer to start with some initial information, generally called input information, and results in the production of output information, which may be translated into physical controlling action, which represents a presumed solution to the stated problem. There are a great variety of generic computer program types. There is also something called software. At this point we will only say that a *program* is a component of *software*. Often the two terms are used interchangeably, and this very unfortunate. We will expand on the differences and similarities soon.

It is relatively common practice to distinguish between *system* programs and *application* programs, or system software and application software. Again, there are nomenclature problems. As used here, *system* does not refer to either use of system concepts or methodology to produce a result, but only programs that are basic to the functioning of a computer *system*. Thus, the term *system program* or *system software* refers to programs or software that enables a computer to *hang together correctly in order to do its thing*. For example, a program or software which functions in a way that allows coordination and control of general computer operations is called an *operating system*.

Operating systems and specific application programs must be written in languages, and these are often called computer languages. As we know, these may be of two generic types. Assembly language and machine language instructions will be understood or interpreted directly by the computer system hardware, in particular a microprocessor, without the need for interpretation or translation. Normally, it is difficult for humans to write code directly in machine language and, as a result of the need for this to be accomplished, a large variety of *high level programming languages* have been developed. We have studied C and Pascal here, but there are many other computer languages, or programming language systems.

Writing computer programs, or computer code, involves primarily the writing of detailed instructions for various parts of the computer that are to be followed exactly in execution of the program. Thus, the performance of a computer system can (rarely) be any better than that allowed by the quality of the programs that have been prepared for it. When a computer system produces an error, the error may be due to an error in programming. It could result from a hardware error, but these are much less common. Alternately, it could result from an error in problem understanding or representation; such that the computer system produces a very good solution to a problem that is not the problem of the client or user who wanted the solution in the first place. This is the one type of error that occurs most often. It is often spoken of as *an error of the third kind*. While *wrong problem errors* may be diagnosed as software systems engineering errors, they are not fundamentally programming errors. This leads to a distinction between programmer productivity efforts directed at enabling programmers to produce higher quality code that can be more easily maintained for a given cost, and efforts directed at the management of the software process—from initial identification of user requirements, to the specification of software and hardware requirements, to production of working code, to the integration of a produced new system into an existing system, to evaluating an existing system to determine the extent to which it is functional in terms of broad satisfaction of user needs.

The first programmer phase in writing a computer program is to define carefully the problem to be solved in terms of *requirements specifications* for the to-be-produced program. This task is often difficult because the specifications of the original problem may be very imperfect, perhaps containing missing elements or even contradictory statements. The software requirements specifications statement should identify the input data, the output data, and the way in which the output is to be related to the input. This is the classic input system-output model of formal systems analysis as represented in Figure 19.1.

Once a software requirements document has been prepared, the next phase is that of identification of an appropriate specific method of realizing the specifications. This phase generally involves the most creative and intellectually challenging aspect of computer programming. During this phase the computer systems analyst often identifies one or more flowcharts that will help organize thought and the specific flow of operations to be performed by the computer and data that will be stored and passed by the computer. On the basis of the flowchart, or perhaps as an input to it, the systems analyst identifies various algorithms that will be needed to implement the requirements specifications.

As they are initially furnished, requirements specifications are generally imperfect in the sense of being incomplete, or containing ambiguities and perhaps even inconsistencies. We have to be very careful with this as there is often an attempt to start coding before we have a very complete picture of what we are coding about and for. To illustrate this, we recall that we wrote a C-language program in our last chapter to find the roots of a polynomial equation $P(x) = 0$. As a specific use of this program, we could attempt to use it to *read a list of*

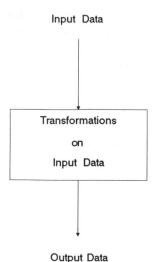

FIGURE 19.1   Simple input/output representation of system development effort.

numbers and print a table of the nth roots of the number. We already have the program, and so we might believe that we have already solved the problem.

Yet there are a number of items still unspecified. First, how do we get the list of input numbers, and how is this list of input numbers to be terminated? We really did not specify this very well at all in the last chapter. We can easily deal with any number of possible terminating approaches. We might have an end-of-line terminator, an end-of-file mark, a special terminating character such as @, or a special number such as 0. But we need to know how it is to be done. In a more general sense, we have not dealt with the person or system that will supply the input. This might be a human, in which case it would be very helpful to have some interactive dialog to elicit the input numbers. Alternately, the input numbers may come from the output of some other program.

In a similar way, we have not specified the range of input numbers for which the program should work. If we know, for example, that the input numbers must always be positive, then we need not be concerned with how to make the program behave if the input number is negative and we are trying to obtain the square root. Also, there was no statement concerning the precision needed. While Newton's algorithm, which we used in the previous chapter, is capable of infinite precision, the finite word length of the computer that we are using will prevent this. Also, there was no specification provided concerning error handling. What should we do in the event of divergence of the algorithm? How should this be detected and flagged to the user? Is it acceptable, for example, to get into an infinite loop such that the computer will have to be *rebooted* in order to get it to do anything else? Finally, we didn't really state the numeric notation used. We implied floating-point decimal, but really did not state this.

Thus we see the need for a program specification document that describes exactly what is to be done by the programming team. At a minimum, this program specification should include identification and description of program name, program structure, program function, program purpose, program input, program output, error handling protocols, and user-computer interaction details. It is important to note here that the program requirements specification describes what the program will do in great detail. *It does not describe anything about* **how** *all of this is to be done.*

While English and other *natural languages* are very useful for communicating ideas; a natural language is not altogether, especially when taken alone, suitable because of the many problems with ambiguities and uncertainties that are unresolved in natural-language statements. There are two other methods of communicating ideas, through *mathematics* and through *graphics*. All three methods of communication are important and a person, or computer, is severely handicapped if communication is not possible in all three generic types of language. This suggests that the most appropriate requirements specifications are comprised of statements in all three languages.

The *program development language* or *PDL* is a useful tool to aid in the development of operational computer programs. The requirements specifications might be viewed as a statement of a computer program at a very abstract level.

After all, the requirements specifications are statements of what the program does, or should do. At the very lowest level of abstraction, we have the program as represented by executable machine-language instructions. It is not unreasonable that there be several interfaces between the program statement at the highest level of abstraction and at the lowest. One level of abstraction is that of the programming language that is used to develop code which a programming-language compiler or run-time interpreter translates into machine-understandable symbols.

We could imagine another level of abstraction between the requirements specification and the production of high-level code. *Computer aided software engineering* tools, or *CASE tools*, are able to take input from program requirements specification and develop computer-program-related specifications. Whether CASE tools include PDLs or are a more abstract set of tools that provides input for a PDL is primarily a point of view. Perhaps the most appropriate view is that CASE tools include PDLs as a *lower-CASE* component. From this perspective, the *upper-CASE* tools would be those components of these tools that more directly interface the requirements specifications portion of the software development effort.

Figure 19.2 presents one view of these levels of abstraction in the production of executable code for problem requirements specifications. We will not be able to present details here of either PDL or CASE tools. References in the Bibliogra-

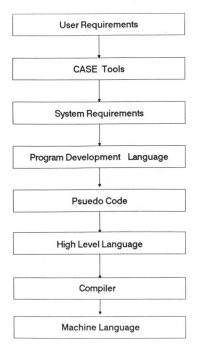

FIGURE 19.2   Some of the many possible flows from established user requirements to executable code.

phy may be consulted for discussions of these contemporary programming support tools.

In general, the development of a computer-system product or service will follow a logical pattern that can be described in terms of a number of sequenced phased activities. Figure 19.3 illustrates a typical sequence of phases. In effect, we have described a system design methodology that consists of seven phases:

1. Requirements specifications identification.
2. Preliminary conceptual design.
3. Logical design and system architecture specification.
4. Detailed design and testing.
5. Operational implementation.
6. Evaluation and modification.
7. Operational deployment.

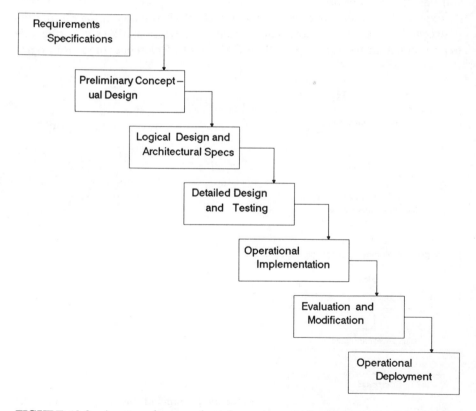

FIGURE 19.3   A seven-phase version of a systems engineering approach to development.

These are sequenced in an iterative manner, as shown in Figure 19.3. The overall systems process is structured as in Figure 19.4, which illustrates an expansion into a number of steps and phases and which accommodates our identified framework for systems methodology. This assumes that within each of the phases we will accomplish formulation, analysis, and interpretation of the problem viewed from the perspective of that phase. This three-step model of activity within each phase is just what we have identified earlier in Figure 19.1. This particular seven-phase systems engineering activity is, in no way, the *unique* set of phases that can be associated with the software life cycle. Figure 19.5, for example, illustrates a slightly different version of these phases.

The requirements-specifications phase of our system design-methodology has as its goal the identification of client needs, activities, and objectives to be achieved by implementation of the resulting design as a product, process, or system. The effort in this phase should result in the identification and description of preliminary conceptual design considerations that are appropriate for the next phase. It is important to note that it is necessary to translate operational deployment needs into requirements specifications in order that these needs be addressed by the system-design efforts. Thus we see that information requirements specifications are affected by, and affect, each of the other design phases of the systemic framework for design.

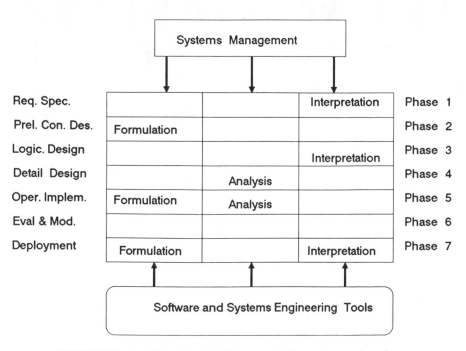

FIGURE 19.4 Methodological framework for system engineering.

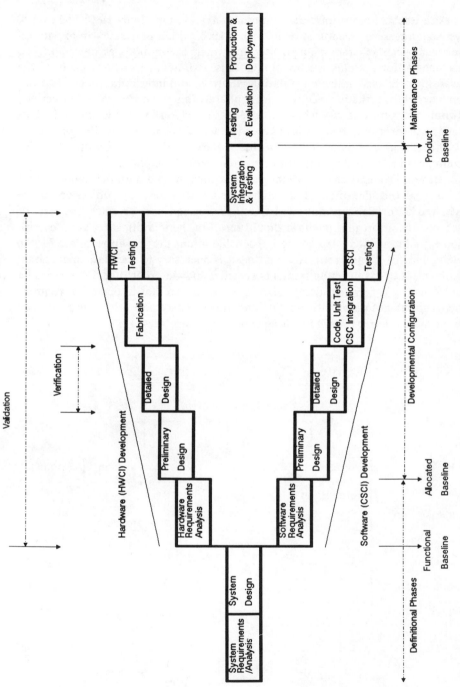

FIGURE 19.5 A phased model of the life cycle of system development.

As a result of the requirements-specifications phase, there should exist a clear definition of design issues such that it becomes possible to make a decision concerning whether to undertake preliminary conceptual design. We see that essentially two primary needs are addressed here. The first is the identification of client or user needs. These are the *user's requirements specifications*. The second is the identification of *program requirements specifications* for the detailed design effort to follow. Figure 19.6 presents a conceptual picture of the transition from user to system requirements.

If the result of *(either portion of)* the requirements-specifications effort indicates that client needs can be met in a functionally satisfactory manner, then documentation is typically prepared concerning specifications for the preliminary conceptual design phase. Initial specifications for the following three phases of effort are typically also prepared and a concept design team is selected to implement the next phase of the design effort.

Preliminary conceptual design typically includes or results in a next-phase effort which leads to specification of the content and associated architecture and general algorithms for the product, process, or system that should result from this effort. The primary goal of this phase is to develop conceptualization of a prototype that is responsive to the requirements identified in the previous phase. Preliminary concept design according to the requirements specifications should be obtained. The desired product of this phase of problem-solving activity is a set of detailed design and architectural specifications that should result in a useful product, process, or system, and the result of the prototype design. There should exist a sufficiently high degree of user confidence that a useful product will result from the problem solving activity, or the entire effort should be redone or possi-

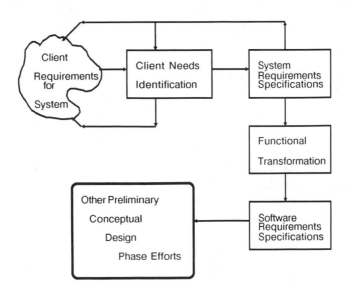

FIGURE 19.6   Transitioning between system development phases.

bly abandoned. Another product of this phase is a refined set of specifications for the evaluation and operational deployment phases of the problem-solving process. In the third phase of effort, these are translated into detailed representations in logical form such that system development may occur. A product, process, or system is produced in the fourth phase of effort. This is not the final solution, but rather the result of implementation of the design that resulted from the conceptual design effort of the last phase. User guides for the product should be produced such that realistic operational tests and evaluations can be conducted.

Evaluation of the design and the resulting product, process, or system is achieved in the sixth phase of the problem-solving process. Preliminary evaluation criteria are obtained as a part of requirements specifications and modified during the following two phases of the design effort. The evaluation effort must be adapted to other phases of the design effort such that it becomes an integral and functional part of the overall design process. Generally, the critical issues for evaluation are adaptations of the elements present in the requirements-specifications phase of the design process. A set of specific evaluation test requirements and tests are evolved from the objectives and needs determined in requirements specifications. These should be such that each objective measure and critical evaluation issue component can be measured from at least one evaluation test instrument.

There are many ways in which we might describe the phases of the life cycle of system effort that result in a product or service. Figure 19.5 illustrates one view of the life cycle of computer system development. This is closely patterned after the U.S. Department of Defense Standard 2167A for software production. It imbeds the notions of programmer productivity that we have been discussing here within concerns for software productivity. Even so, there is more to be done to insure large-scale and scope productivity of a system development project. At the front end are many concerns relative to capturing meaningful problems from the client for, or user of, the system to be developed. At the other end are needs associated with system integration and transitioning to new environments. Figure 19.6 presents some needs relative to these issues.

After a program has been coded, it must be tested to see that it is correct in the sense of satisfaction of the requirements specifications. This is known as software *validation*. Another commonly used term is software *verification*. Essentially, this refers to the effort required to insure that the result produced at the end of any phase of life cycle development is in accordance with the output of the phase that proceeded it. Figure 19.5 illustrates both the validation and verification notion.

Coding errors can slip into a program in a number of ways. They may occur because of an incomplete statement of the problem requirements specifications, such as not noting that special error-handling techniques would be needed to cope with the input requirement to take the square root of a negative number. Errors may also result from a misunderstanding of the constructs of the assembly or high- level programming language that is used to produce code. Errors can result from a careless mistake, and careless mistakes can be encouraged by poor programming practices such as including many unstructured GOTOs in program code. Alternately, we may have a fundamental error in the algorithm that we use as a basis for code implementation.

The process of testing programs, in terms of diagnosis or finding errors, detecting the causes for the errors, and correcting them, is called *debugging*. Debugging often takes a very large fraction of program development time. Yet debugging is only a small part of verification and validation. Figure 19.7 presents a distribution of costs and effort across the life cycle of a typical software effort. It shows that major costs are incurred in the latter portions of the effort. Yet it is the initial portions that determine whether the correct problem, in terms of user needs, has been identified.

The most important user-oriented criterion for judging a system-development effort is the evaluation of whether or not it produces correct results. We should explicitly note here that *correct* is a relative term and not generally an absolute one. In the broadest possible sense, correctfulness includes usability. If the user cannot, for any of a variety of reasons, use a system the system is not correct.

Another computer performance criterion is program efficiency. Running a program on a computer requires two resources: computing time and storage requirements for program and data. An efficient program should generally use no

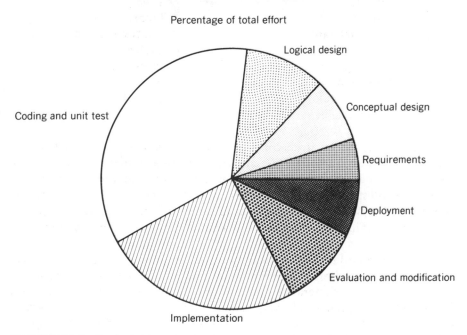

Conventional effort consumption

Percentage of total effort

Logical design

Conceptual design

Coding and unit test

Requirements

Deployment

Evaluation and modification

Implementation

FIGURE 19.7   Typical effort distribution across the phases of software systems design.

more computer time or storage space than necessary. This consideration is of major importance in those situations where computer equipment is expensive or where rapid performance is needed, such as in real-time systems. In many cases, there is a trade-off between execution time and storage resources. Usually, improvements in program execution time occur at the expense of increased storage requirements.

There are many other attributes that contribute to software productivity. Some of them are:

Acceptable	Manageable
Accessible	Modifiable
Accountable	Modular
Accurate	Operable
Adaptable	Portable
Appropriate	Precise
Assurable	Reliable
Available	Repairable
Clear	Reusable
Complete	Robust
Consistent	Secure
Correct	Self-contained
Documentable	Survivable
Documented	Testable
Effective	Timely
Efficient	Transferable
Error-tolerant	Understandable
Expandable	Usable
Flexible	User-friendly
Generalizable	Valid
Interoperable	Verifiable
Maintainable	

An important goal in efforts concerning metrics for software and system productivity is to develop attribute measures for performance features such as those just listed so that we can meaningfully evaluate software and system performance. We will structure these and other attributes such as to obtain a hierarchy of performance measures that enable us to determine the capability of a specific software product in terms of operational functionality, transition capability, and revisability.

If it is determined that the software product, process, or system cannot meet user needs, perhaps through an operational evaluation, the systemic design process for software reverts iteratively back to an earlier phase and effort continues. An important by-product of evaluation is determination of ultimate performance limitations for an operationally realizable system and identification of those protocols and procedures for use of the result of the design effort that enable maximum user satisfaction. Often, operational evaluation is the only realistic way to establish meaningful information concerning functional effectiveness of the result of a design effort. Successful evaluation is dependent upon explicit development of a plan for evaluation developed before initiation of the evaluation effort.

The last phase of a system design effort concerns final acceptance and operational deployment. This description of design methodology contains a strong process flavor. For our purposes, a process is the integration of a methodology with the behavioral concerns of human judgment in a realistic operational environment. Our description of systems design in this section has emphasized the methodological concerns and, perhaps to a lesser extent, operational environment concerns. The goal in all of this is to produce software, and systems and processes which incorporate software, that *measure up to high standards*.

19.2   PROBLEM-SOLVING STRATEGIES—SYSTEMS ENGINEERING

Generally, a problem is presented in what is often called a *problem statement*. This defines the problem and states the objective that is to be achieved in the problem solution. We prefer the use of the term *issue formulation*, which has the potential advantage of making it explicitly clear that there is purposeful human effort involved in doing this.

Regardless of the way in which the problem solving process is characterized, and regardless of the type of process or system that is being designed, all characterizations will necessarily involve:

1. *Formulation of the issue*—in which the needs and objectives of a client group are identified, and potentially acceptable issue alternatives, or options, are identified or generated.
2. *Analysis of the alternative designs*—in which the impacts of the identified options are evaluated.
3. *Interpretation and selection*—in which the options are compared by means of an evaluation of the impacts of the problem solving alternatives. The needs and objectives of the client group are used as a basis for evaluation. The most acceptable alternative is selected for implementation or further study in a subsequent phase of design.

Our model of the steps of the fine structure of the systems process, shown in Figure 19.8, is based upon this conceptualization. As we have indicated here, these three steps can be disaggregated into a number of others. Without question, this is a formal rational model of the way in which problem solving is accomplished. Even within this formal framework, there is the need for much iteration from one step back to an earlier step when it is discovered that improvements in the results of an earlier step are needed in order to obtain a

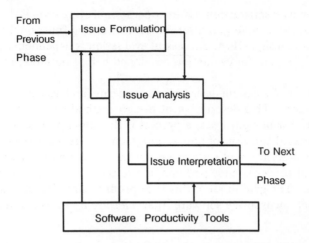

FIGURE 19.8   The three fundamental fine-grain steps of problem solution.

quality result at a later step of the design effort. Also, this description does not emphasize the key role of information and information requirements determination, which is concentrated in the formulation step, but which exists throughout all steps of the problem-solving process.

More importantly, this morphological framework, in terms of phases of the design process and steps within these phases, does not emphasize the different types of information and different types of support that are needed within each step at the various phases. During the issue-formulation step, the support that is needed tends to be of an affective, perceptive, or gestalt nature. Intuition-based experiential wisdom will play a most important role in this. During the analysis step, the need is typically for quantitative and algorithmic support, typically through use of one of the formal methods for programmer productivity enhancement. In the interpretation step, the needed effort shifts to a blend of the perceptive and the analytical.

Within each of our seven phases of software systems engineering, there will generally be a number of steps. The most economic characterization of these involves, as we have already noted, three activities: issue *formulation, analysis* of proposed solutions, and *interpretation* of these solutions in terms of objectives for the task at hand such as to enable evaluation and selection of a proposed alternative. Each of the steps of the fine structure of software systems engineering is repeated at each of the phases in the software life cycle. In the accompanying figure, some of the typical activities that are associated with each step of the seven- step structure are shown. The precise nature of the activities will be very much a function of system design activity, however. Nevertheless, we believe that the three- or seven-step characterization of the design process is ubiquitous across the seven phases of design and acquisition of general and imbedded system software. It is primarily the specific activities within each step, and particularly the time that is required to accomplish them, that varies across corresponding steps within the seven-phase software (system) design and acquisition process. For example, Figure 19.9 illustrates how this disaggregation might proceed for the logical design- and system- architecture-specification phase of the software life cycle.

Through the process of associating the formal steps of problem solving we obtain a morphological box for software systems engineering, as we have already discussed illustrated in Figure 19.4. We have just identified a number of activities, illustrated in very general terms in Figure 19.4, whose accomplishment should do much to result in the design of trustworthy software. To determine the specific activities to be accomplished within each of these boxes is one of the major methodological concerns in software systems engineering. It is important to note that there is intended to be iteration and feedback from later to earlier stages when deficiencies are observed. The process envisioned is not a linear sequential process, and the flow of activities is cornucopia like, within the steps of each phase as well as within the phases themselves. There is, at least normatively, much iteration and feedback among the steps and phases of the life cycle of computer software development.

19.3 EXAMPLES OF THE SYSTEMS APPROACH: SEVERAL WELL-KNOWN PROBLEMS

The advantages of this approach are easily cited through reference to a specific example. Suppose that we are presently in Los Angeles and wish to visit a friend

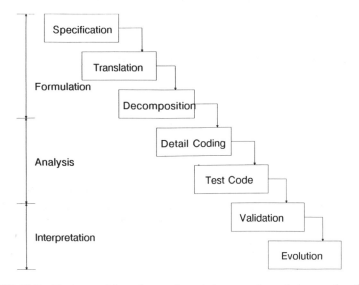

FIGURE 19.9 Decomposition of one phase into a number of steps and activities.

in Manchester, England. Several approaches to problem solution pose themselves. Almost intuitively, we would first look at ways to fly to England, most probably to London. From there, we would probably look at a convenient way to fly or catch a train to Manchester where we would, very likely for the first time, look at a detailed map of streets to find the location of our friend. We would probably never even think of the alternative to request street maps of the world and then begin to look for our friend's home.

Let us consider another similiar problem. Suppose that we agree to accept $36.52 for an item that we wish to sell, and the purchaser gives us a $100 bill. We subtract these two numbers and realize that we owe the person $63.48 in change. Most of us would sense that we should give the purchaser the maximum number of $20 bills, three in fact, to reduce the amount of money then owed to $3.48. Then we would return three $1 bills such that we would owe $0.48. Although what we do from this point forward might differ a bit from person to person, we might well give the person a quarter, two dimes, and three pennies. The amount that we owe in return for the $100 is then reduced to zero and the transaction is complete.

It is interesting to conjecture how we might instruct a computer to go about this solution process. First, we might say that we owe an amount A and that the largest valued single piece of money that is smaller than A is B. The solution algorithm is simply stated in *pseudocode* of an undefined but easily understandable nature:

```
/* Program to Solve P(A) */
if A = 0;
   then do nothing
   report that problem is solved with no
     additional money
return
else
   choose max B≤A /* as we have just
     described */
   pay B
   solve A-B
   replace original A with A-B
   return
end
```

What we see here is a very simple example of a *recursive* problem solution. There are instances in which recursion is extremely useful in problem solving, and other cases where it is not especially useful. Without question, recursion is one of the most valuable of tools problem solving. We have, in fact, used it several times in our efforts to this point, although we have not explicitly discussed the subject.

Recursion is, simply stated, a function that calls itself. It must therefore occur in a loop which must have a way of terminating. Figure 19.10 presents several

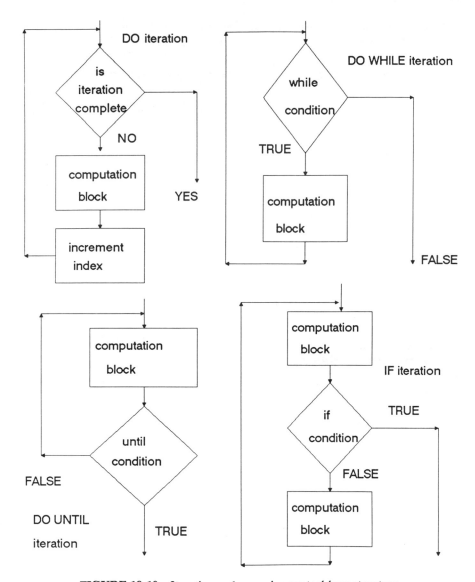

FIGURE 19.10   Iterative and recursive control loop structure.

types of control structures which may be used for recursion. There must be three fundamental components to a recursive relation:

1. some sort of test to determine whether or not the problem is simple enough for a direct, non-recursive, solution;
2. a solution algorithm for the problem posed; and
3. a termination condition that will cause to branch from the recursive loop when the solution is complete.

Probably the most often-used recursive relation is the factorial function M! which we have previously used, but not defined. It is defined by

$$M! = M(M-1)! \qquad \text{for } M \geq 1, \quad 0! = 1$$

Another well-known recursive relation is that which defines the Fibonacci numbers. This is

$$F_N = F_{N-1} + F_{N-2} \qquad \text{for } N \geq 2, \quad F0 = F1 = 1$$
$$F_N = 1, 1, 2, 3, 5, 8, 13, 21, 34, 55, \quad \ldots$$

A very simple, actually trivial, recursive program in C is given by

```
/* counter.c   recursive countdown */
main()
{
  int index;

  index = 6;
  count_dn(index);
}
count_dn(count)
  int count;
{
  count--;
  printf("\nThe value of our count is now %d",
    count);
  if (count > 0)
    count_dn(count);
  printf("\nNow our count is %d", count);
}
```

In this program the variable *index* is initially set equal to 6. It is used as the argument to the function *count_dn*. The function acts only to decrement the variable. It also prints it out in a message. If the variable is not zero, it calls itself, and then decrements itself again. Finally, the variable will reach zero, and the function will not call itself again since the count is now not greater than zero. Instead, it will return to the main program and then to DOS. We could have obtained precisely the same operations by having six copies of the function "count_dn" available and then calling all of them, one at a time in sequence.

This is not what really happens of course, although it is a reasonable analogy. When we called the function from itself, all of the variables and all of the internal flags needed to complete the function were stored in a block somewhere. The next time the function calls itself, it performs the same operations. It creates and stores another block of everything it needs to complete that function call. The program continues making these blocks and storing them away until it reaches the last function. At that point, the program starts retrieving the blocks of data. It uses them to complete each function call. As we recall from earlier discussions, the blocks are actually stored on a part of the microprocessor that is called the *stack*. This is a part of memory carefully organized to store data for housekeeping efforts, such as those described.

We may use indirect recursion as well as the direct recursion that we have just described. Indirect recursion occurs when a function A calls the function B, which in turn calls A, which in turn calls B, and so on. Also, there is no reason to not have three functions calling each other in a circle, or four, or more. At some point, however, something must go to zero, or reach some other predefined number in order to terminate the recursive loop. If this does not occur, we will have an infinite loop. This may cause the program to continue on forever. More likely, however, the stack will fill up and overflow, and the resulting error will stop the machine. Needless to say, this is not a pleasant way to end a long evening's computations.

A rather interesting use of recursion is in implementation of the *Tower of Hanoi* program. This is a relatively straightfoward game in which there is a platform with three needles and a number, often variable from problem to problem, of disks. Each disk has a different diameter and all of the disks are stacked in order from the smallest diameter on top to the largest diameter on the bottom. The object of the game is to move the stack of disks from the left-most tower to the right-most tower in precisely the same smallest-on-top to largest-on-bottom orientation. The constraints affecting movement of the disks are that only one disk may be moved at a time, and at no time may a larger disk rest on top of a smaller disk. Figure 19.11 presents a picture of the initial and goal states for this problem.

The solution to the Tower of Hanoi may be developed as an iterative, or a recursive solution. The iterative solution is of a much more brute force nature than the recursive solution. Let us look at it first. Figure 19.12 represents the complete problem space for the Tower of Hanoi problem for the case of three disks. Clearly, this would become an impossible picture to draw if there were 64 disks, as there were in the initial version of the problem. Given Figure 19.12, or its equivalent as a computer representation, we could easily go about locating where we are, in the lower left-hand corner of the problem space triangle, and where we want to be, which is the lower right corner of the problem-solving triangle. By inspection of this directed graph equivalent, we can determine the minimum number of possible moves to go from the start to the end state. It is clearly seven. There are many applications for graph theory in computer-based problem solving. It is a very important tool for the solution of realistic problems. The *traveling salesman* problem is a very famous one that has been approached using graph theory constructs.

A recursive solution to this problem is generally more efficient, especially for

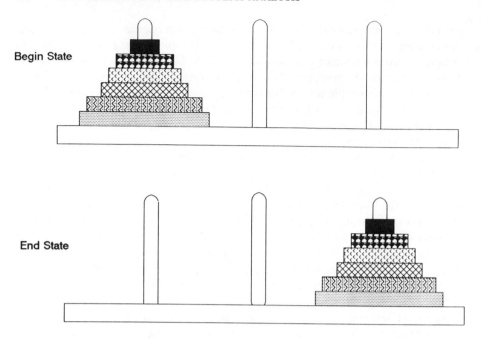

Begin State

End State

FIGURE 19.11 Tower of Hanoi problem.

a very large stack of disks. The iterative solution to the problem is obtained essentially by drawing all possible paths and then choosing the one that is best, or at least that works. Obtaining a recursive solution is very dependent upon being able to *see* the nature of the recursion that is going to work. Actually, we can guess this from the iterative solution, or through the very creative artifice of regarding all but the largest disk as a single new equivalent disk. Then we need to develop the solution for the two disk problem. This is very simple indeed, as shown in Figure 19.13. Just because we visualize this solution for the two disk problem does not mean that we can solve the bigger problem this way. A little thought however indicates that we can and must be able to do things this way in that the problem of moving the stack of N-1 disks to the middle needle is needed. To do this, we need to be able to move N-2 disks to the right most needle, and so forth on down to the case where we only move a single disk.

Solution to the Tower of Hanoi problem by recursive techniques involves three steps with the disk aggregation shown in Figure 19.13. We will use the terminology, actually a procedure call `move(N,a,b,c)` to denote moving N disks from needle a to needle b, using c for storage of other disks. The three steps from initial to goal state shown in Figure 19.13 are just

1. `move(N-1,1,2,3)`
2. `move(1,1,3, )`
3. `move(N-1,2,3,1)`

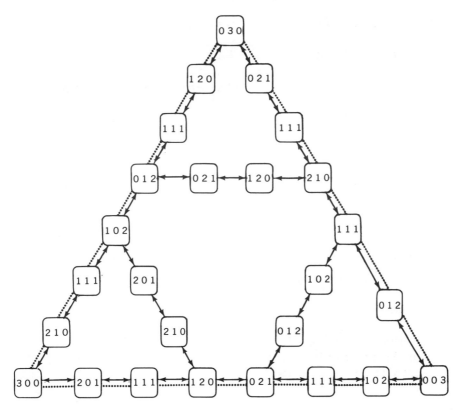

FIGURE 19.12 A complete enumeration of the problem space. (a,b,c) = Number of disks on needles (left, center, right).

To obtain the general recursive solution, we first specify the needle that we will use to store the disk pile that contains all of the disks except the largest. For example, in order to move the largest disk from needle 1 to needle 3, all of the other disks must be on needle 2. So, we really need to associate four parameters with the move procedure call: the number of disks to move, the initial state, the final state, and the temporary needle (if any) used for storage.

A C-language program that will resolve the Tower of Hanoi problem is relatively simple. One such recursive program is:

```
/*   hanoi.c   Tower of Hanoi problem recursive
   solution   */
int moves = 0;
main(argc, argv)
   int argc;
   char *argv[];
{
```

```
  int total, from, to, using;

  if (argc != 5)
  {
    printf("\nusage: hanoi number from to
      using\n");
    exit(1);
  }
  total = atoi(argv[1]);
  from = *argv[2] - 0x30;
  to   = *argv[3] - 0x30;
  using= *argv[4] - 0x30;
  move(total, from, to, using);
  printf("\n\ntotal moves = %d\n", moves);
}
move(n, f, t, u)
  int n, f, t, u;
{
  if (n > 0)
  {
    move (n - 1, f, u, t);
    printf("\n %d -> %d", f, t);
    moves++;
    move (n - 1, u, t, f);
  }
}
```

Much more complicated programs than this could be written. Most of the extra code is used for housekeeping chores and to implement a nice graphics display. Turbo C, for example, contains a relatively sophisticated implementation, with the source code for the problem on the Turbo C distribution disk.

As we have noted in Chapter 17, the most fundamental data structure is the *array*. Arrays are defined as primitives in almost all programming languages. They represent a fixed number of data items which are stored consecutively and which are accessible through use of an appropriate index. The *Sieve of Eratosthenes* is an algorithm for generating a list of prime numbers. There are several ways in which this could be done. A prime number is a positive number that cannot be divided by any number than itself and one. One of the problems in this chapter will present a simple Pascal program to calculate the prime numbers. Here we take a somewhat more efficient approach that first generates a set of candidate prime numbers by using the relation

```
    prime = 2i + 3        for i =0,1,2,3,4,5,...
```

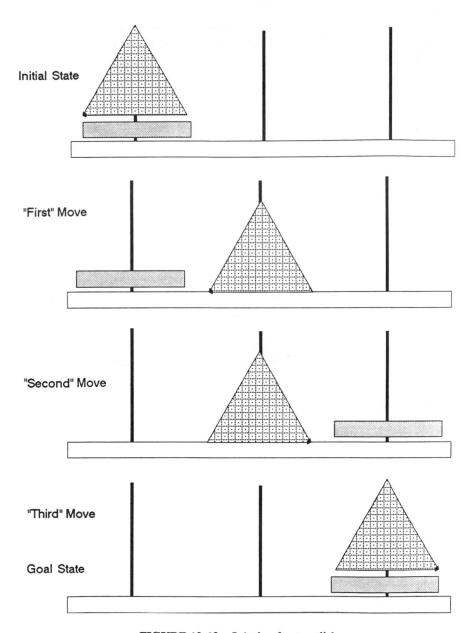

Initial State

"First" Move

"Second" Move

"Third" Move

Goal State

FIGURE 19.13   Solution for two disks.

Ultimately, this relation will generate nonprime numbers, as they will be numbers that will be devisable by 3. Thus the first odd multiple is 3 * prime, which has index j such that

$$3 \text{ prime} = 2j + 3 \tag{1}$$

The next problem will be 5 prime $= 2k + 3$. To obtain a list of the nonprime numbers in this, we rewrite eq. (1) as

$$3(2i + 3) = 2j + 3$$
$$j = (6i + 6)/2 = 3i + 3 = 2i + 3 + i = \text{prime} + i$$

Consequently, the next index, k goes with 5 prime as

$$5(2i + 3) = 2k + 3$$
$$k = (10i + 12)/2 = 5i + 6 = i + 2(2i + 3) = 2 \text{ prime} + i$$

We can sketch the intersection of these numbers, and this will allow us to visualize the numbers that are not prime numbers. Figure 19.14 indicates the reasoning involved.

The C-language program to implement this algorithm is:

```
/* Sieve of Eratosthenes   */

#include <stdio.h>
#define TRUE 1
#define FALSE 0
#define SIZE 8190
#define SIZEPL 8191
char flags[SIZEPL];
int i, prime, k, count, iter;
main(argc, argv)
   int argc;
   char *argv[];
{
   int list = FALSE;
   if (argc > 1)
     if (argv[1][0] == '-')
       if (argv[1][1] == 'l')
          list = TRUE;
```

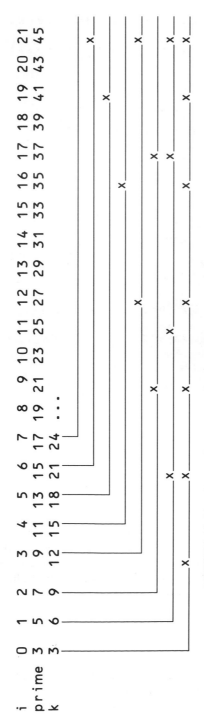

FIGURE 19.14 Illustrative computation numbers along prime row without x are prime numbers.

```
printf("Hit return to do 10 iterations");
getchar();
for (iter = 1; iter <= 10; iter++)
{
   count = 0;
   for (i = 0; i <= SIZE; i++)
     flags[i] = TRUE;
   for (i = 0; i <= SIZE; i++)
   {
      if (flags[i])
      {
        prime = i + i + 3;
        if (list == TRUE && iter == 10)
        {
          printf("%7d", prime);
          if ((count + 1) % 10 == 0)
            puts("");
        }
        k = i + prime;

        while (k <= SIZE)
        {
          flags[k] = FALSE;
          k += prime;
        }
        count++;
      }
   }
}
   printf("\7\n%d primes.\n", count);
}
```

The algorithm just delineated is typical of those that exploit the fact that an item of an array can be efficiently addressed. Using a linked list instead of an array here would be a very poor choice, as we would then be unable to get from any (array) position to any other quickly. Thus we see that choice of solution algorithm can be very important indeed.

19.4 CONCLUSIONS

We believe that a potential advantage to the morphological box sketched here in Figure 19.4 is that each of the steps of the fine structure of the process have the same name across all of the phases. As we have previously discussed, the specific activities to be accomplished within each cell of this morphological box depend upon the specific phase of effort being undertaken. However, it also is very much a function of the overall task to be accomplished, the environment into which this task is imbedded, and the experiential familiarity of the user group and the systems engineering group with the task and the environment.

One of the fundamental consequences of application of the systems, or scientific, process to various problem-solving endeavors is that large problems are decomposed, or disaggregated, into a sequence of smaller problems. The implicit belief in this is that somehow it will be easier to solve the smaller problems, *and to reaggregate the solution to these such that we obtain the solution to the initial large problem,* than it will be to directly solve the larger problem. This idea is a very fundamental one in all of science and engineering, and perhaps a fitting one with which to close our discussions.

PROBLEMS

1. The following is suggested as a Pascal program to obtain a recursive solution to the Tower of Hanoi problem:

```pascal
program HanoTower (input,output);
   var
      numdisk : integer;
   procedure move (N,a,c,b:integer);
      begin
         if N>0
            then
               begin
                  move(N-1,a,b,c);
                  writeln('Move from a to c);
                  move(N-1,b,c,a)
               end
      end
begin
   read (numdisks);
   move (numdisks,1,2,3)
end.
```

Polish this program such that the structure is more indicative of the information flow. Correct any errors that you find and improve the logic. Contrast and compare the Pascal solution with the C solution. How does the execution time differ between the two programs?

2. A simple Pascal program to determine the prime numbers for the Sieve of Eratosthenes is

```pascal
program primenumber (input,output)
const N=5000;
```

```
var a : array[1..N] of boolean;
   i,j : integer;
begin
a[i]:=false, for i:=2 to N do a[i]:=true
for i:= 2 to N div 2 do
   for j:=2 to N div i do a[i*j]:=false;
for i:1 to N do
   if a[i] then write (i:4);
end.
```

Polish this program such that the structure is more indicative of the information flow. Correct any errors that you find and improve the logic. Contrast and compare the Pascal solution with the C solution. How does the execution time differ between the two programs?

3. Write a *complete* problem description and propose a systemic solution to the Tower of Hanoi problem using the system development approach outlined in Section 19.2.

BIBLIOGRAPHY

We have not supplied many references in our discussions in this text. This is primarily because of the introductory nature of our work as well as the fact that most of our discussions are relatively self-contained. In almost every case there has been much more said about a given topic that we can possibly say here. This is simply an annotated bibliography of some of the fundamental works relevant to our efforts in this text. This serves both to acknowledge the intellectual debt that we have to others in the field as well as to suggest sources of additional material.

Aho, A. V., J. Hopcroft, and J. Ullman. *Data Structures and Algorithms*, Reading, MA: Addison-Wesley, 1982.
This well-written book provides a near classic introduction to the very important subject of data structures and related algorithms.

AT&T UNIX (System 5 Release 3.0). *UNIX System User's Manual (Release 5.0)*. Murray Hill, NJ: AT&T Bell Laboratories, 1987.
This reference work is a standard for use of the UNIX operating system. We have not emphasized UNIX in our efforts, as there is generally limited present availability of this operating system for 8088-, 80286-, and 80386-based machines. UNIX and C are very closely associated as much of the operating system was written, in a bootstrapping-like manner, in C.

Burks, A. R. and A. W. Burks. *The First Electronic Computer: The Atanasoff Story*. Ann Arbor, MI: University of Michigan Press, 1988.
This book provides an excellent historical overview of the development of what many consider to be the first digital computer.

Caldwell, S. H. *Switching Circuits and Logical Design*. New York: Wiley, 1958.
This is a seminal classic work on the theory of switching circuits.

Dahl, O. J., E. W. Dijkstra and C. A. R. Hoare. *Structured Programming*. New York: Academic, 1972.
This is a first and classic textbook reference to the use of structure in programming languages.

Dijkstra, E. W. GoTo Statement Considered Harmful. *CACM*, **VII** (March), 147–148, 1968.
This classic work presents the authors view on potential and real programming difficulties that result from undisciplined use of GoTo-type absolute address statements. These are essential at assembly and machine levels, but are normally best avoided in high level languages.

Evans, Jr., A. A Comparison of Programming Languages: Ada, Pascal, C. In *Comparing and Assessing Programming Languages*, Englewood Cliffs, NJ: A. Feuer and N. Gehani (eds). Prentice-Hall, 1984.
This chapter in an edited work provides a very useful comparative overview of the

advantages and disadvantages of the two programming languages we emphasize in this book, C and Pascal, and a Pascal-like language—Ada.

Feuer, A. and N. Gehani. A Comparison of the Programming Languages C and Pascal. *ACM Computing Surveys*, **14**, (1) 73–92, March 1982.
An overview of the edited book noted next, which also contains this paper.

Feuer, A. and N. Gehani (Eds.). *Comparing and Assessing Programming Languages*. Englewood Cliffs, NJ: Prentice-Hall, 1984.
This book has a good overview and comparison of programmning languages.

Feibel, W. *Using Quick C*. New York: Osborne McGraw-Hill, 1988.
This is a very readable introduction to the Microsoft Quick C and Microsoft C compilers.

Freeman, P., *Software Perspectives*. Reading MA: Addison-Wesley, 1987.
An interesting, somewhat philosophical overview of problem solving and software engineering. For the most part, it is written from a systems engineering perspective.

Gehani, N. *C for Personal Computers*. Rockville, MD: Computer Science Press, 1985.
This is a close to users-guide-type presentation of details concerning the Lattice C compiler and the Microsoft C compiler.

Grogono, P. *Programming in Pascal*. Reading, MA: Addison-Wesley, 1978.
This is a near classic and very readible book concerning structured programming in Pascal. It also contains a number of very useful discussions concerning computer problem solving in general.

Grogono, P. and S. H. Nelson. *Problem Solving and Computer Programming*. Reading, MA: Addison-Wesley, 1982.
This very well-written and generally easy to read book provides much useful discussion concerning problem-solving strategies.

Hamming, R. W. *Numerical Methods for Scientists and Engineers*. (2nd ed.). New York: McGraw-Hill, 1962.
This represents one of the classic works in the important computer science and engineering subject of numerical analysis.

Hancock, L. and M. Krieger. *The C Primer*. New York: McGraw-Hill, 1982.
A useful introductory treatment of the C programming language.

Harbison, S. P. and G. L. Steele, Jr., *A C Reference Manual*. Englewood Cliffs, NJ: Prentice-Hall, 1984.
This is a useful and relatively complete reference guide for the C programming language.

Hoare, C. A. R. Quicksort. *Computer Jl.*, **5** (1) 10–15, 1962.
This classic paper discusses the then-new quicksort algorithm that we have also developed here.

Hoare, C. A. R. and N. Wirth. An Axiomatic Definition of the Programming Language Pascal. *Acta Informatica*, **2** 335–355, 1973.
This represents one of the first published descriptions, from an axiomatic perspective, of the Pascal programming language.

Johnson, L. W. and R. D. Riess. *Numerical Analysis*, 2nd ed. Reading, MA: Addison-Wesley, 1982.
One of the standard numerical analysis textbooks.

Keister, W., A. E. Richie, and A. Washburn. *Electronic Switching Systems*. New York: Van Nostrand, 1951.
This is a very interesting classic work on electronic switching circuits, primarily for telephone switching systems. It provides some valuable historical insignt into this area.

Kelly, A. and I. Pohl. *A Book on C*. Menlo Park, CA: Benjamin Cummings Publishing Co., 1984.
Here is another useful introduction to details of the C programming language.

Kempf, J. *Numerical Software Tools in C*. Englewood Cliffs, NJ: Prentice Hall, 1987.
This is one of the few numerical methods books written for the C programming language. It is very worthwhile reading.

Kernighan, B. W. and P. J. Plauger. *The Elements of Programming Style*. New York: McGraw-Hill, 1974.
Here is another classic concerning structured programming and a systems approach to computer problem solving.

Kernighan, B. W. and P. J. Plaugher. *Software Tools*. Reading, MA: Addison-Wesley, 1976.
This classic book is a precursor of what has now become known as software engineering.

Kernighan, B. W. and P. J. Plaugher. *Software Tools in Pascal*. Reading, MA: Addison-Wesley, 1981.
This is, more or less, an adaption to the previously noted book on the Pascal programming language.

Kernighan, B. W. and D. M. Ritchie. *The C Programming Language*. 1st ed., 1978; 2nd ed., 1988. Englewood Cliffs, NJ: Prentice-Hall.
The first edition of this book represents the first widely published definition of the C programming language. The second edition of the book contains a discussion of the proposed *ANSI Standard for C*. Both editions are currently available, as there is no adopted standard for the language and many existing compilers do not follow the proposed standard.

Kernighan, B. W. and R. Pike. *The UNIX Programming Environment*. Englewood Cliffs, NJ: Prentice-Hall, 1984.
This new classic work is especially good relative to its interface to programming system developers.

Knuth, D. E. *The Art of Computer Programming: Vol. 1, Fundamental Algorithms, 1973; Vol. 2, Seminumerical Algorithms, 1981; Vol. 3, Sorting and Searching*. Reading, MA: Addison Wesley, 1983.
These three volumes represent one of the most definitive and referenced treatments of fundamental algorithms useful for computer science.

Langsam, Y., M. J. Augenstein, and A. M. Tenenbaum. *Data Structures for Personal Computers*. Englewood Cliffs, NJ: Prentice Hall 1985.
This introductory book demonstrates the use of structured Basic for the development of various data structure algorithms. Despite common wisdon in many computer science circles, it is quite possible to write effective and efficient programs in Basic, and this book discusses how to do this.

McGettrick, A. D. and P. D. Smith. *Graded Problems in Computer Science*. Reading, MA: Addison-Wesley, 1983.
A useful collection of problem solutions and problem solution strategies.

Microsoft C. *Microsoft C Compiler Reference Manual* (for 8086 and 8088 Microprocessors and the MS-DOS Operating System), Redmond, WA: 1984.
The documentation for the Microsoft C compiler is generally good and is recommended as one place to start in becoming familiar with this language.

Pollack, L. and B. J. Cummings. *Programming in C on the IBM PC*. Englewood Cliffs, NJ: Prentice-Hall, 1984.
This short book contains useful discussions of programming in C, specifically for MS-DOS computers.

Polya, G., *How to Solve It*. Princeton, NJ: Princeton University Press, 1973.
This classic problem solving book is still insightful.

Press, W. H., B. P. Flannery, S. A. Teukolsky and W. T. Vetterling. *Numerical Recipes: The Art of Scientific Computing*. Cambridge, MA: Cambridge University Press, 1986.
This lengthy book provides, in handbook-like fashion, a compendium of existing knowledge about numerical analysis and coding of numerical algorithms in Fortran and Pascal.

Press, W. H., B. P. Flannery, S. A. Teukolsky, and W. T. Vetterling. *Numerical Recipes in C: The Art of Scientific Computing*. Cambridge, MA: Cambridge University Press, 1988.
This book is essentially a duplicate of the one noted above, except that all of the (extensive) effort has been redone in C. One, or both, of these books will prove to be very useful for anyone who has numerical type programming to do—for a living or as a hobby.

Ralston, A. and P. Rabinowitz. *A First Course in Numerical Analysis*, 2nd ed. New York: McGraw-Hill, 1978.
Another classic work in numerical analysis.

Rice, J. R. *Numerical Methods, Software, and Analysis*. New York: McGraw-Hill, 1983.
A more pragmatic look at numerical methods than available in most textbooks.

Rosler, L. The Evolution of C-Past and Future. *AT&T Bell Lab. Tech. J.*, **63** (8), Part 2, pp. 1685–1700, 1984.
An interesting discussion of where C is now and where it is likely to go.

Sedgewick, B. *Algorithms*. Reading, MA: Addison-Wesley, 1983.
This well written introduction should be very helpful to those undertaking further serious study of the material we present in Chapters 17–19.

Standish, T. A., *Data Structure Techniques*. Reading, MA: Addison-Wesley, 1980.
A useful, pedagogically sound introduction to data structures.

Tenenbaum, A. M. and M. J. Augenstein. *Data Structures Using Pascal*. Englewood Cliffs, NJ: Prentice-Hall, 1981.
A near classic work that presents a very readable discussion of data structures in Pascal.

Wirth, N. *Algorithms + Data Structures = Programs*. Englewood Cliffs, NJ: Prentice-Hall, 1976.

A classic work in the field. Provides much interesting perspective concerning theories of how computer programs should be constructed.

Wirth, N. The Design of a Pascal Compiler. *Software-Pract. and Exp.* **1**, 309–333, 1971a.

Wirth, N. The Programming Language Pascal. *Acta Informatica.* **1**, 35–63, 1971b.

Wirth, N. *Systematic Programming: An Introduction*. Englewood Cliffs, NJ: Prentice-Hall, 1973.

The aforenoted three books provide much rich historical perspective concerning the development of the Pascal programming language, written by the *father* of the language.

INDEX